Language for Study

LEVEL 2

Tamsin Espinosa   Clare Walsh   Alistair McNair

Series editor: Ian Smallwood

CAMBRIDGE
UNIVERSITY PRESS

CAMBRIDGE
UNIVERSITY PRESS

University Printing House, Cambridge CB2 8BS, United Kingdom

One Liberty Plaza, 20th Floor, New York, NY 10006, USA

477 Williamstown Road, Port Melbourne, VIC 3207, Australia

4843/24, 2nd Floor, Ansari Road, Daryaganj, Delhi – 110002, India

79 Anson Road, #06–04/06, Singapore 079906

Cambridge University Press is part of the University of Cambridge.

It furthers the University's mission by disseminating knowledge in the pursuit of education, learning and research at the highest international levels of excellence.

www.cambridge.org
Information on this title: www.cambridge.org/9781107694668

First published 2012
20 19 18 17 16 15 14 13 12 11 10 9 8 7 6 5

Printed in Great Britain by CPI Group (UK) Ltd, Croydon CR0 4YY

A catalogue record for this publication is available from the British Library

ISBN 978-1-107-69466-8

Acknowledgements
The authors and publishers acknowledge the following sources of copyright material and are grateful for the permissions granted. While every effort has been made, it has not always been possible to identify the sources of all the material used, or to trace all copyright holders. If any omissions are brought to our notice, we will be happy to include the appropriate acknowledgements on reprinting.

Author acknowledgements
The authoring team would like to thank Clare Sheridan, Ian Morrison, Nick Robinson, Nik White, Sarah Curtis, Chris Capper and Ian Collier for their constant help and support throughout the whole project. We also offer our grateful acknowledgement to Sarah Clark, Fred Gooch and Neil McSweeney for their advice and contributions to the manuscripts. Finally, we would like to thank all ELT and academic skills staff and students across Kaplan International Colleges for their assistance in trialling the materials during development and for their valuable feedback and suggestions.

Publisher acknowledgements
The authors and publishers would like to thank the following people who reviewed and commented on the material at various stages: Olwyn Alexander, Michael McCarthy, Jenifer Spencer and Scott Thornbury.

Design and illustrations by Hart McLeod, Cambridge

Photo Acknowledgements
p.4© Neustockimages/istockphotos.com, ©Christine Osborne Pictures/Alamy, ©Huw Jones/ Alamy, ©Steven May/Alamy; p.7 © Neustockimages/ istockphotos.com; p.51 ©Christine Osborne Pictures/ Alamy; p.108 ©Huw Jones/Alamy; p.158 ©Steven May/ Alamy; p.159 © Jeff Griffin, ©Onur Kocamaz, ©Anandha Krishnan, ©Gergana Valcheva

Language for study Contents

Map of the book

Understanding

	Speaking Part A	Writing Part B
1 Gender issues	Recognizing different types of numerical data Understanding and using language to simplify numerical data	Recognizing and using verbs and adverbs for describing trends Using nouns and adjectives to show trends Using prepositions to describe trends
UNIT TASK	Dealing with numerical data	Describing graphics
2 Water	Understanding discourse markers Follow lab instructions	Identifying text structure Identifying different functions in report introductions Identifying recommendations
UNIT TASK	Following a discussion	Reading to make a recommendation
3 Progress	Recognizing and using time expressions to show sequence Understanding the use of repetition, reformulation and rhetorical questions Using context to understand the meaning of new vocabulary	Using definite and indefinite articles Recognizing and using conditionals in descriptions of a process Recognizing and using prepositions with common verbs in academic writing
UNIT TASK	Describing a process	Timed error correction
4 Art, creativity and design	Recognizing speaker attitude Understanding signposting expressions to improve comprehension Understanding the relationship between parts of a talk	Understanding register variations in academic and non-academic vocabulary Understanding the use of affixes in academic vocabulary Understanding nominalisation
UNIT TASK	Listening to attitude to information	Reading texts with high-frequency academic vocabulary

Appendices

Investigating

Reporting

Part C	Speaking Part D	Writing Part E
Using punctuation correctly in references Paraphrasing while note-taking	Using appropriate verb tenses for describing trends Comparing data using the discourse markers *while* and *whereas* Comparing data using multiple values and fractions	Following tense patterns in literature reviews Building paragraphs using *it* as a subject Building paragraphs using determiners to link ideas Writing definitions of key terms using participle phrases
Note-taking and referencing	**Analysing and discussing statistical data**	**Using participle phrases in definitions**
Understanding the language of research questions Understanding the language of research titles Understanding the language of lab manuals and reports	Using expressions to manage group dynamics Starting and finishing seminars	Matching sentence structure with purpose Using the past passive to report procedures Structuring a technical (lab) report
Discussing the effectiveness of a scientific experiment	**Holding a seminar**	**Reporting a science experiment**
Recognizing how writers use connotation to shape opinion Recognizing and using vocabulary for describing research methods	Using tenses to describe past actions and experiences Using tenses to describe future actions Using language to show a contrast between reality and expectation Using pausing to show attitude	Understanding the use of the first person in academic writing Recognizing and using synonyms and parallel expressions to compare and contrast other writers' ideas
Using vocabulary to describe research methods	**Improving your speaking and discussion methods**	**Taking notes to compare sources**
Recognizing key research terminology Understanding the language features of research reports Writing about research limitations	Describing and commenting on research findings Forming indirect questions Using appropriate pronunciation and language when agreeing and disagreeing	Recognizing and using the structure and grammar of abstracts Writing an abstract using concise language
Discussing research designs	**Conducting a class survey**	**Writing an abstract**

Unit 1 Gender issues

Unit overview

Part	This part will help you to …	By improving your ability to …
A	**Understand data presented in lectures**	• recognize different types of numerical data • understand and use language to simplify numerical data.
B	**Understand and evaluate data and graphics**	• recognize and use verbs and adverbs for describing trends • use nouns and adjectives to show trends • use prepositions to describe trends.
C	**Keep accurate records of your research**	• use punctuation correctly in references • paraphrase while note-taking.
D	**Contribute to discussions**	• use appropriate verb tenses for describing trends • compare data using the discourse markers *while* and *whereas* • compare data using multiple values and fractions.
E	**Write standard academic reports**	• follow tense patterns in literature reviews • build paragraphs using *it* as a subject • build paragraphs using determiners to link ideas • write definitions of key terms using participle phrases.

Understanding spoken information

By the end of Part A you will be able to:

- recognize different types of numerical data
- understand and use language to simplify numerical data.

1 Recognizing different types of numerical data

> Many students find dealing with numerical data one of the most difficult aspects of listening to lectures. In order to help you understand and note down numerical data quickly, it is important that you are aware of the different ways in which it is presented.

1a Work in pairs. Discuss why writers or lecturers refer to data.

1b Work in pairs. Complete the second column of the table with the numerical data in the box below.

5.4	5th	4/5	2005	54%	5,400

Types of data	Example	Examples in context (Exercise 1e)
1 cardinal numbers (counting numbers)		
2 ordinal numbers (ranking numbers)		
3 decimals		
4 percentages		
5 fractions		
6 year (of publication)		

1c **1** How do we pronounce the figures and symbols in the box below?

' . '	'%'	0	104	2/3	2010	3.142	5/8	9/10

2 The numbers *0, 104* and *2010* all have more than one pronunciation.

    a What are the alternative pronunciations for these numbers?

    b Can we use the alternative pronunciations for each number in any context or only in specific situations?

3 How do we pronounce the numbers after the ' . ' in a decimal?

4 With ordinal numbers, when are these abbreviations used?

    –th   *–st*   *–nd*   *–rd*

1d You are going to listen to some extracts from a lecture on some of the differences male and female children experience in their education in the developed world, with a particular focus on the UK. Before you listen, work in small groups and discuss these questions.

    1 Are there any differences in the way in which girls and boys are educated in your country? Consider the following.

       • quality of education

       • duration of education

       • expectations of families

       • exam results

    2 Do you expect it to be the same, or different, in the UK?

1.1

1e Listen to extracts from a lecture on education in the UK. In each extract, the lecturer refers to numerical data. Make a note of the data in the third column of the table in 1b.

1f Check your answers with a partner.

1g Work in groups. You are going to listen to a longer extract from the same lecture. Before you listen, look at a student's lecture notes and predict the following.

    1 What type of data might you expect to hear for each point (e.g. ordinal number, percentage)?

    2 Do you have any idea of what the numbers could be (for your home country or for the UK)?

Notes
• UK male–female ratio studying degree programmes = 1) _____
• Male–female wage differences: School leavers (M)
• First 10 yrs. work = earn 2) _____ less
• After 10–15 yrs. work = no difference
Uni graduates (M)
• After 30 yrs. work = earn 3) _____ more
• 2006 survey = 4) _____ all snr academic posts held by M.

1.2

1h Listen to the extract and complete the missing information (1–4) in the notes in 1g.

1i Check your answers with a partner. Is any of the information surprising? Why / Why not?

2 Understanding and using language to simplify numerical data

Many lecturers help their audience by simplifying numerical data to communicate key points more effectively. Preposition or adverb phrases such as: *about, around, a little over, just under, roughly*, etc. signal simplified data. There are three common ways of simplifying specific data:

- rounding numbers up or down to give an approximate value in place of the specific one (e.g. *75%* ... in place of *76.3%*)
- using a fraction in place of a specific value (e.g. *About three-quarters* ... in place of *76.3%*)
- giving a subjective estimate of the size of the value (e.g. *many women / the majority of professors* ... in place of *76.3%*)

2a Work in pairs. You are going to listen to an extract from a lecture about the numbers of male and female students studying engineering in UK universities. Before you listen, discuss these questions.

1 In your country, is it common for female students to study engineering?

2 Are there some subjects which male students typically prefer and others which are typically studied by female students? Why do you think this is?

3 Do you expect the situation will be the same in the UK?

1.3

2b Listen to the extract. How well balanced is the student population in this university?

2c Listen to the extract again. As you listen, write the numbers you hear below.

Notes
% male engineering undergrads: 30 yrs ago = _____
% increase female eng. undergrads: over last 20 yrs = _____
All courses – ratio females enrolled = _____

2d Check your answers to 2c with a partner. Did you note down the same numbers?

2e Look at this transcript from the extract and identify:

- any words or phrases used to signal that a piece of data has been simplified
- two different ways in which data has been simplified.

Certainly, engineering has traditionally been a male-dominated field: about 90% of engineering undergraduates here were male 30 years ago. However, have things changed? Well, they have. Proportions of female students have increased by over 20% over the last twenty years, though the ratio of female students remains well under half on all degrees and still around a quarter on most. And this is a university which prides itself on its male-to-female ratio!

Words and phrases which introduce simplified data

2f Work in pairs. Add the signalling words and phrases from the transcript in 2e to the first two columns of this table. Then add any other signalling words that you can think of.

<	≈	>
	about	

Rounding up or down to give approximate values

> Lecturers can simplify numbers by using approximate values of figures rather than the exact number. Depending on their purpose, these might be very approximate (e.g. *around 50%* for an exact figure of 45%) or more specific (e.g. *around 49%* for an exact figure of 48.6%).

2g You are going to listen to some extracts from a lecture about some gender differences in the workplace. Work in pairs. Look at these notes. What approximate values could the lecturer give for the underlined data? Discuss your ideas.

Extract	Notes
A	*consistent increase in female employment rates, 2008: <u>69%</u> women / <u>81%</u> men employed.*
B	*2008: <u>48.73%</u> of workforce female.*
C	*at age 50, graduate women earn average <u>£13.89</u> per hour. Men without degrees <u>£13.63</u> per hour.*
D	*2005 female graduate proportion: <u>71%</u> education, <u>65.8%</u> arts and humanities, <u>56.8%</u> business and law, <u>39%</u> science, <u>25.2%</u> engineering.*
E	*<u>25.93%</u> women employed in education, <u>26.2%</u> public services.*

1.4

2h Listen to the extracts and complete these sentences with the approximation of the data used by the lecturer.

A

In one sense, women are enjoying much better career opportunities than ever before: female employment rates have increased consistently over the last few decades, until in 2008 _____ /_____ % of UK women were in work (men were slightly ahead, with _____ /_____ % in work, but the gap is closing fast).

B

Furthermore, a greater percentage of the workforce across the EU and the UK is now made up of women – in 2008, for instance, the UK workforce was split almost evenly, with women making up _____ /_____ % of all people in work.

C

By the age of 50, the gap was even starker: university-educated males earned _____ /_____ / £_____ an hour, with university-educated women again earning more or less the same as men who did not have a degree – _____ / £_____ .

D

_____ /_____ % of all education degrees awarded in 2005 went to women, about 66% of graduates in the arts and humanities were female, and _____ /_____ % in business and law. However, the number of female graduates in sciences, maths and engineering courses was far lower, with _____ /_____ % of science graduates being female, and a mere 25% in engineering.

E

_____ /_____ % of all working women are employed in education of one form or another, and _____ another _____ % are employed in public services, and women vastly outnumber men in these types of job.

2i Check your answers with a partner.

2j Add any other phrases for simplifying data to the table in 2f.

Using fractions

> The final technique commonly used is to simplify data as fractions.

2k Complete these descriptions by choosing a suitable word or phrase from the box below.

a	~~of~~	of	out of	of	in

1 70% ____*of*____ undergraduate students may be female in future years.

2 Over two-thirds _____ undergraduate students may be female in future years.

3 Under _____ third of students on most education courses are male.

4 Over two-thirds _____ students on most education courses are female.

5 Approximately one _____ ten primary school teachers in the UK is male.

6 Over nine _____ ten primary school teachers in the UK are female.

2l Work in pairs. Complete these grammar notes, using the examples in 2k to help you.

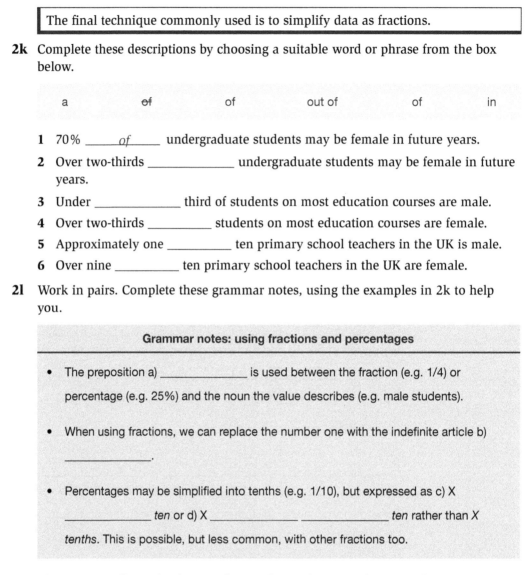

Grammar notes: using fractions and percentages

- The preposition a) _____ is used between the fraction (e.g. 1/4) or percentage (e.g. 25%) and the noun the value describes (e.g. male students).

- When using fractions, we can replace the number one with the indefinite article b) _____.

- Percentages may be simplified into tenths (e.g. 1/10), but expressed as c) X _____ *ten* or d) X _____ _____ *ten* rather than X *tenths*. This is possible, but less common, with other fractions too.

1.5

2m Phrases, as well as adverbs, are also used to make generalisations about quantities. Listen to a final extract from the same lecture. Which phrases match these meanings?

1 *Most of* (MEng and PhD students of Engineering)

2 *Very few* (female software engineering students)

2n Work in pairs. Can you think of any other synonyms for the phrases above?

2o Check your answers with a partner.

> **LESSON TASK** **3 Dealing with numerical data**

3a Work in pairs. Each student should read one of the tables in **Appendix 1** to find the answer to these questions.

Student A – Read Table 1 and answer this question.

In 2007, which nation had the most even distribution of senior female academics across all age groups?

Student B – Read Table 2 and answer this question.

Which academic fields saw the greatest growth in female PhD researchers between 2001 and 2006?

3b Write a short summary of the information in the table, using approximate data.

3c Use your summary to explain the information in the table to your partner.

3d Review the information you have learned about the gender gap so far in this unit. In small groups, discuss the following question. Use approximate language to help support your opinions.

'How significant is the gender gap in education?'

4 Review and extension

Using numerical data

4a Listen to a lecturer giving a summary of some statistics, in turn taken from another lecture. The lecture deals with the gender gap in education in the United States. Write notes on the lecturer's summary, and hand them to your teacher in the next class.

4b Find a chart or table which presents information about the gender gap. Take notes of the data shown on the graphic you have found. Find ways to simplify the data by using preposition and adverb phrases, approximations and fractions.

4c Practise delivering the information in your graphic to your classmates at the beginning of the next class.

Understanding written information

By the end of Part B you will be able to:
- recognize and use verbs and adverbs for describing trends
- use nouns and adjectives to show trends
- use prepositions to describe trends.

1 Recognizing and using verbs and adverbs for describing trends

1a Numerical data is often used to show evidence of trends. Work in small groups. Discuss these questions.

1 What is a trend? Complete the definition below.

> A trend is...

2 In academic writing, what is the benefit of showing trends in information?

> To recognize trends in academic texts, and to improve understanding of and ability to use graphic representations of trends, it is important to understand the language used to describe them.

1b You are going to read an extract from a text on gender in higher education in the UK. Before you read, discuss these questions in your group.

1 In your country, do more women study now than 30 years ago? Why / Why not?

2 Do you expect the ratio of male:female students will change in the next twenty years? Why / Why not?

1c Read this extract. Would you change your answers to the questions in 1b?

> The percentage of all students who are male has fallen from around 55% in the mid-1980s to just under 50% at the time of writing. Analysts predict that university campuses will increasingly be dominated by female students, with their numbers expected to rise consistently for the next twenty years.

1d The extract in 1c describes the trend in the proportion of students who are female from the mid-1980s to approximately 2030. Write the infinitive form of the two verbs the writer uses to show the trend in the correct column of the table below. Then, in your group, think of other verbs you could add to all three columns of the table.

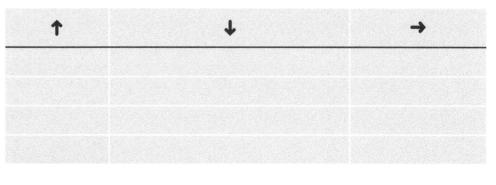

↑	↓	→

1e Work in pairs. The graphs below reflect more ways of describing trends in a range of academic disciplines. Match the verbs (1–8) with the parts circled in red in the graphs (a–h). Make a note of any trends that you think could be described by more than one verb, then discuss with your partner which of the two verbs might be best.

1 peak _a_

2 level off ____

3 dip ____

4 plummet ____

5 recover ____

6 crash ____

7 fluctuate ____

8 climb ____

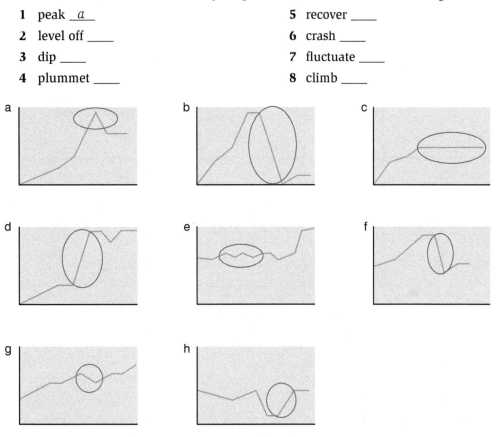

1f Add the verbs in 1e to the table in 1d. Discuss the verb *fluctuate* with a partner. Explain where you think it belongs, and why.

1g Work in pairs. You are going to read a text comparing male and female wages in the UK since 1999. What do you expect the text to show? Discuss these questions.

1 Do women earn less than men? If so, by how much do you think this is (as a percentage)?

2 Do you think the situation has changed since 1999? If so, how?

1h Read the text to answer the questions in 1g.

> There can be no doubt that men are paid more than women, and this aspect of the gender gap receives a lot of media attention. However, evidence suggests that the gap between women's and men's pay is closing slowly. Figures from the Annual Survey of Hours and Earnings in 2009 show that women were paid just 74% as much as men in 1999, but this had gone up to 78% by 2006, climbing sharply between 2001 and 2002. Unfortunately, this trend has not continued since 2006: female earnings as a percentage of males' remained stable until 2007 and then declined very slightly to 77.8% in 2008. It is hoped that they will not drop further, but that the percentage of women's pay will grow again in the future.

1i Underline any verb in the text which describes a rising, falling or stable trend.

> Adverbs used to describe trends can show changes in degree (the amount of change), or in time (the speed of change).

1j Identify the adverb phrases that are used with the verbs to describe trends.

1k Work in pairs. Add more adverbs used to describe trends to the two tables below.

Degree of change	
Large: sharply,	**Small:** slightly,

Speed of change	
Fast: rapidly,	**Slow:** slowly,

1l You are going to read an extract from research where women working in different sectors were questioned on how their pay has changed over time **(Appendix 2)**. Work in three different groups. Each group should read a different extract (1, 2 or 3). As you read, underline any more adverbs used to describe trends and add them to the tables in 1k.

1m Get into groups with students who read the other two extracts. First, summarise the main idea of the extract which you read for the other students. Then share the adverb phrases you found in your extracts and add them to correct places in the tables in 1k.

1n Work in pairs. Look at the graphic on p.18, which shows how women's and men's pay in the administration department of one company changed between the years 1990 and 2000. Answer these questions.

    1 Have women's and men's pay increases followed the same trends?

    2 Which years have seen the biggest differences between men's and women's pay?

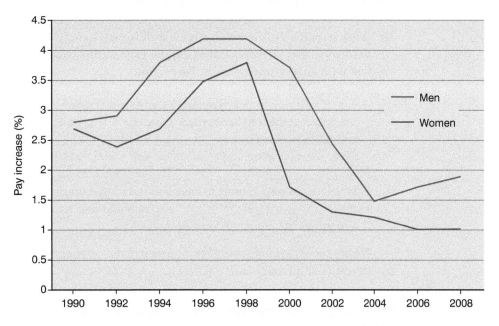

Figure 1: Male and female pay increase administration 1990–2008

1o Work in pairs. Read this text describing the graphic. Complete the text by choosing appropriate phrases from the options below. If necessary, change the tense of the verb to ensure that it is grammatically correct.

1 drop more swiftly   4 recover slightly

2 fall dramatically   5 dip slightly

3 ~~increase sharply~~

> Figure 1 shows that pay increases for males and females followed similar trends over much of the last twenty years: pay generally **1)** <u>increased sharply</u> up to the late 1990s and then **2)** _____ in the early 2000s. However, while women's pay remained stable from 2006, men's pay started to **3)** _____, with pay rises back up to almost 2% in 2008. Women's pay also appears to have suffered more in the early 1990s, where pay rises **4)** _____ in 1992, and around the year 2000, where it **5)** _____ than men's.

2 Using nouns and adjectives to show trends

> Most of the verbs and adverbs you studied above have an equivalent noun and adjective form which may also be used to describe trends. Describing a trend using a verb–adverb or adjective–noun combination allows you to emphasize different aspects of the same data.

2a Work in pairs. Compare this text with the text in 1h. Discuss how some verbs and adverbs have been changed to nouns and adjectives. Underline any changes in the text below.

> … Figures from the Annual Survey of Hours and Earnings in 2009 show that women were paid just 74% as much as men in 1999, but this had gone up to 78% by 2006, with a sharp climb between 2001 and 2002. Unfortunately, this trend has not continued since 2006: female earnings as a percentage of males' remained stable until 2007, but then saw a slight decline to 77.8% in 2008 …

2b Work in pairs. This text describes Figure 1 (1n) using adjectives and nouns rather than verbs and adverbs. Transform the expressions you used in 1o to complete this text with an appropriate adjective or noun.

Figure 1 shows that pay increases for males and females followed similar trends over much of the last twenty years: there was a **1)** <u>sharp</u> **2)** <u>increase</u> in pay up to the late 1990s followed by a **3)**_____ **4)** _____ in the early 2000s. However, while women's pay remained stable from 2006, men's pay started to see a **5)** _____ **6)** _____, with pay rises back up to almost 2% in 2008. Women's pay also appears to have suffered more in the early 1990s, where there was a **7)** _____ **8)** _____ in pay rises in 1992, and around the year 2000, where they saw a greater decrease than men's.

2c Check your answers with a partner.

3 Using prepositions to describe trends

3a Read the three extracts from 1l (**Appendix 2**). Underline the verbs and nouns used to describe trends.

3b Check your answers with a partner.

3c Work in pairs. Circle the prepositions which follow the verbs and nouns you underlined in 3a. Discuss when these prepositions are used.

by   in   of

3d Complete these sentences with a preposition from the box above.

1 Nationally, recent years have seen a steady rise _____ the number of female students remaining in full-time education from 16 to 18.

2 Unsurprisingly, the number of female students applying for university places has also increased _____ a few per cent more than male students.

3 In fact, it is expected that numbers of female students will see an increase _____ about 20% in the next decades.

4 Though there has been a drop _____ the number of university places overall, some courses are trying harder than ever to attract female students.

5 Some evidence suggests that female students are more likely to complete their course than male students: female drop-out rates have seen an increase _____ less than 0.5%, whereas male drop-out rates have seen an increase _____ up to 1%.

6 Like male students, many female students are now choosing to stay at home during their studies, as doing so may lead their living costs to be reduced _____ up to 50%.

4 Describing graphics

4a Work in small groups. Write a text describing the main trends in a graphic. After you have written your text, you will pass it to another group who will have to use your description to draw a graphic.

- Group A, write a description of Gender gap graph 1 in **Appendix 3**.
- Group B, write a description of Gender gap graph 2 in **Appendix 4**.

4b Swap your descriptions with members of the other group, and use the space below to draw the graphic from their description.

Graphic 1

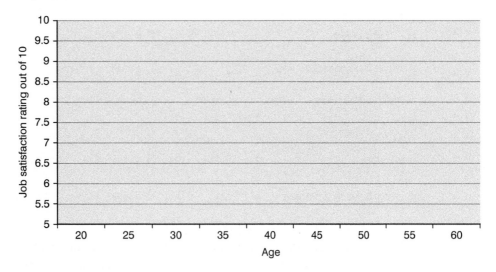

Figure 2: Female nurse job satisfaction rating /10

Graphic 2

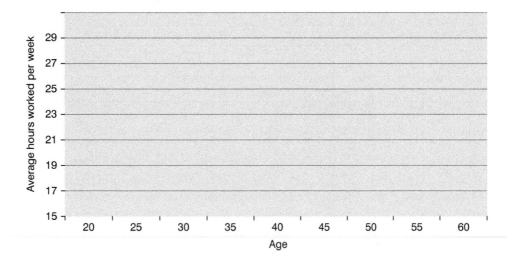

Figure 3: Average hours worked per week by public sector females aged 20–60

5 Review and extension

Verbs to describe trends

5a In addition to those you studied above, many other verbs and expressions are used to describe trends in a range of different academic disciplines. Some of the most common are shown here. Use a dictionary to find their meaning and then add them to the table in 1d (p.14). Draw a simple line graph to show the meaning of each word. For example, *boom*:

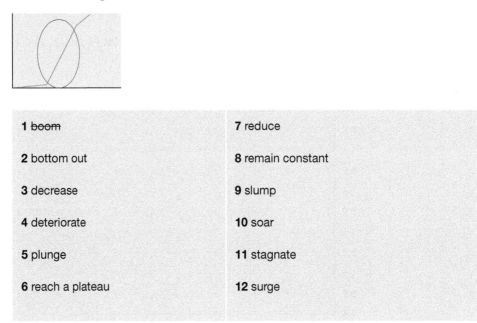

1 ~~boom~~	**7** reduce
2 bottom out	**8** remain constant
3 decrease	**9** slump
4 deteriorate	**10** soar
5 plunge	**11** stagnate
6 reach a plateau	**12** surge

5b Look at *stagnate, reach a plateau, remain constant* and *bottom out*. They all describe similar states, but have slightly different connotations. Describe which ones have a positive, negative or neutral connotation.

5c Use the graphic below to complete a short text describing the trends shown, using suitable verbs from 5a and any other language studied in this part.

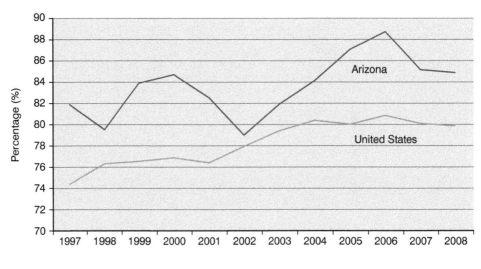

Source: Bureau of Labour Statistics, 2009

Figure 1: Women's earnings as a percentage of men's. Full-time wage and salary workers, Arizona and the United States, 2000–08 annual average.

According to Figure 1 ...

The language of trends

5d Update your personal vocabulary logbook with the language you have learned in this part. You should include: **verbs** and verb phrases to describe trends; **adverbs** and adverb phrases used when describing trends; **nouns** to describe trends; **adjectives** used when describing trends.

Show your vocabulary records to your teacher at the beginning of your next class.

By the end of Part C you will be able to:
- use punctuation correctly in references
- paraphrase while note-taking.

1   Using punctuation correctly in references

1a   Writers refer to the sources they have used both in their text (*in-text citations* or *in-text references*) and at the end of their work (*the list of references*). In your group, discuss these questions.

1   What information should be provided in in-text citations?

2   In what order should this information be provided?

3   In a list of references, what information should be provided for a book?

4   In what order should this information be provided?

5   In a list of references, what different information should be given for

  A An article in a journal?

  B A web page?

> Writing in-text citations and references is an area of academic writing where presentation rules are very strict. As a student, you are expected to follow them correctly and consistently. Accuracy is particularly important in this area – if you do not reference accurately, you may be accused of plagiarism.

1b   Work in pairs. The following punctuation markers are important in writing in-text citations and references. Match the names (1–11) with the markers (a–k).

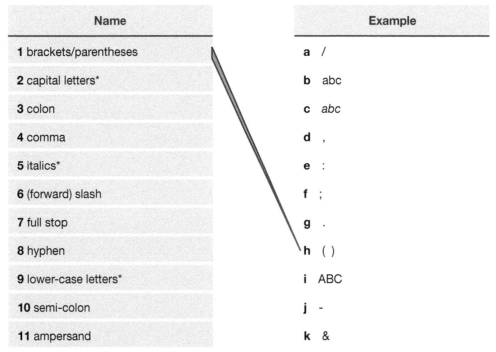

Name		Example	
1 brackets/parentheses		**a**	/
2 capital letters*		**b**	abc
3 colon		**c**	*abc*
4 comma		**d**	,
5 italics*		**e**	:
6 (forward) slash		**f**	;
7 full stop		**g**	.
8 hyphen		**h**	( )
9 lower-case letters*		**i**	ABC
10 semi-colon		**j**	-
11 ampersand		**k**	&

Note: capital letters, lower-case letters and italics are strictly a feature of typography rather than punctuation, but are important in the layout of references.

Using punctuation correctly in a list of references

1c Work in pairs. Study these entries from a list of references written in Harvard format, then select from the boxes the appropriate words to complete the rules which follow.

> Huyer, S. (2006). *Gender, Science and Technology for sustainable development: Looking ahead to the next ten years. Report of the Meeting of the Gender Advisory Board of the UN Commission on Science and Technology Development*; 12–13 December 2006. Paris: UNESCO.
>
> Jacobs, J. (1999). The Sex Segregation of Occupations: Prospects for the 21st Century. In G.N. Powell (Ed.), *Handbook of Gender and Work* (pp.125–41). Newbury Park: Sage.
>
> Lapping, C. (2005). Antagonism and overdetermination: the production of student positions in contrasting undergraduate disciplines and institutions in the UK. *British Journal of Sociology of Education, 26*(5), 657–671.
>
> Van Langen, A., & Dekkers, H. (2005). Cross-national differences in participating in tertiary science, technology, engineering and mathematics. *Comparative Education, 41*(3), 329–350. Retrieved from http://premia.iacm.forth.gr/docs/ws1/papers/Van%20Langen1.pdf

Punctuation rules in references

Capital letters are used:

acronym	publishers'	publication	months	initials

- As the first letter of authors' family names
- For authors' **1)** _____
- As the first letter of places of **2)** _____
- As the first letter of **3)** _____ names
- As the first letter of **4)** _____ and days of the week
- Where used in the titles of articles, books, journals, etc. (see note below)
- For each letter in an **5)** _____ (e.g. UNESCO).

Full stops are used:

title	web address	after	end	book

- After authors' initials
- **6)** _____ the year of publication
- After the first **7)** _____ given (book, article in a journal, web page)
- At the **8)** _____ of the reference except when the last information given is a **9)** _____
- Where originally found in titles of books, articles, etc.
- After the abbreviation Ed. in an edited book and p. (page) or pp. (pages).

Brackets (parentheses) are used:

pages	year	volume number	issue number

- Around the **10)** _____
- With journal articles, around the **11)** _____ .

Colons are used:

> publisher   place of publication   book title   author's name

- For books, in between the **12)** _____ and the **13)** _____
- Where originally found in titles of books, articles, etc.

Commas are used:

> issue number   family name   volume number   journal title

- After the author's **14)** _____
- With journal articles, after the **15)** _____ and after the **16)** _____
- Where originally found in titles of books, articles, etc.

Hyphens are used:

> between start and end pages   between place of publication and the publisher's name

- **17)** _____
- Where originally found in titles of books, articles, etc.

Italics are used:

> books   journals   journal articles

- For the titles of **18)** _____ and **19)** _____ .

Ampersand is used:

> between authors' names   in titles

- In place of the word 'and' **20)** _____ .

1d Compare your answers to 1c with another pair. Do you agree on the same rules?

> Many students find the use of capital letters in titles confusing. This is not helped by the inconsistency you will find in the academic texts you read, where you will probably find all of the following:
>
> - The first letter of all words in the title is capitalised (this is particularly common with shorter titles).
>
>   **Example** *World Gender Report*
>
> - Just the first letter of the first word in the title is capitalised (this is particularly common with longer titles).
>
>   **Example** *Cross-national differences in participating in tertiary science, technology, engineering and mathematics*
>
> - The first letter of the first word in the title is capitalised, and then the first letter of all content words is capitalised, but the first letter of all function words (prepositions, articles, etc.) is lower case.
>
>   **Example** *The Sex Segregation of Occupations: Prospects for the 21st Century.*

1e Work in pairs. Rewrite these references, adding the necessary punctuation. The titles are correctly punctuated already.

1

office for national statistics
2009
Annual Survey of Hours and Earnings (ASHE) – 2009 results
retrieved from wwwstatistics.gov.uk/statBase/product.asp?vlnk=15313

2

kate purcell and peter elias
2003
Researching Graduate Careers Seven Years On: education, skills and economic restructuring
research project funded jointly by ESRC and ECSU

3

united states department of labor
2009
Quick Stats on women workers, 2009
retrieved from www.dol.gov/wb/stats/main.htm

Using punctuation correctly in in-text citations

1f Work in pairs. From your knowledge of what is included in an in-text citation, discuss which punctuation markers you think are necessary. Write notes in the table below.

Punctuation marker	When it is used
Full stop	After 'p' for page numbers.

1g A student used two of the sources in 1e while writing an essay. Look at the correctly written in-text citations below. Read the citations and make any changes or additions to your notes in 1f.

- Attending university helps to increase earnings (Purcell & Elias, 2003, p.11).

- Women tend to work in lower-paying fields (United States Department of Labor, 2009; Office for National Statistics, 2009).

2 Paraphrasing while note-taking

Writing correct references for the sources you have used in your study is only useful as long as you have also kept a record of the ideas within those sources. Learning to paraphrase at the note-taking stage will help you to organize your writing more clearly and express your own ideas (reducing the risk of plagiarism).

2a As part of their research into the gender gap, three students made notes on the following.

1 why the percentage of the workforce who are female overall is lower than that of men

2 why the percentage of working-age women who have jobs is lower than that of working-age men

Work in pairs. Discuss what you think some of these reasons could be.

2b Look at an original source below. How many of the ideas you discussed in 2a does it mention? Does it include any other information?

Original source:

European Commission Advisory Committee on Equal Opportunities for Women and Men. (2010). *Opinion on The Future of Gender Equality Policy after 2010*. Retrieved from http://ec.europa.eu./social/main.jsp?catld=418&langid=en

[Extract from p.9]

Enhancing reconciliation of work, private and family life

2.1 Need for more effective reconciliation policies

Childcare is still unequally divided between women and men. Women are still taking on most of the childcare and, at the same time, many women are in paid employment.

The double burden of paid work and unpaid work within the family, together with a possible lack of support care services, are some of the reasons behind the declining fertility rate in Europe and can be identified as one of the main barriers to women's full participation in the labour market and decision making at all levels.

2.2 Maternity, paternity, parental and family leaves and flexible working patterns

Maternity, paternity, parental and family leave are effective measures, amongst others, to encourage the sharing of family caring responsibilities between both partners in a relationship. However, barriers still exist which discourage their use. Women take up parental leave more than men and several studies show that men can be discouraged from utilizing this right, due to women's lower income and the persistence of gender stereotypes which can influence women's and men's behaviours and roles in caring responsibilities[7].

[7] See EAC Opinion on New Forms of Leave (Paternity Leave, Adoption Leave and Filial Leave), July 2008.

2c Work in pairs. Look at the three students' notes. Discuss what features of good note-taking they have used.

Student 1

- Need to divide work / home tasks better
- Though many women have paid jobs, also undertake maj. of care wk → 'double burden'
  - One factor which prevents equal participation in labour market
  - May result in ↓ fertility rate
- Lack of support care services an issue
- Need to encourage more equal take-up of family leave / flexitime
- Currently maternity leave most pop
  - Why? Women gen. paid less / stereotypes

Student 2

Main point	Supporting point(s)
Unequal division of care work	• ♀ do most on top of paid jobs • poss. insufficient support services • prevent ♀ fully taking part in lab. mkt / decisions
Family leave / flexitime	• should enable duties to be shared / discouraged • ♂ do less: higher pay? stereotypes?

Student 3

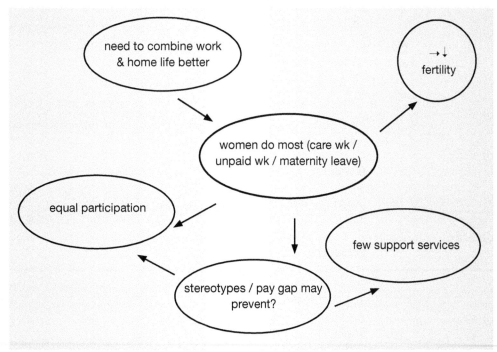

2d Are the notes written in the students' own words (paraphrased) or do they copy the source?

2e Work in small groups. Discuss why it is better to paraphrase when making notes. Consider:

- understanding of the content
- avoiding plagiarism.

2f Report your ideas back to the class.

2g Work in small groups. In Level 1 of this series you studied a number of language techniques which can help you paraphrase and summarise texts. Try to recall these techniques and write notes.

2h Which of the techniques in 2g can you find in each student's notes in 2c?

2i Read an extract from a text about flexible working arrangements and answer these questions. According to the author:

1 does everybody have a right to flexible working arrangements?
2 what are the benefits of flexible working arrangements for employees?
3 what are the benefits of flexible working arrangements for employers?

> Rial, M. (2009). *Work and the Family*. London: Clyde Forbes Education. [Extract from p.7]
>
> Difficulties balancing work and family life are often cited as reasons behind the gender pay gap. However, many women and men now have a legal right to request flexible working hours to enable them to plan their working schedule around family commitments. This should enable both men and women to share the responsibilities of childcare or indeed care for other dependent relatives. Statistics suggest that this can be beneficial to the employer as well, increasing productivity and encouraging employees to remain with the company. Unfortunately, there is no legal obligation for employers to grant flexible working arrangements, so access to them remains somewhat of a lottery. Of course, there also are some industries in which such arrangements are impractical – education, for instance, or client-facing businesses open 9–5.

2j Work in pairs. Look at the extracts from notes five different students took on this text. Discuss these questions.

1 What paraphrasing techniques are used?
2 Which paraphrase do you think is most effective and why?
3 Which two students' notes are incomplete or misrepresent points from the original text and how?

Student A
Diff. balancing career and home life = often given as reasons for gender pay gap, but many are now entitled to ask for flexible working hours – helps male ♣ females look after family members.
Flexible hours positive for company too: employees work harder ♣ stay in jobs (Rial, 2009, p.7).

Student B
Acc. Rial (2009, p.7), reason for gender hole = diff. weighing home life ♣ career.
However, ♂ and ♀ now have right to flex. working hrs so they can balance work and parenting better.
Also good for employers: productivity and retention increase.

Student C
Flexible hours can be beneficial to employer, increasing productivity and discouraging employees from leaving.
Unfortunately, no legal obligation to grant flexible working hours, not practical in some industries (Rial, 2009, p.7).

Student D

Gender pay gap may be explained due to ♀'s diffs managing home life + career.
However, resp. cd be managed by ♀ and ♂: both legally entitled to ask employers for flex. wking hrs.
Stats indicate such agreements encourage retention and raise productivity: employers thus benefit too (Rial, 2009, p.7).

Student E

According to Rial (2009, p.7), reasons behind gender pay gap: work + family life difficult to balance:.
Solution? Flexible working hours — enable men/women to care for children + other relatives.
Employer can also benefit: employees more productive and loyal.

2k Work in small groups. Compare your answers to the questions in 2j. Discuss which of the notes (A–E) you think are most successful. Why?

> **LESSON TASK**   **3 Note-taking and referencing**

3a Work in pairs. You are going to take notes for this essay.

Outline the distinctions between men's and women's wealth (including pay and pensions), with a particular focus on how these distinctions are different depending on a woman's age.

You have found the two sources below to help you. Read the source texts, underlining or highlighting the key points you wish to select.

Source 1

Author: United States Department of Labor
Year: 1999
Web page title: Futurework: Trends and Challenges for Work in the 21st Century.
URL: www.dol.gov/oasam/programs/history/herman/reports/futurework/report/chapter2/main2.htm

Men and women. Although the pay gap between men and women workers shrank by more than one-third between 1979 and 1998, women have yet to achieve parity with men. Overall, women's earnings have risen from 63 percent to 76 percent of men's earnings. While earnings of young women are nearly on par with young men (at about 91¢ on the dollar), older women lag further behind comparably aged men. Women 45 to 54 years old earn just 67 percent of what men earn, and women 55 to 64 years old earn just 66 percent.

The pay gap between men and women can be explained primarily by three factors. Roughly one-third of the pay gap between men and women is due to differences in labor market experience and, to a lesser extent, educational attainment. Women have roughly the same average educational attainment as men, and their test scores are roughly comparable (though women tend to score slightly higher in verbal areas while men do so in math). Differences in courses taken by men and women contribute somewhat to the differences observed between college-educated men and women, but not to those between men and women with high-school or less education. Work experience levels are lower among women, many of whom withdraw temporarily from the labor force to rear children.

Another 28 percent of the gap reflects differences in the occupations and industries in which men and women work and differences in their union status. Women continue to be concentrated in certain occupations (e.g. teaching and clerical work) and industries (e.g. retail trade and services). Some of this concentration, or "segregation," no doubt reflects women's choices, while some likely reflects barriers they continue to face in gaining entry to male-dominated fields.

More than 40 percent of the pay gap remaining between men and women cannot be explained by differences in the characteristics of female and male workers or the jobs they hold and is often interpreted as discrimination.[12] Discrimination can take many forms, such as being hired less frequently in high-wage firms, receiving less training and fewer promotions, particularly into the executive suite, and being assigned to lower-paying jobs within the same occupations. For example, in 1998, waiters earned 22 percent more than waitresses.[13]

Women workers also face a pension gap. Fewer than 40 percent of all women working in the private sector are covered by a pension, compared with 46 percent of men, and only 32 percent of current female retirees receive a pension, compared with 55 percent of men. The lower earnings of women contribute to lower pensions when they retire. The average pension benefit received by new female retirees is less than half that of men.

Source 2

Authors: Horstmann, S., Hüllsman, J., Ginn, J., Leitner, S., Leppik, L., & Ratajczak-Tucholka, J.
Year: 2009
Title: *The Socio-Economic Impact of Pension Systems on Women*
Place of publication: Brussels
Publisher: European Commission Directorate-General for Employment, Social Affairs, and Equal Opportunities.

Elderly women in the EU are more affected by poverty than men. In more than half of the Member States, the at-risk-of-poverty rate of women above 65 years of age is above 20%. Poverty rates of women in the EU have in fact worsened over the last years: the average rate for the EU 25 has increased slightly from 19% in 1999 by two percentage points to 21% in 2006. The poverty rates of women above 75 years of age are even higher, with an average of 24% (EU 25) and 26% (EU 15).

Information on the situation of both women and men as regards individual income is rather limited. Income data is mainly available on a household level, readjusted to the number of household members (equivalized) and based on the assumption that the household income is equally shared by household members. The information derived from this household level data does not allow for conclusions to be drawn regarding actual income of individual household members. There are different calculation methods to weight the income, but the general problem is that the concept of equal sharing of resources might overestimate the income of women and that the actual number of poor women is larger than household income data reveals.

EU-SILC data allows for an analysis of individually attributable income, which excludes, however, certain income components, such as means-tested benefits provided at household level. Thus, individually attributable income represents part of the actual income of individual household members. Individually attributable income of women is in general lower than individually attributable income of men.

Available EU-SILC data shows that income from pensions is by far the most important component of income and is even more important for elderly women than for elderly men. In many countries, pension income constitutes up to 90% of the total income of elderly women.

3b Make notes on the key points, being careful to remember the techniques reviewed in this section. Include in-text citations to show where your points have come from. Include a final list of references giving details of the two sources.

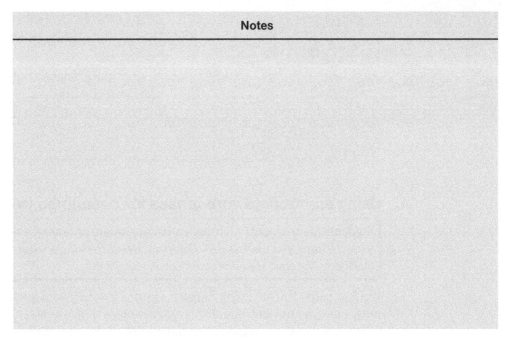

3c Work in pairs. Give feedback on each other's notes. Think about the following features:

- quantity/quality of relevant information
- note-taking technique
- paraphrasing technique
- in-text citations
- list of references.

4   Review and extension

Referencing

4a Make a list of references containing all of the sources you have used to help research a topic you are currently working on. Ensure that you pay attention to punctuating the list of references correctly.

4b Work in groups of three. Look at the Harvard-style references written by a student How many punctuation errors can you find?

1   Altbach P Reisberg L & Rumbley L (2009). *Trends in global higher education: Tracking an academic revolution*. Report prepared for the UNESCO 2009 World Conference on Higher Education. Paris United Nations Educational, Scientific and Cultural Organization. Retrieved from http//unesdoc.unesco.org/images/0017/001831/183168e.pdf

2   Giesecke, j and Schindler, s. 2008. Field of Study and Flexible Work: A Comparison between Germany and the UK. *International Journal of Comparative Sociology*. 49. pp.283, 304. Doi: 10.1177/0020715208093078.

3   JACOBS, J. 1996. Gender Inequality and Higher Education, *Annual Review of Sociology*. 22, pp.153:185.

Reporting in speech

By the end of Part D you will be able to:

- use appropriate verb tenses for describing trends
- compare data using the discourse markers *while* and *whereas*
- compare data using multiple values and fractions.

1 Using appropriate verb tenses for describing trends

Students often support their points using graphic or other numerical data during presentations and discussions. Selecting the correct verb tense is important in clarifying the time frame which the data refers to.

1a Work in pairs. You are going to listen to some extracts from a seminar discussion on the gender gap in education, focusing on women's involvement in STEM subjects (science, technology, engineering and maths). Before you listen, discuss these questions and write notes below.

1 How popular are STEM subjects among women in your country? What are some of the reasons for their (lack of) popularity?

2 How might you expect women's involvement in STEM to have changed over the last 30 or 40 years in the UK?

3 What might encourage more women to study STEM?

Notes
1
2
3

1.7

1b Listen to two students, Jenny and Martin, during the seminar. Use ideas from their discussion to add to your notes in 1a.

1c Check your answers with a partner.

1d The discussion between Jenny and Martin covered time frames from the 1970s to the future. It includes examples of most of the verb tenses shown in the table below. Look at the excerpts from their conversation in **Appendix 5** and complete the second column of the table with examples of the tenses you find.

Tense	Example	Reason for use
Past perfect	I wondered where this <u>had come</u> from.	
Past simple		
Past continuous		
Present perfect		
Present perfect continuous		
Present simple		
Present continuous		
Past perfect continuous		
Ways of referring to the future	1	
	2	
	3	
	4	

1e Work in pairs. Why was each tense used in its context? Refer back to the transcript in **Appendix 5** to complete the third column of the table in 1d with this information.

    a a trend that occurred at a stated time in the past

    b a trend that occurred before a stated time in the past

    c a current state

    d a future prediction

    e an action or state that occurred recently (no specific time is given), and which is still important

    f a current trend

    g an action or state that occurred at a stated time in the past

    h a trend that started in the past and continues to the present

    i a cautious future prediction / future consequence of present action or state

    j a prediction of a future trend

    k an action or state that occurred before a stated time in the past

    l a prediction of when a future event will have finished

1f Complete this passage using appropriate tenses from the table in 1d. Then check your answers with a partner. More than one answer may be possible in some cases.

> Although far more women than men study education, statistics show that male science and maths teachers **1)** <u>have</u> always **2)** <u>outnumbered</u> (outnumber) females. This may be one of the reasons why fewer women choose to study STEM subjects at university.
>
> In a 2007 survey, one school noted that before it **3)** _____ (employ) a female physics teacher in 2003, only 3% of its female students **4)** _____
>
> **5)** _____ (apply) to study physics or related studies at university, but after they **6)** _____ **7)** _____ (take on) the female teacher this figure
>
> **8)** _____ (rise) to 8%. Male pupils, and a school's wider community, also
>
> **9)** _____ (benefit) from having more female teachers in science and maths, because this **10)** _____ (help) break down stereotypes in society. In fact, recent reports suggest that the curriculum **11)** _____ even
>
> **12)** _____ (change) as a result of female STEM teachers, who are making it more relevant to issues affecting both genders. However, some are concerned that this focus on education **13)** _____ now in fact **14)** _____ (weaken) women's position in STEM. They fear that rather than showing women succeeding in traditionally male-dominated careers such as engineering, it reinforces the stereotype that women **15)** _____ (be) better in caring jobs such as teaching. A recent study of women in engineering showed that although the number of female engineers
>
> **16)** _____ **17)** _____ (increase) since the 1980s, this rise
>
> **18)** _____ not **19)** _____ (be) as steep as that of women teaching STEM.

1g Answer the questions (1–6) for this graph. Write at least one full sentence for each answer, using a suitable verb tense.

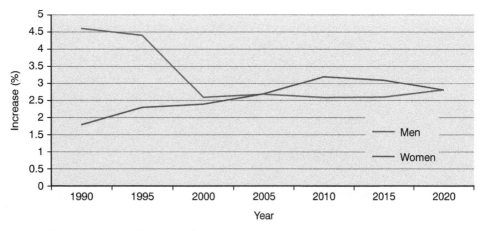

Figure 1: Pay increases by gender

1 What is the general trend shown in women's pay increases from 1990 to 2015?

_____

2 What is the general trend shown in men's pay increases from 1990 to 2015?

_____

3 When did men's pay increases drop most significantly?

_____

4 What was the trend in men's pay increases before it fell in 1995?

_____

5 What was the trend in women's pay increases before it began to fall in 2010?

_____

6 What predictions can be made regarding future pay increases?

_____

1h Work in small groups. Use the data in Table 1 on p.36, as well as any other information you have gathered during your studies, to discuss the changing position of women in SET in the UK (sciences, engineering and technology – a common alternative to STEM) and to make predictions about future trends. Write notes below. You will return to these notes in a later exercise.

Table 1: Proportion of women SET graduates by subject; Great Britain; autumn quarters, 1997, 2000 and 2004

	1997	2000	2004
Medical-related subjects	66	70	71
Biological sciences	47	47	58
Medicine	36	38	43
Agricultural sciences*	22	28	43
Technology	13*	24	35
Physical/Environmental sciences	22	24	29
Mathematical sciences and computing	27	25	25
Architecture and related studies	18	20	21
Engineering	4	4	7

Source: Labour Force Survey (n.d.) in Marriott, B. (2006). *Special Feature: Scientists, Engineers and Technologists in Great Britain.* Retrieved from http://www.statistics.gov.uk/articles/labour_market_trends/SET.pdf

Working age (16–59/64) and single subjects only.

Note: * Denotes estimates that are based on small sample sizes and are therefore subject to a margin of uncertainty. They should therefore be treated with caution.

Notes
General trends in 1990s and 2000s: Situation of women in SET at specific points in time: • 1997 – • 2000 – • 2004 –   Future predictions regarding women in SET:

2 Comparing data using the discourse markers *while* and *whereas*

2a In 2010, some students discussed the data in 1h. Listen and find out which trends they mention.

2b Check your answers with a partner.

> The discourse markers *while* (or *whilst*) and *whereas* are used to show contrast between two ideas within the same sentence.
>
> ***Example***
>
> (Contrasting two ideas in the same sentences.)
>
> *While the graph confirms that women's participation in STEM subjects is increasing overall, the table suggests that in some cases this isn't actually happening.*

2c Listen again. This time, complete the extracts below with one word in each gap that each student uses to show a contrast.

    1 _____ the graph confirms that women's participation in STEM subjects is increasing overall, the table suggests that in some subjects this isn't actually happening.

    2 _____ the proportion of female students might be rising there, it's doing so very slowly.

    3 ... numbers are very low in some subjects, _____ in other subjects the proportion of women appears to be booming.

    4 And what about the fact that, _____ women do still form the minority in most of the subjects listed, they outnumber men by far in medical-related subjects ...

2d Work in pairs. Look at the answers you wrote in 2c, and answer these questions.

    1 Where are *while* and *whereas* placed in the sentence and in relation to the ideas they are contrasting?

    2 What discourse marker(s) could you use if you wanted to show contrast between two separate sentences?

2e Refer back to the notes you made in 1h. Review the differences you found between 1997, 2000 and 2004. Describe three interesting contrasts in the data, using *while* and *whereas*.

e.g. While the number of women studying engineering has increased, the overall number of women studying this subject is still very small.

1

2

3

3 Comparing data using multiple values and fractions

Numbers are also often compared and contrasted by using multiple values and fractions. For example, in the Audio you heard:

- almost <u>three times as many</u> women now study technology as in 1997
- isn't it strange that the proportion of women in medicine is much lower – just about <u>half as many</u> as those studying medical-related subjects

Use Table 1 in 1h to compare the following, using multiples.

1 The proportion of women studying engineering in 1997 compared to 2004.

2 The proportion of women studying architecture and related subjects in 2004 compared to those studying engineering in 2004.

3 The proportion of women studying architecture and related subjects in 2000 compared to those studying engineering in 2000.

4 The proportion of women studying physical/environmental sciences in 2004 compared to the proportion of women studying medicine in 2004.

▶ LESSON TASK 4 Analysing and discussing statistical data

4a Prepare for a group discussion about women in STEM. Work in small groups. Identify any trends in the data on pp.39–40. Identify any contrasting data – either within this information or contrasting with research you have previously done on the topic.

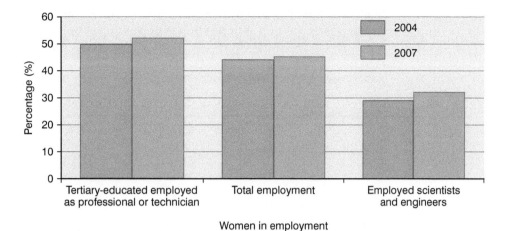

Women in employment

Figure 2: Proportion of women in the EU-25 for different employment categories in 2004 and 2007.

Source: European Commission She Figures, 2009

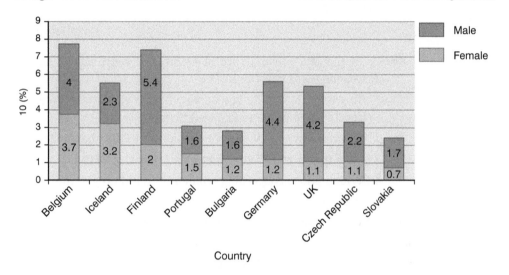

Country

Figure 3: Proportion of scientists and engineers in total labour force by sex, 2004

Source: European Commission She Figures 2006

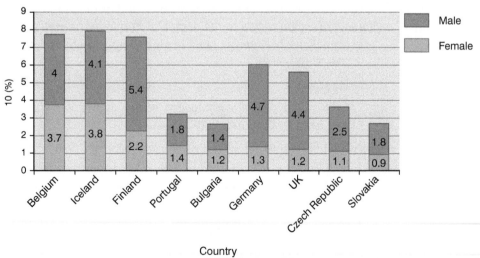

Country

Figure 4: Proportion of scientists and engineers in the labour force by sex, 2007

Source: European Commission She Figures, 2009

Table 2: Gender pay gap by selected occupations in the EU-25, in 2006

Occupation	Gender pay gap
Legislators, senior officials and managers	30
Corporate managers	30
Managers of small enterprises	28
Professionals	
Physical, mathematical and engineering science professionals	22
Life science, health, teaching and other professionals	33

Source: European Commission She Figures, 2009

4b Using the data you analyzed in 4a, support your ideas in a group discussion, answering these questions.

1 To what extent to do you agree with the view that women's position in STEM continues to be overshadowed by men's?

2 In what ways has women's position in STEM changed?

3 How would you predict women's postion in STEM to change in the future?

4 Which issues concerning women in STEM do you think need addressing most urgently?

4c Join with another group. Discuss the questions in 4b, with reference to the data.

5   Review and extension

Verb tenses and comparing and contrasting data

5a Take some of the data you have found during your own studies (ideally data that you will use to support a discussion or oral presentation). Write five sentences to show the main trends in the data, and to refer to important events at specific points in time. Refer back to the table in 1d to help you check that you have used the correct verb tenses.

Examples

The data shows that the number of women applying to study engineering was in fact falling between 2005 and 2008.

30% of women applied to study engineering in 2005, whereas only 23% did in 2008.

1 _____

2 _____

3 _____

4 _____

5 _____

5b Identify some of the contrasts in this data and write five sentences using *while* and *whereas*.

1

2

3

4

5

Bring your data to the next class. Your teacher might ask you to present some of the contrasts orally to the class.

Stative and dynamic uses of verbs

5c Read the sentences and for each sentence underline the verb form you think is correct.

1 Many women currently *believe / are believing* STEM to be a route to more secure employment.

2 An understanding of what factors *influence / are influencing* job satisfaction is critical for a number of reasons.

3 Clark and Oswald (1996) *drew / were drawing* a link between earned income and satisfaction.

4 It is widely accepted that women *tend / are tending* to have greater job satisfaction than men (Mueller & Wallace, 1996; Clark & Oswald, ibid; Hammermesh, 2000; Donohue & Heywood, 2004).

5 If women *do not have / are not having* such high expectations of salary or career advancement as men do, then it follows that they will be more satisfied with less attractive earnings and career outcomes.

6 However, as Hammermesh (ibid) notes, job expectations and actual work experiences *change / are changing* during the course of a career.

7 In a study of job attitudes among US lawyers, Mueller and Wallace (ibid) *find / are finding* that the perception of fair pay between male and female workers is a significant element of female job satisfaction.

8 In conclusion, there is widespread agreement that a gender / job-satisfaction gap *does exist / is existing*.

5d Work in pairs. Compare your answers to 5c and give reasons for your answers.

> There are many verbs which are normally used to express a state (e.g. *believe*) – rather than an action (e.g. *walk*) – and so are very rarely (or never) used in continuous tenses. Some examples are in the table below.

5e Can you add any verbs to the list in this table?

believe	
belong	
like	
mean	
own	
seem	
remember	
understand (and synonyms, e.g. see)	
want	

Unit 1

Part E

Reporting in writing

By the end of Part E you will be able to:

- follow tense patterns in literature reviews
- build paragraphs using *it* as a subject
- build paragraphs using determiners to link ideas
- write definitions of key terms using participle phrases.

1 Following tense patterns in literature reviews

Literature reviews are one of the most common types of academic writing. They may be a significant part of an academic report or you may be asked to write one on its own in order to demonstrate your understanding of the current state of knowledge on a topic.

Academic knowledge is constantly developing, ideas are tested and improved upon, or rejected and replaced, and new ways of thinking about old problems are constantly suggested. Therefore ideas can be quickly superseded. As a rule, the tense that a writer uses indicates whether the information they are reporting is still relevant or not.

1a Work in pairs. Look at the example sentences below. In each one, decide which of the work referred to is:

1 considered more current by the writer

2 considered out of date by the writer.

A Barnes (2009) notes that women tend to have higher job satisfaction than men, though this claim is strongly rejected by Da Silva (2010).

B Cutler (1996) has stated that women are more likely to report higher job satisfaction if most of their colleagues are female. Leib (2007), however, observes that women in high-profile 'masculine' jobs are likely to have similar job-satisfaction views to the men around them.

C Cox (1986) famously claimed that women's higher job satisfaction was the result of lower expectations than men. Recent studies, however, suggest that womens' expectations are similar to their male peers (see for instance White and Levine, 2002).

1b Work in pairs. Discuss which tenses should probably be used for each of the following: ideas which are currently accepted; ideas which are out of date; or either. Put a tick (✓) in the correct box.

Tense	Use		
	Current idea	Out of date	Either
Present simple			
Present perfect			
Past simple			

1c Work in pairs. You are going to read an example literature review on the topic of job satisfaction and the gender gap. Before you read, discuss these questions.

1 What is *job satisfaction*?

2 What factors typically contribute to a person's job satisfaction?

3 From the research you have done so far, how might job satisfaction differ according to gender?

1d Ignoring the underlined words, read the literature review (see **Appendix 6**). Which of the ideas you discussed in 1c are mentioned?

1e Work in pairs. Look at the literature review again. Answer these questions.

1 Which tenses are the underlined verbs?

2 Which of the ideas reported in the literature review does the writer think are more current and relevant?

1f Work in pairs. Discuss whether you think the following information is current or out of date. Give reasons for your answers.

1 Barwell (1976): clear differences between male and female achievement in science and arts subjects in UK schools.

2 Gracie (1982): girls prefer arts and humanities subjects over maths and science.

3 Cox (2010): girls prefer arts and humanities subjects.

4 McGuinness (2012): a growing number of female students enter university to study sciences.

1g Write a short paragraph in the space below, referring to each of the sources above. Use the tense that indicates your feeling about the information.

> There are changing trends in the subjects that male and female students tend to pursue.

2 Building paragraphs using *it* as a subject

Paragraphs in literature reviews tend to include three main categories of information:

a summary of a commonly accepted position in that field, or which summarises the belief of the majority of researchers in that field

b an argument, comment or conclusion by the writer of the literature review on an issue covered by one or more other writers in the literature

c a reference to a specific example or examples and detail(s) taken from one or two key studies on the topic which is being reviewed.

2a Work in pairs. Study the second paragraph from the example literature review (**Appendix 6**). Answer these questions.

    1 Which of the above categories (a–c) are the underlined parts (1–3) examples of?

    2 What does the language at the beginning of underlined parts 1 and 3 have in common?

> [1] It is widely accepted that women tend to have greater job satisfaction than men (Mueller & Wallace, 1996; Clark & Oswald, 1996; Hammermesh, 2000; Donohue & Heywood, 2004). This is often explained in part as being due to women having low expectations of what they will be able to earn, or how likely they are to be promoted. If women do not have as high expectations of salary or career advancement as men do, then it follows that they will be more satisfied with less attractive earnings and career outcomes. However, [2] as Hammermesh (2000) notes, job expectations and actual work experiences change during the course of a career, and so [3] it is unlikely that male and female expectations are uniformly different. This would seem to undermine Clark's claim for low expectations, though findings from a large body of studies following Clark suggest that it is at least part of the reason.

2b Answer these questions.

    1 In the first sentence, *it* is the subject of a passive sentence. Why is a passive used in this case?

    2 What other (adverbs and) verbs with a similar meaning to *widely accepted* could be used here?

> The structure *it* + *be* (+ adverb) + adjective / past participle verb + *that* is often used to introduce a comment, e.g. *It is unlikely that male and female expectations are uniformly different. It* is considered a preparatory subject here: in English, writers tend not to place long clauses at the beginning of a sentence. In itself *it* has no meaning, but it allows the writer to place a longer clause at the end of the sentence.
>
> For example, the sentence below contains two key ideas:
>
> 1 (widely accepted) + 2 (women tend to have greater job satisfaction than men)
>
> This information can be organized in two ways:
>
> 1 That (women tend to have greater job satisfaction than men) is (widely accepted).
>
> 2 It is (widely accepted) that (women tend to have greater job satisfaction than men).
>
> The first sentence puts the longer clause at the beginning, and so is less common in written English.

2c Work in pairs. Discuss how using *it* as preparatory subject helps make the text more academic in style.

2d Look at the example literature review in **Appendix 6** and identify other places where *it* is used as a subject.

> *It* is also used as a preparatory subject in fixed expressions with *seem, appear* and *follow*.
>
> **a** *It seems that* + subject + verb …
>
> **b** *It appears that* + subject + verb …
>
> **c** *It follows that* + subject + verb …

2e Which of the expressions a–c above can you find in the example literature review in **Appendix 6**?

2f Report on the information below, using *it* as subject in the ways shown above. Rewrite the underlined sections only.

1   <u>Many different studies have shown that girls perform better than boys in school</u>. <u>Some data suggests that boys are still outperforming girls in maths, however</u>.

2   Children educated in single-sex schools consistently do better in exams. Parents are therefore increasingly choosing to send their children to such schools. <u>However, there is little evidence which shows that educating boys and girls separately is the reason why their exam results are better</u>.

3   Recent studies indicate that the gender pay gap is now closing much more slowly than in the past. <u>This trend will probably continue unless new laws are enforced to ensure equal pay</u>.

4   <u>Many people believe that boys are more likely to play truant from school</u>. In fact, data suggests that girls choose to miss classes more often than boys. <u>However, boys certainly miss more classes due to suspensions and exclusions because of bad behaviour</u>.

3   Building paragraphs using determiners to link ideas

3a In Unit 3 of *Language for Study 1*, you looked at some of the ways in which academic writers use language to link their ideas. Write as many as you can remember below.

Linking words

3b Look again at the second paragraph of **Appendix 6**. How are the words in bold used to link ideas?

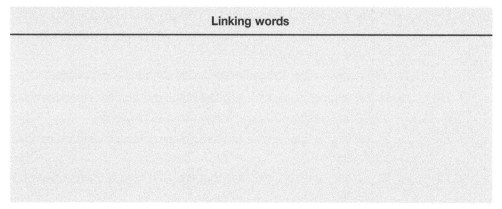

Clark and Oswald (1996) were the first to create a model of the factors involved in job satisfaction. **They** drew a link between earned income and satisfaction, but also introduced the importance of expectations: greater job satisfaction is found where the gap between actual and expected wages is small. Clark and Oswald therefore claimed that the amount of money earned is not, by itself, the most important element of job satisfaction. **This** has become particularly significant in the debate about the sources of women's satisfaction at work, and explanations for the so-called gender/job-satisfaction paradox.

3c Look again at **Appendix 6**. Answer these questions.

1   What other examples of the use of pronouns and determiners to link ideas can you find? Put a circle around them.

2   What parts of the text do they refer back to? Highlight or underline them.

3d Rewrite the two pairs of sentences below to make the links between ideas more efficient.

> **1** Bells and Neri (2008) theorise that one of the reasons for the wage gap is that women are less likely to ask for a pay rise than men. Bells and Neri suggest that the reason women are less likely to ask for a pay rise than men is that they are more likely to consider others' needs before their own.

> **2** One of the earliest researchers to look at the education gap in developing countries was Blum (1984), who suggested that trends then seen in more developed countries would eventually be seen in developing countries as well. However, the theory that more developed countries would eventually see the same trends as developed countries is now much contested.

4 Writing definitions of key terms using participle phrases

4a Work in pairs. Discuss this question.

Why is it important to provide definitions of key terms in academic writing?

> Definitions can be introduced in a number of ways.
> - Phrases such as x *can be defined as* y.
>   *Truancy can be defined as unauthorised absence from school.*
> - Defining relative clauses such as *which, who*, etc.
>   *Truancy, which means an unauthorised absence from school, ...*

4b Work in pairs. Write a definition of *poster,* using the relative pronoun *which*.

> Although relative pronouns can be used to define key terms successfully, shorter phrases are more commonly used in their place. Compare the two definitions of a seminar:
> **1** *A seminar is a type of class which requires students to contribute their ideas based on their research of a topic.*
> **2** *A seminar is a type of class requiring students to contribute their ideas based on their research of a topic.*

4c Rewrite the definition you wrote in 4b, using a participle phrase (*-ing* form).

4d How might you alter the definition of the term 'lecture' below in order to replace the defining clause with a participle phrase?

A lecture is a type of class which is held in order to transmit key information about a topic to students. Students are not usually expected to contribute their ideas.

> A lecture is a type of class ...

4e Work in pairs. Define these terms using participle phrases.

1 gender

2 wage gap

3 'soft' subjects

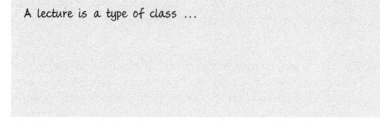 **LESSON TASK**   **5** **Using participle phrases in definitions**

5a Practise defining terms using participle phrases. There is a list of words and phrases below which have been taken from **Appendix 6**. Work in teams. Choose six of these words and write definitions for them on a piece of paper, using a participle phrase.

> **Example (income)**
> This is a term meaning the money coming into a person's bank account yearly through company pay and any investments the person may have.

Words to define		
policy-makers	working conditions (n)	performance (n)
turnover costs (n)	happiness (n)	wages (n)
paradox (n)	expectation (n)	to earn (v)
salary (n)	career (n)	earnings (n)
flexible (adj)	lawyers (n)	fair (adj)
significant (adj)	uniform (adj)	professional jobs (n)
higher education (n)	colleagues (n)	to investigate (v)
critical (adj)	campaign (n)	promotion (n)

5b Exchange papers with another team. Read the six definitions and try to guess which words they have defined.

6 Review and extension

6a Annotate a copy of a literature review which you are currently working on as part of your studies. Make comments (either throughout the text or numbered at the end of the text) on:

1 Your choice of verb tense: which tense have you used and why? This should reflect the guidelines you saw in this class. You might also like to include some reflective comments on how easy/difficult you found these choices to make.

2 Your use of *it* as a subject in passive constructions and as a preparatory subject.

3 Your use of linkers.

6b Choose five academic terms which you are currently using in your studies and write definitions of these, using participle phrases.

Unit 2 **Water**

Unit overview

Part	This part will help you to …	By improving your ability to …
A	**Follow discussions between multiple speakers**	• understand discourse markers • follow lab instructions.
B	**Read for a purpose**	• identify text structure • identify different functions in report introductions • identify recommendations.
C	**Develop your ability to do academic research**	• understand the language of research questions • understand the language of research titles • understand the language of lab manuals and reports.
D	**Participate in group discussions**	• use expressions to manage group dynamics • start and finish seminars.
E	**Write academic reports**	• match sentence structure with purpose • use the past passive to report procedures • structure a technical (lab) report.

Understanding spoken information

By the end of Part A you will be able to:

- understand discourse markers
- follow lab instructions.

1 Understanding discourse markers

> Discourse markers are words and phrases which help conversations and discussions run smoothly. These words and phrases help speakers to signal what kinds of information they want to express. Some discourse markers can have more than one function. For example, speakers may use *Well* to show that they are thinking about what to say next (and would therefore prefer not to be interrupted), or to introduce a new topic to the conversation, or before they make a list of examples.

1a Work in pairs. Discuss these questions.

1 Where do you think most water is used in your country: in the home, in agriculture or in industry?

2 How is water used in these three areas? Make a list of the different purposes for each.

2.1

1b Two students are discussing question 2 from 1a. Listen and complete their conversation with these common discourse markers.

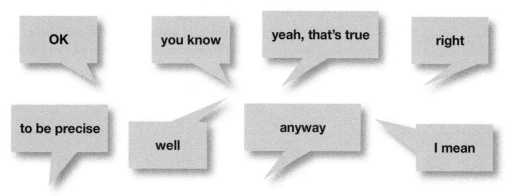

OK   you know   yeah, that's true   right

to be precise   well   anyway   I mean

Student A: 1) _____, domestic use is very high. **2)** _____, especially if people waste water.

Student B: 3) _____. **4)** _____, over 20 per cent of household water's wasted. That's a lot, isn't it?

Student A: True. **5)** _____, now what about industrial water use? **6)** _____, that can be kind of wasteful too. What makes them use so much?

Student B: 7) _____, things like cleaning equipment and washing down factories is a big factor. And chemical companies use a lot, **8)** _____.

Student A: Then there's industrial cooking and food preparation.

Student B: 9) _____, but chemical companies use more. For things like cosmetics and soap and cooling their processes down and stuff.

Student A: 10) _____, let's get some of this information written down, shall we?

1c The table below describes some typical functions of discourse markers. Use the discourse markers from the dialogue in 1b to add examples to the table. Some discourse markers can have more than one function.

Some different functions of discourse markers	
Signal when a speaker wants to speak Well	Signal the end of a topic / a change in topics
Show that you understand what has been said	Signal more information is added

1d You will listen to two students, Mark and Jennifer, discussing ideas on the topic of their next assignment, the impact of drought. Before you listen, work in pairs to discuss these questions.

    1 Which of these natural disasters do you think have the most impact? Why?

        drought   earthquake   volcanic eruptions

    2 How would you define 'drought' for the purposes of an assignment discussing the impact it has?

    3 Tell each other about any droughts that you have read about or experienced. What caused them? How long did they last?

    4 What are the effects of drought? Make a list of at least four consequences.

1e Now listen to the discussion and make notes on Mark's and Jennifer's answers to the four questions in 1d. Then discuss how far their ideas agree with your own.

2.2

1f Now look at the transcript of the discussion in **Appendix 7**. Some of the discourse markers the speakers used have been underlined. Discuss which function(s) they carry out in the conversation. Add any new ones to the table in 1c.

1g In academic writing, *so* is usually used as a linker of cause and effect. However, it is often used in conversation with a number of different meanings and functions. Match the conversational functions of *so* (a–e) with the examples of their use (1–5).

a to signal a change in topic

b to bring a conversation to a close

c to signal an approximation

d to strengthen the meaning of an adjective or adverb

e to show that you agree with some previous information

1 'I found that article about industrial water usage so difficult to understand.'

2 A: … and this means that water will soon be scarce.

B: So, what about food? Will that be similar?

3 'It looks like the population will grow by 20% or so.'

4 A: Look, I think there's a mistake here!

B: So there is!

5 'So, see you at the lecture theatre at 10.'

2 Following lab instructions

2a Match the common objects found in a chemistry or biology laboratory (1–8) with the definitions (a–h).

1 bench	**a** a tube-shaped device which burns gas to heat things in science experiments
2 Bunsen burner	**b** a shallow, flat-bottomed plate with sides and a loose cover, used to grow bacteria
3 flask	**c** an instrument for measuring temperature
4 microscope	**d** an instrument for measuring weight
5 petri dish	**e** the table where scientists work
6 scales	**f** a small glass bottle, often with a long neck
7 test tube	**g** a small, glass, tube-shaped container that is closed and rounded at one end and open at the other, used to mix, heat and store chemicals
8 thermometer	**h** a device that uses lenses to make very small objects look larger, so that they can be examined and studied

2b Work in pairs. Which objects from 2a might be used in each of these experiments (1–5)? Discuss your ideas.

1 an experiment to identify which one of several unknown liquids is water

2 an experiment to find the melting point of ice

3 an experiment to find if heat destroys nutrients in different solid foods

4 an experiment to identify microbes in sea water

5 an experiment involving the heating and condensing of water

2c Listen to a science teacher giving instructions to their students. Which of the experiments in 2b is being described?

2d Listen to another teacher giving instructions to their students. Which of the experiments in 2b is being described?

2e Match the verbs taken from the instructions *for the two experiments* (1–10) with the phrases they collocate with (a–j). More than one answer may be possible.

1 set up	**a** the first sample
2 fill	**b** the Bunsen burner
3 hold (it) over	**c** the resulting temperatures
4 boil	**d** the results
5 repeat	**e** the process
6 plot	**f** any possible reasons
7 compare	**g** the equipment
8 comment on	**h** the flask
9 support with	**i** a stand
10 turn on	**j** the Bunsen burner

2f Listen to Audio 2.3 and Audio 2.4 again to check your answers.

➤ LESSON TASK **3 Following a discussion**

3a Work in pairs. You are going to listen to and then take part in a seminar discussion about how best to manage future world water problems. Before you listen, complete these tasks.

1 Demand for water is predicted to increase considerably over the next twenty years or so. Make a list of the major reasons for this.

2 Discuss whether you think the main demand for water in the next fifteen to twenty years will come from urban or rural areas. Make brief notes on why you think this.

3 Get into groups of four and share ideas for tasks 1 and 2 with students from another pair.

3b Look at the information given on p.56 from a UN source. Does this information change any of the ideas you discussed in 3a? Use the information to add data to support any of the points you made.

Urbanisation 2008   Urbanisation 2030

Urban population
Rural population

Figure 1: Global urbanisation projection

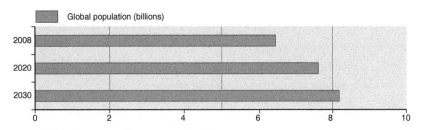

Global population (billions)

Figure 2: World population projection

Water consumption – sources and methods

- Worldwide, agriculture accounts for 70% of all water consumption, compared to 20% for industry and 10% for domestic use. In industrialized nations, however, industries consume more than half of the water available for human use. Belgium, for example, uses 80% of the water available for industry.

- Freshwater withdrawals have tripled over the last 50 years. Demand for freshwater is increasing by 64 billion cubic metres a year (1 cubic metre = 1,000 litres).

- The world's population is growing by roughly 80 million people each year.

- Changes in lifestyles and eating habits in recent years are requiring more water consumption per capita.

- The production of biofuels has also increased sharply in recent years, with significant impact on water demand. Between 1,000 and 4,000 litres of water are needed to produce a single litre of biofuel.

- Energy demand is also accelerating, with corresponding implications for water demand.

- Almost 80% of diseases in so-called 'developing' countries are associated with water, causing some three million early deaths. For example, 5,000 children die every day from diarrhoea, or one every 17 seconds.

3c Look at the seminar handout in **Appendix 8**. Add any further information to your notes from 3a.

3d Listen to the first part of the seminar. Make notes on the economic benefits of access to water and the problems which result from a lack of access to water.

3e Work in pairs. Use your notes to discuss the personal and economic benefits of improving access to water discussed by the speakers.

3f Read the fact file at the top of p.56 and make notes to support your position on each of the main seminar issues in **Appendix 8**.

2.5

Harnessing and managing water

The budget of any nation dedicated to maximising and protecting water should include:

- river-basin development
- storage
- flood-risk management
- environmental protection and pollution management
- water services to households, commerce, industry and agriculture
- waste-water treatment
- maintenance of existing pipes
- research, monitoring and legislation (including compliance and enforcement of laws).

Past problems – countries have over-invested in new facilities, but failed to manage and maintain existing facilities.

Current supra-national targets of a $15 billion a year investment represents half of the financing needed just to meet the needs of supplying clean water, not the needs of sewage treatment.

Costs of not managing water efficiently

Worldwide, the majority of natural disasters are water-related.

Flood damage – both casualties (600,000 between 1960 and 2006 in Asia-Pacific alone) and infrastructure damage ($8 billion in Asia-Pacific)

Yearly economic loss due to extreme events rose ten times 1950s–1990s, mostly water-related.

Subsidence (Tianjin in China lost $27 billion between 1959 and 1993. In China more than 45 cities are under threat).

3g Work in groups to continue the seminar discussion. Choose one person to continue leading the discussion. You should be prepared to report back on the findings of your group.

4 Review and extension

Discourse markers

4a Read part of a discussion between three students about what you should do when you take part in a seminar (on the next page). First, work in pairs and try to suggest which discourse markers might be possible in each gap. Then listen and complete the blanks.

2.6

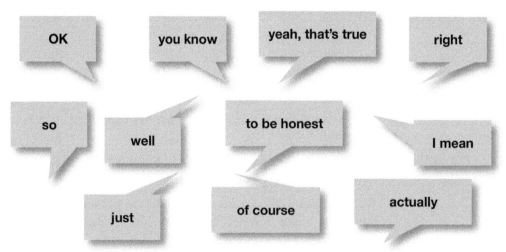

Ali:	What do you think, Simon?
Simon:	1) _____, let's see. 2) _____, I don't find it very difficult: I just listen along and try to understand what I'm hearing. Isn't that 3) _____ what everyone else does? ... Ali?
Ali:	4) _____ no, I think there's more to it than that ... 5) _____, of course just listening quietly is important.
Simon:	Yeah, 6) _____.
Olive:	I always think—
Ali:	But there are other things you can do as well. Sorry, go on, Olive.
Olive:	I always think it's a good idea to, before the seminar, read up on the topic and get familiar with it because—
Ali:	Yeah, yeah, 7) _____.
Olive:	... because, 8) _____, sometimes it's more difficult to know what's going on if it's a topic—
Simon:	If it's a topic you're not familiar with, 9) _____.
Olive:	10) _____, knowing the main points of what you're likely to be discussing makes it easier to follow so you're not trying to listen and think, and understand at the same time. How are you with that, Ali?
Ali:	Yeah, I'd agree with that. 11) _____ what about recording the discussion, is that a good idea?

> *Then* is most often used to show that one event happened after another. However, it can also be used as a discourse marker, especially when it is combined with other words.

4b Match the examples of *then* as discourse marker (1–4) with the functions (a–d).

1 **Right then**! Let's start with the political effects, shall we?

2 **Well then**, it seems that we all agree on at least one thing – that water is vital to all aspects of life.

3 All right, we'll try a search on the Internet. Let's each have a look on the computer tonight **then**, and meet again tomorrow to compare results.

4 Well, it appears to be a rural problem. But **then again** things are changing so rapidly, it could soon become the next big urban problem.

   a often used to introduce a summary of what's been said

   b used to correct something said previously

   c used to introduce a new topic

   d used to show a summary or conclusion

Understanding written information

By the end of Part B you will be able to:
- identify text structure
- identify different functions in report introductions
- identify recommendations.

1 Identifying text structure

Different types of report

Almost all reports follow a specific structure, according to their type.

1a Match these common types of report (1–5) with their definitions (a–e).

1 laboratory report	**a** This gives information about a project, or new facility or system, with an analysis of whether it was effective or not. It will often give measures for improvement.
2 feasibility study	**b** This gives details of how a problem was investigated, including the methods used, the results found and any conclusions or recommendations that can be learned.
3 evaluation report	**c** This describes in detail the procedure followed and the results obtained from a scientific experiment.
4 recommendation report	**d** This looks at a number of circumstances, options and solutions to decide if a proposed action is possible (such as whether a new school can be built in a certain location).
5 research report	**e** This tends to compare two or more options to decide which one is best (such as which of two markets would be best to launch a new project in).

1b Read text extracts A–D below and decide which type of report (defined in 1a) each one is.

A

Hydroelectricity is the production of electrical power by taking advantage of the power of flowing water. It is one of the oldest and most commonly used forms of renewable energy. Hydroelectricity accounts for around 20% of total world energy production and 88% of global renewable power.

B

Ontario has considerable hydroelectric resources which can be developed, and it is hoped that the new Niagara Dam will be able to meet the needs of the growing economy. The Niagara Dam project will produce enough electricity to supply power to over 160,000 homes in the area and will be the first to have a system to capture water which spills over the main structure.

C

The pressure of water through the system was increased by 5 litres/second at intervals of two minutes, and the effects on output measured by electronic sensors.

D

It is clear that the Llanwirn installation is operating at high levels of efficiency. Hydroelectric power is available 24 hours a day. Because of the consistent nature of the supply, relatively low water levels are required to meet the daily total amounts and therefore have low impact on the surrounding environment.

1c Below is a summary of the parts of some different kinds of report. Put the parts in the order you would expect them to follow.

Feasibility study	**Recommendation report**
a evaluation of the plan	a analysis of one possibility
b recommendation whether to proceed with the plan or not	b recommendation whether to use one option or not
c presentation of a proposed plan	c analysis of a second/third, etc. possibility
d requirements that the proposed plan must satisfy	d identification of the problem needs to be solved
Order: 1_____ 2_____ 3_____ 4_____	Order: 1_____ 2_____ 3_____ 4_____
Evaluation report	**Research report**
a justification of why the project was necessary and what existed before it	a what conclusions can be drawn
	b an analysis of the results
b recommendation(s) for future improvements/steps	c a discussion of what the results could mean
c evaluation of how successful performance is from different viewpoints	d description of what research method(s) was/were used
d present performance measures	e the research question and what was investigated
Order: 1_____ 2_____ 3_____ 4_____	Order: 1_____ 2_____ 3_____ 4_____ 5

> Knowing the typical structure of an academic text, and using the subheadings to help you identify different sections, can help you find information more quickly.

1d Work in pairs. You are going to read a report about a system of water supply known as rainwater harvesting (RWH). Discuss what you think this might involve.

1e The report is entitled 'Opportunities in Rainwater Harvesting'. Look at the sub-headings from the report below (A–I) and put them in the order you would expect to find them.

Subheading	Order
A agricultural rainwater harvesting	
B conclusions	
C domestic rainwater harvesting	
D introduction	1
E problems and constraints hampering rainwater harvesting	
F quality of harvested rainwater	
G references	
H rainwater harvesting techniques	
I rainwater treatment for domestic rainwater harvesting	

1f Which parts of the report (A–I) would you read to find this information?

   1 The common uses for rainwater after it has been collected.

   2 Reasons why RWH is not as widely used as it could be.

   3 A comparison of the different methods of cleaning rainwater for drinking.

   4 Typical forms of pollution in collected rainwater.

   5 Information about different filtration techniques.

   6 The conditions needed for collecting rainwater for farming.

   7 Different types of rainwater storage for use in homes.

   8 Information on the costs of storing rainwater.

1g Now read the report in **Appendix 9**. Check your predictions for the two activities above as quickly as possible.

2   Identifying different functions in report introductions

2a Work in pairs. Discuss these questions and make notes summarising your answers.

   1 Historically, there has been a strong link between rivers and the development of towns and cities. Why do you think this was so?

   2 What might be the benefits to cities of investing in improving their riversides and river infrastructure today?

2b Skim read this introduction to a feasibility study to check your ideas from 2a.

Urban rivers as factors of urban (dis)integration

1 Introduction

Rivers have had a crucial part in the emergence of human society, being strongly present in almost every single stage of the human journey. The city was born in between rivers, and throughout history most cities tended to be founded about or near rivers, with notable events along the river course chosen for location, such as the meeting of two rivers, sharp bends, high points overlooking the river, islands or on the river mouth. This is explained in great part by the fact that both agricultural and industrial activities were, up until very recently, heavily dependent on a close and ever-available water source. Trading also relied on waterways.

The emergence of environmental issues and urban sustainability has highlighted new themes for debate: water quality improvement, waterfront rehabilitation and regeneration of riversides, the restoration of natural rivers and streams as part of improving the quality of the urban landscape. Old industrial areas on the margins of rivers are seen as an opportunity to improve the aesthetics of public urban spaces.

In this paper, the relation of the integration between a city and its river is explored at both national and regional scales, to assess the integration of river and city in each location. Firstly, the factors relevant to the city-river system will be identified, in terms of its description, characterization and measurement. It is believed that a better understanding of the current city-river structure, rather than the historical relation, will contribute to a better formulation of policies to enhance the city-river integration and to understand the limits to that integration. The Portuguese subsystem of rivers will be analyzed. The second part of the paper explores the possibilities for greater local integration.

Adapted from:

Silva, J.B., Serdoura, F., and Pinto, P. (2006, September). *Urban rivers as factors of urban (dis)integration.* Paper presented at the 42nd ISoCaRP Congress, Istanbul, Turkey. Retrieved from http://www.isocarp.net/Data/case_studies/789.pdf

2c Work in pairs to answer these questions.

1 What is meant by urban *(dis)integration* in the title? Why might rivers be a cause of disintegration?

2 What is the function of each paragraph? Skim the paragraphs quickly and match them with the correct function (A–C).

   A explaining the structure of the text

   B explaining issues that affect rivers today

   C explaining historical importance

2d Which paragraph would you look at to find this information?

1 the main factors that need considering when evaluating river/city environments

2 the reasons why cities have developed around rivers

3 the main types of urban river improvement currently popular

4 the parts of rivers which attracted settlement in the past

2e Read the introduction again more carefully to check your answers to 2c and 2d.

> Introductions to feasibility studies, recommendation reports and evaluation reports are often similar because they often use the same standard phrases to structure their introductions.

2f Complete the second example of each function with a phrase from the introduction in 2b.

Function	Examples
explaining historical importance	• Historically, there has been a strong link between ... • (X) have _____ crucial _____ in ...
explaining issues that affect rivers today	• Recent research has indicated that ... • _____ of (X) has highlighted _____
explaining the structure of the text	• The main aim of this report is to ... • _____ to (X) will be identified.

3 Identifying recommendations

3a Work in pairs. Discuss these questions.

1 How much water do you drink a day?

2 How much water should a healthy adult drink each day?

3 What factors might affect the amount of water an adult needs to drink each day?

3b Quickly skim read the conclusions to three different reports (extracts A–C) to find which one makes recommendations about the amount of water an adult needs to drink. Then read that extract more carefully and decide how accurate your answers to 3a were.

A

The water quality and conditions of use for greywater and rainwater systems presented in this report are designed to compensate for the lack of a specific standard for their installation and use in the UK. It is recommended that such a standard should be developed possibly by adopting the standard already produced by NSF International in the USA for waste-water recycle/reuse and water conservation devices (this is currently under revision). The resulting standard should be application specific (i.e. based on the category of use of the recycled water) and should incorporate the water quality criteria and conditions of use proposed in this report. It is also recommended that action should be taken to accredit test houses to certify systems using the new standard.

Source: Mustow, S. & Grey, R. (1997). *Greywater and rainwater systems: recommended UK requirements – Final report 13034/2*, DEFRA (p.14). Online at: http://dwi.defra.gov.uk/reesrach/completed-research/reports/dwi0778.pdf

B

In conclusion, we make no recommendations based on how much water people should be drinking each day simply because our hydration needs can be met through a variety of sources in addition to drinking water. The fact is that water is not the only choice for hydration, because people can rehydrate from a number of other foods and beverages such as coffee, tea, juice, fruit and various vegetables. We conclude, therefore, that because people can get adequate amounts of water from their normal drinking behaviour patterns based on daily beverage consumption, they should therefore let their thirst guide them. However, we have shown that water and salt intake are interrelated and we do make a number of specific recommendations regarding salt intake. Healthy 19- to 50-year-old adults should consume 1.5 grams of sodium and 2.3 grams of chloride each day (which is 3.8 grams of salt) and this is required to replace the amount lost every day through perspiration. On the other hand, there needs to be an upper limit of sodium intake due to the effect of sodium on blood pressure and its associated diseases (including stroke and coronary heart disease). We strongly recommend that the maximum average upper limit should be 5.8 grams of salt, although older people, African Americans and other susceptible groups should consume lower levels than this.

C

From the point of view of cost and sustainability, water reuse is to be recommended over desalination. However, public perception of water reuse is a significant issue. Despite the fact that reused water can be purified to a level far higher than ordinary tap water, without public support such a system would be likely to fail, which could have negative consequences for a tourist resort such as Amal Palms, which relies greatly on its public image as an exotic holiday destination. Water reuse for human consumption at the present time seems to be at odds with Amal Palms's image, and is therefore not recommended. However, a combined system of desalination for drinking water and water reuse for irrigation of the grounds may be possible if care is taken to promote the system to visiting guests in a positive way.

3c Now read all three extracts again and identify any phrases used to make a recommendation. Make a list of your answers. The first one (from extract A) has been done for you.

> It is recommended that such a standard should be developed …

3d Work in pairs and compare your list of phrases. Then identify which ones include:
- an active verb form
- a passive verb form
- a verb–noun collocation.

3e Discuss with your partner whether you think the language used makes a difference to the kind of recommendation given.

3f Discuss the difference in meaning between these two recommendations.

- Water reuse for human consumption is not recommended.
- No recommendations are made about using reused water for human consumption.

> **LESSON TASK** **4 Reading to make a recommendation**

4a Work in small groups. Discuss what is meant by the term 'river development'. List all the areas that you think 'river development' might include.

> e.g. lowering pollution levels

4b You have been asked to prepare and write a report discussing the investment in river development in Portugal. A group of experts has already identified the variables involved in making this kind of decision (see below). Work in a small group to discuss and make notes on why these variables are likely to be important.

Feature	Why is this a significant factor?
population and size of the city	e.g. population density important – needs to be large number of people living in area round river for investment to be economic + more local money/taxes available to help finance
river flow	
risks from the river	
bridges	
site of the river	
distance from the sea	

4c Read parts 4 and 5 of the report about urban rivers in Portugal to check your answers to 4b. Add any new information you did not note to your table.

4 The metrics of city-river systems

4.1 Geography and morphology

The recent century has seen a growth in the coastal areas of Portugal, which explains why almost 90% of the cities with rivers are located up to no more than 60km from the sea. Closeness to the sea suggests favourable conditions for the physical and functional integration of the city and river because of the easy access to the water.

4.2 The urban dimension

Generally, most cities with rivers in Portugal have relatively stable populations, with the exception of Lisbon. Rivers play an important role in stabilizing the population. In general, cities with a lower density of population to area may be less suitable for urban river development.

4.3 The river dimension

The Portuguese water system is dominated by four Iberian rivers, the Minho, Douro, Tagus and Guadiana. The river Tagus is an important one as it has ten cities located along it. The river Douro and river Leca have four cities, and the Boco, Ave, Ferreira and Tamega have four cities along their banks. The more cities along a river, the more beneficial investments in improving the water.

The amount of water that flows is also important. The absence of water in small rivers and streams can make impossible or less interesting some activities by people either on water or on their margins, weakening the possibilities for development. In other cases, fast-flowing rivers and rivers prone to flood have a psychological effect on the people, affecting their perception of their safety. A flow of less than 500m^3 per second makes the use of the river viable. Anything above 600m^2 per second may suggest a threat.

5 The city–river relationship

The position of the river relative to the city can be divided into three main types:

Diametral: where both banks are built up – that is, the river cuts through the centre of the city

Eccentric: is used to describe those cities that have clearly a more developed bank, but create a smaller nucleus on the other side of the bank

Tangential: means the river passes outside the city, bordering it on one side.

Diametral   Eccentric   Tangential

In addition to this, further classification was needed of estuaries.

Cities in estuaries: are characterized by exceptionally wide rivers near the mouth. This leads to a naturally lower number of crossings. These cities can have water surfaces up to 42 times larger than average, creating inner 'seas'. This influences enormously the way the city relates to the river, not unlike a seafront. In general, the closer the river to the sea, the more likely the population is to benefit from investment in the river.

An important factor in choosing to develop the river is also the number of crossings. Bridges are important because they allow people to see and to have sensorial contact with the river. Their two main functions are:

Linking: where people can cross the river

Contact zones: where people can wait over the water, watch and enjoy the view.

The width of the river is also important. A river begins to be perceived as a physical barrier when bridges need to span further than 220–330m. Anything greater than this tends to be less pleasant to cross by foot and tends to be traffic oriented.

Adapted from:

Silva, J.B., Serdoura, F., & Pinto, P. (2006, September). *Urban rivers as factors of urban (dis)integration* Paper presented at the 42nd ISoCaRP Congress, Istanbul, Turkey. Retrieved from http://www.isocarp.net/Data/case_studies/789.pdf [pp.5-12]

4d The Portuguese government is considering investing in the development of a river near one of three cities, Tomar, Lisbon or Vila Nova de Gaia. Choose one of these three cities to investigate. Use the information in 4c and the data about each city on p.68 to decide to what extent your city would be suitable for investment in river development. Make notes of your reasons in this table.

City name:	
Suitability factors	**Unsuitability factors**

Tomar

Population:	43,000
Size of the urban area:	350km^2
Name of river:	Tagus
Flow of river:	500m^3 per second
Risks from river:	Dams along route prevent flooding in the city.
Bridges:	five bridges
Site of river:	diametral
Distance from sea:	less than 60km
Leisure possibilities:	picturesque Roman Bridge

Lisbon

Population:	2.4 million
Size of the urban area:	958km^2
Name of river:	Tagus
Flow of river:	500m^3 per second
Risks from river:	Dams along route prevent flooding in the city.
Bridges:	Two main bridges plus rail and tram crossings. The 25th April Bridge is the longest suspension bridge in Europe, the Vasco de Gama bridge is the longest bridge in Europe at 17.2km long
Site of river:	located at the estuary
Distance from sea:	0km
Leisure possibilities:	possibilities of hosting the Olympic Games in the future

Vila Nova de Gaia

Population:	289,000
Size of the urban area:	200km^2
Name of river:	Douro
Flow of river:	714m^3 per second
Risks from river:	Dams along the route prevent flooding in the city.
Bridges:	two main bridges plus rail crossing
Site of river:	eccentric
Distance from sea:	0km
Leisure possibilities:	seventeen blue flag beaches over seventeen km of seaside

4e Work with students who analyzed different cities from you. Share information about the cities and then agree which of the three cities should receive the investment and why.

4f You need to prepare and present a short report to a committee justifying your decision. The report will have the following stages. Make notes on the different stages and think about the language that you are going to use for each part.

Stage	Notes and language
Brief historical background	
Justification for the investment	
Aims and structure of the report	
Variables considered	
Analysis of the first city	
Analysis of the second city	
Analysis of the final city	
Recommendation	

4g In your groups, give a brief oral report of your findings to the rest of the class.

5 Review and extension

Text structure

5a Number these sentences in the order you would be most likely to see them in a feasibility study.

☐ **a** A second option is to build a new pipe in a new location. This also has disadvantages.

☐ **b** In conclusion, it is felt that the option of constructing a new pipe would be preferable to repairing the existing pipe. However, many factors still need to be resolved before work can begin.

☐ **c** Today we face the situation where some major cities, such as London, are supplied by the same pipe that was built over a hundred years ago to cope with much smaller population needs.

☐ **d** Clean water supply has always been the main consideration when developing urban areas.

☐ **e** So, as can be seen, a wide range of factors need to be addressed. The first option is to repair and widen the existing pipe.

| f | This paper will define the factors which need to be considered in analysing the options. It will then go on to analyze the options available to the city of London in replacing its water supply pipe. |
| g | Factors which will affect the choice of pipe have been characterised into three main groups, demographic, geographic and technical considerations. Each of these will be defined below. |

Locating information

5b Read the text below. In which passage (A–D) are each of the following stated?

1 A disastrous consequence of the decrease in the water level caused by the drought.

2 The problem may have a negative effect on the surrounding eco system.

3 Harvests have gone to waste as a result of the transportation problems.

4 Previously water from an alternative source flowed into the river.

5 The local people use the river to transport crops to market.

6 A further disaster may occur as a result of this drought.

7 The lack of rain has caused problems with electricity and lighting.

8 There are few alternative means of transport for the villagers.

Drought in the Amazon Region

A

The rivers and tributaries of the Amazon are crucial to the people who live around them. They are their only connection with the world. There are often no roads in or out of the village and the forests are too dangerous to pass through. The Amazon provides a vital economic and social link to these towns and communities.

It is often crucial for the local economy, too, not only through fishing, but through the use of boats to sell goods such as sugar in neighbouring towns.

B

But river levels have been falling recently and parts of the river are no longer navigable by ships and ferries.

The area has become increasingly volatile in recent years. Only three months before the drought, the area flooded, leaving over 100,000 people homeless. In the past, water levels in the river have been less dramatic because melting ice from the Andes has refilled the area. However, as a result of global warming, the glaciers at the top of the mountains have reduced greatly in size, a trend which is likely to increase in future years.

C

Now over 26 cities are on high alert caused by shortages of energy and water. Huge tankers that are no longer able to move up the rivers were the sole source of fuel and oil in the region. This has led to fuel rationing and power cuts lasting as long as twelve hours a day in some areas.

Crops in the region have been affected by the drought – what produce there is lies rotting on the banks of the dried-up river. Many parts of the region are now only accessible by air. Food shortages in the towns have meant that the cost of food has increased, with some products selling at five times the price before the drought.

D

The lack of water also poses a threat to the local wildlife. For example, the rare pink dolphin is under threat, and many other endangered species depend on these rivers. The authorities have placed the land around on red alert, principally because the dried vegetation poses a high risk of fire, which may have further detrimental effects on local flora and fauna. The drought is likely to have a devastating effect for many years to come.

The language of reports

5c Complete this introduction to a short report on regulating water levels for shipping purposes by writing the verb in brackets in the correct tense and voice (active or passive). In some cases, you will need to include adverbs with the verb phrase. Sometimes, more than one correct answer is possible.

Waterways **1)** _____ (play) a crucial role in the transport of people and goods historically. Rivers **2)** _____ (only recently / replace) by roads and air transport as the fastest and most efficient means of moving things long distances.

In many parts of the world today this **3)** _____ (still / be) the case. The emergence of Asia as a main production base **4)** _____ (renew) the importance of shipping as the cheapest means of transporting large numbers of goods. Many people living in poorer countries still **5)** _____ (rely) on waterways for their day-to-day contact with those outside the community.

In this paper, various means of regulating river levels **6)** _____ (discuss). The first part **7)** _____ (outline) traditional methods of water level regulation. The second part **8)** _____ (consider) projects currently under development. Finally, the report **9)** _____ (recommend) a course of action.

Investigating

By the end of Part C you will be able to:
- understand the language of research questions
- understand the language of research titles
- understand the language of lab manuals and reports.

1   Understanding the language of research questions

> When beginning some research and deciding on the area you wish to investigate, you may need to formulate your own research question; this will be essential to your research proposal. However, there are some differences between research questions based on secondary research and those formulated for primary research.

1a   Work in small groups and discuss these questions.

1   What is the difference between primary and secondary research?

2   What resources do you need for each type of research?

3   For you in your present situation, would the following research questions (A–E) relate mainly to primary research (P) or secondary research (S)?

   A   How has privatisation affected domestic water supply costs in the United States?

   B   How do patterns of water consumption differ from rural to urban areas?

   C   To what extent are international students at [your college name] aware of different world water problems?

   D   What are the social and economic impacts of building wells in villages in sub-Saharan Africa?

   E   What were the immediate effects of the sanitary revolution in the UK in the 1900s?

Primary research questions

1b   Here are some research questions some students have used for small-scale primary research projects. Match the question phrases (1–6) with the correct endings (a–f).

1	To what extent do	a	students aware of the environmental issues surrounding bottled water?
2	What are	b	advertising a major factor in the student purchase of bottled water?
3	What factors	c	students use bottled drinking water?
4	Is	d	the major factors in student purchase decisions of bottled water?
5	To what degree does	e	home culture affect international student attitudes towards buying bottled water?
6	To what extent are	f	affect student purchases of bottled water?

1c Complete two examples of effect/impact research questions by rewriting the groups of phrases into the correct order.

1 [in the Pacific] [of rising sea levels] [on low-lying land] [the environmental impacts] [what are]

_____?

2 [does] [have] [in children under five] [in sub-tropical climates] [on levels of malaria] [rainfall variation] [what effect]

_____?

1d Use the words in the box below to describe the structure of the two research questions.

> additional information / details   auxiliary verb (if required)   main verb
>
> object of investigation   question phrase   subject of investigation

> A noun phrase is a noun (e.g. *impacts, land, sea levels*) whose meaning is made more specific to a particular context by adding words before the noun (e.g. ***the** environmental* impacts, *low-lying land, rising sea levels*) and/or phrases after the noun (e.g. *the impacts **of rising sea levels***). Noun phrases may be the subject or object of a sentence.
>
> A preposition phrase is a preposition followed by another phrase, often a noun phrase (e.g. ***on** low-lying land, **of** rising sea levels*).

1e Identify what kind of information in the completed research questions is represented by:

- a preposition phrase
- a noun phrase.

1f You would like to do some research about student water usage, using the other students in your class as the source of data. Brainstorm a list of possible primary research questions you could investigate.

1g Think of the subject that you intend to study at university. What research question would you like to investigate? Write your question and then discuss your ideas with the others in your class.

2 Understanding the language of research titles

2a Below are some titles of research reports and presentations. Decide which area of study they are most likely to be related to (business, environmental science, biology, etc.).

1 Is entry to the Tanzanian water supply market a feasible option for the Euro Water Company at the present time?

2 The effects of manipulation on the genes of rice plants and saltwater plants in the production of rice grain which will tolerate saline conditions

3 The environmental impacts of rising sea levels on low-lying islands in the Pacific, and an evaluation of the political responses to these problems

4 Redistribution of wastewater acidity using microbiotic fuel cells

5   Water management in rice production

6   The relationship between rainfall distribution and malaria incidence in tropical West Africa

7   Pathogens in water – absent or present?

8   Predicting health risks from recreational water contact

9   The oxidation of two pesticides in natural waters by ozonisation – a comparative study

10 The impact of price on residential water demand

2b Are research titles usually statements or questions?

2c Work in pairs. Look at the grammatical structure of the research titles in 2a again. First, identify the noun phrases and put brackets around them as in the example below. If there is no noun phrase, bracket the noun. Then decide which noun phrases / nouns belong to preposition phrases and draw a circle around them. Then compare your answers in small groups.

NP [The effects of manipulation] PP on NP [the genes of rice plants] and NP [salt-water plants] PP in NP [the production of rice grain] which will tolerate NP [saline conditions]

2d Work in pairs to answer these research title questions.

1   What other grammatical features do you notice in these research titles?

2   Can you identify any common patterns in the structure of these titles?

2e Write the different parts of these questions in the correct order.

1   does / on the activity levels / have / What effect / of water micro organisms / a variation in temperature / ?

_____

2   does / depth / the surface tension / affect / of liquids / How / ?

_____

3   of female natterjack toads / What is / of differing food types / the impact / on the growth rate / ?

_____

3   Understanding the language of lab manuals and reports

3a Match the science projects (1–6) with the general area of science that you would associate them with.

	Chemistry	Physics	Biology
1 developing a fat-free potato chip			
2 carbon dating objects			
3 DNA engineering			

4 new flexible mobile phone cells	
5 identifying the structure of atoms	
6 developing plant-based plastics	

> Although there are many useful subject-specific dictionaries, it is still a good idea to create your own vocabulary logbook with words you come across as you study. Many subjects generate new terminology quickly, and it can take several years for new words to enter a dictionary.

3b Here are some sentences which appear in a science lab manual. Discuss with a partner what the meaning of the words and phrases in bold might be.

    1 Saltwater will then be carefully measured and added **at intervals**.

    2 This is an experiment to **determine** the solubility of sodium chloride.

    3 Temperature is the only factor which will be **manipulated** in this experiment.

    4 We **hypothesized** that the fluoridation of water would lead to decreased muscle mass.

    5 We tested the effects of fluoridation by **varying** the concentrations in water supply.

    6 Ten **specimens** of Rana pipiens were placed in a 12mg/L solution of fluoride.

    7 Ten **control** frogs were given unfluoridated water.

    8 The difference in means was not **significant**.

    9 **Inconsistencies** in the effects of pollution on the frogs were found.

    10 The results here presented have serious **implications** for those involved in testing water treatment operations.

3c Match the words and phrases (1–10) in 3b with their definitions (a–j).

    a something which is examined because it is a typical example of things of this type

    b to make a change in the amount, degree, level or rate of something

    c to suggest a possible explanation for something which has not yet been proved

    d a sample which does not receive the treatment or procedure which the experiment is investigating, in order to provide a comparison with the test sample

    e important or noticeable

    f something which behaves in an irregular pattern or in an unexpected way

    g repeated after particular periods of time

    h something that will have further consequences

    i to find something out through an investigation

    j to change something in order to influence the results of a particular test run

A benefit of recording your own vocabulary in a logbook while you carry out your own experiments is that you can add information on how to use the word (which prepositions are often used with the word, other words it commonly collocates with, synonyms and antonyms, etc.).

3d Complete these extracts from a lab report with the correct prepositions.

Fluoridation of water has been found to have negative effects **1)** _____ certain species of frog. This experiment will test the effects **2)** _____ pollution **3)** _____ frogs. Fluoride was added **4)** _____ water at different levels of concentration. The water was heated **5)** _____ 18 degrees C and was maintained **6)** _____ this temperature in both the test tank and the control tank. The frogs were induced to jump **7)** _____ clapping loudly behind them. This was repeated three times and the jumping distance was defined **8)** _____ the combined total of the three jumps. The mean jump **9)** _____ the test group was shorter than the control group. This will have serious implications **10)** _____ the conservation of these species.

3e Which verb can collocate with all three nouns in each group?

analyze	carry out	confirm	observe

1 _____	research an experiment an investigation	2 _____	your hypothesis your suspicions an earlier theory
3 _____	the data the results the stats	4 _____	a change the specimens no difference

3f Work in pairs. You have been asked to test this simple hypothesis. Discuss the experiment you would design to test this hypothesis.

Carbon dioxide freezes at a lower temperature than ice.

3g Look at the notes below, which describe an experiment to test the hypothesis in 3f. Change the words in italics to a more suitable word for a lab report by choosing from the box.

carry out	observed	flask/tube	confirm	hypothesis	at intervals

We decided to **1)** *do* _____ a research project to test the **2)** *possible explanation* _____ that carbon dioxide (CO_2) freezes at a lower temperature than water (H_2O). Carbon dioxide gas will be put into a sealed **3)** *glass* _____, and the temperature will be lowered gradually in a freezing chamber. The temperature will be recorded **4)** *after particular periods of time* _____, and when ice crystals start to form on the sides of the glass it will be recorded. The experiment will be repeated with H_2O, with the freezing temperature being **5)** *watched* _____. We predict that the results will **6)** *agree with* _____ our original hypothesis.

Understanding the scientific method

3h Work in pairs. Below are key concepts relating to the scientific method. Use a dictionary to check the meaning of each word.

the scientific method	variables	independent variable	dependent variable	control
pilot study	inductive reasoning	generalisation	validity	reliability

3i Read through this description of the scientific method. Add the sentences or phrases (A–J) to the blanks (1–10) in the passage.

A ... manipulated or changed in some way

B These are small-scale tests of the experiment which help to ensure that there are no major problems in the design of the experiment

C ... is one which gives the same – or very similar – results each time it is repeated

D ... by carrying out measurement and observation to test hypotheses and predictions about the world

E ... independent variable

F ... the conditions of each experiment must be exactly the same so that only the independent variable affects the plant growth

G ... things which can change and affect each other in some manner

H ... must be able to make sure that they are studying only the variables that they want to study

I ... generalisations ...

J ... dependent variable

The scientific method

Much academic research attempts to follow the scientific method, meaning that researchers generate knowledge on a topic **1)** _____. However, it would be misleading to claim that observation always precedes hypotheses – in fact, the scientific method is a continuing cycle: hypotheses and predictions are developed, then tested and the results observed, then the results of these tests and observations are used to develop new hypotheses or strengthen existing ones. In this way scientists are able to develop knowledge about the way the real world works.

The scientific method relies on data as the basis of all knowledge. In many disciplines, the observation and measurement of data are carried out through tests or experiments. Experiments can be carried out in a number of ways depending on the discipline. For instance, in the natural sciences such as physics, chemistry and biology, experiments would normally be carried out in laboratories, while in disciplines such as social sciences, questionnaires might be given to participants in a survey.

The researcher is interested in observing the relationship between variables, or **2)** _____. Some variables are manipulated or deliberately changed by the researcher, and the effects of this change on other variables are observed. Independent variables are elements in an experiment which are **3)** _____. The researcher then observes the effect of this change on the dependent variable. For instance, in a study of the amount of water required for plant growth, researchers might vary the quantity of water given to several plants in order to see how well each plant grows. The quantity of water given to each plant is the **4)** _____; the amount that each plant grows by is the **5)** _____.

The design of experiments is critical to their validity. The researcher **6)** _____. For instance, in the research about plant growth, other variables such as temperature, soil quality, and light – which could affect the results – must be controlled: **7)** _____.

For this reason, pilot studies are often carried out before a main study. **8)** _____.

The data, or findings, from a piece of research are related to the real world through inductive reasoning: the researcher interprets the data and evidence that they have gathered, and uses this limited information to make 9) _____ about how the world works. For instance, in the study of plant growth, the researcher might study only 30 plants, but then use the data they have gathered to make a general hypothesis about how water quantity affects the growth of all plants of that type. The researcher can then use this hypothesis to make predictions about how plants will grow depending on the quantity of water they are given.

Scientists tend to be cautious about what they discover. They do not accept claims and hypotheses based on a single study; instead, studies are often repeated to build up enough evidence to be reasonably certain that the hypotheses are correct. The ability to repeat experiments in order to test the hypotheses and predictions is vital for good science, therefore the reliability of experiments is essential. A reliable experiment 10) _____. Experimental results which are not reliable must be abandoned.

3j Work in pairs. Think of an experiment to test the effectiveness of swimming as a recreational activity in reducing high blood pressure. What problems with the experimental design would you have, having read the information above? Use some of the language you have studied in this unit to complete the table below.

State your hypothesis:

Issue	Problems	Action to improve this
reliability		
validity		
sample size		
dependent variable		
independent variable		
other variables which need to be controlled		

3k Report back to the class on your ideas. Check that wherever possible you are using the terminology of scientific research.

> **LESSON TASK** **4 Discussing the effectiveness of a scientific experiment**

In this section, you will use the language you have studied to discuss the validity of an experiment using water.

4a Work in small groups. Discuss these questions.

A Most soft drinks are a solution. What kinds of things are dissolved in them?

B Make a list of at least five other kinds of solutions you commonly come into contact with, or make, in everyday life.

C What happens if you put a spoonful of sugar into a cup of tea? What happens if you put ten spoonfuls in?

D Most scientific experiments are done using distilled water. What is this? Why is it used for this purpose?

4b Work in pairs. Use words from this word family to complete the sentences (1–5).

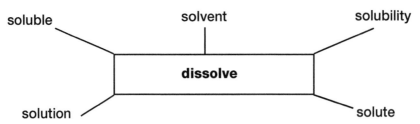

1 _____ describes something that can be dissolved.
2 A _____ is the liquid in which a solute is dissolved to make a solution.
3 _____ is the extent to which something can be dissolved.
4 A _____ is a solid added to the solvent.
5 A _____ is the result of adding a solute to a solvent.

4c Create similar diagrams for these words.
- saturate
- dilute

4d Here are the introduction and background to a simple experiment involving water. Underline any of the word forms above. Check the meaning of some of these by using the context given.

> Saturated solutions are achieved when enough solid material is added to a liquid medium to prevent any more material from dissolving in the liquid.
>
> For instance, copper sulphate makes a dilute solution when it is added to water. The solution becomes increasingly concentrated as greater quantities of the solute (in this case, copper sulphate) are added, until finally the water reaches a point where it is unable to dissolve any more. This state is known as a saturated solution and the point where nothing else can dissolve is called the saturation point.

4e Look at the hypothesis and materials section of an experiment to test the solubility of salt (sodium chloride, or NaCl) in water. Work in pairs to formulate a research question for the experiment.

> ### The experiment
> Research question
>
>
> Hypothesis
> That the saturation point of water will increase as temperature increases.
> Materials
> electronic scales, distilled water, glass jars and sodium chloride (salt), thermometer, bunsen burner, tripod, spoon

4f Work in pairs. Using the materials given, discuss and make notes on the procedure you would use to carry out the experiment. Write these in the form of numbered instructions that other students could follow. Compare your ideas with another pair by using your notes.

Procedures

e.g.
1 Pour some distilled water into a glass jar.

4g Here is part of a lab report, showing the method followed by a group of students. Discuss how effective you think the experiment would be if done like this. Make notes in the table below identifying any problem areas and areas for improvement.

Method

About 1 cm of water was poured into four different jars. The uncovered jars were then heated to different temperatures (30 °C, 37 °C, 40 °C and 55 °C) and each placed on a tripod. To control the variables, salt was carefully added to each jar at the same time. A spoonful of salt was added, one spoonful at a time, and the solution was stirred vigorously so that the salt could dissolve. Spoonfuls were added until a saturation point was created (i.e. no more salt would dissolve). The jars were then weighed and the weight of each jar was compared to see which one had dissolved the most salt.

Issue	Problems	Action to improve this
reliability		
validity		
sample size		
independent variable		
dependent variable		
other variables which need to be controlled		

4h Work in two groups. Use the information about equipment and background provided to discuss how you would carry out the experiments below.

Group A – Experiment A

Group B – Experiment B

Experiment A

Background

If you are a swimmer, or know anything about diving and underwater exploration, you will be aware that there seems to be a relationship between deeper water and pressure. Design an experiment that could help you prove or demonstrate what this relationship is.

Materials

- large tin, oil drum or plastic container (cylindrical in shape)
- hammer and nails for making holes
- ruler (or tape measure)

Experiment B

Background

You may have noticed that objects which don't float seem to weigh less when they are underwater than when they are held outside the water. For example, if you pick something up from a swimming pool floor, it seems to be lighter than when you pick it up normally on land. Design an experiment that could help you prove that this is true.

Materials

- full bucket of water
- pan (or similar) to catch overflow water
- scales
- object which doesn't float but which also doesn't sink right to the bottom

4i Write up the first part of the lab report (below) as if you had done the experiment.

Title: Experiment to demonstrate ...

General background / Introduction

Research question

Hypothesis	
Materials	
Method	

4j Exchange lab reports with a pair who did a different experiment. Critically analyze their experiment using this table and give them any feedback.

Issue	Problems	Action to improve this
reliability		
validity		
sample size		
other possible variables		

5 Review and extension

The language of scientific research

5a Match the words (1–8) with the definitions (a–h).

1 reliable	**a** a false drug to ensure that psychological effects are not being measured
2 valid	**b** a relationship between two or more variables
3 correlation	**c** something that will have further consequences
4 causality	**d** testing what you claim to be testing
5 placebo	**e** something which is examined because it is a typical example of things of this type

6 population	**f** a relationship of cause and effect
7 specimen	**g** likely to produce the same results if the test were repeated
8 implications	**h** the number of subjects (people or things) involved in the study

5b Here are some procedure instructions for an experiment to test the effect of water level and capillary action of water up a tube. Fill in the blanks with words from the box.

> examine   half fill   tape   repeat   pour   plot   ~~wrap~~   make   record   place   pull out

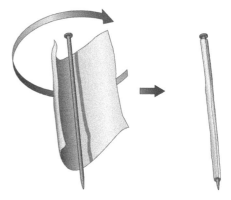

1 _____Wrap_____ a plastic sheet around a knitting needle.

2 _____ the edges so that a narrow tube is formed, then _____ the knitting needle.

3 _____ sure the plastic tube is not bent and is open at both ends.

4 _____ the glass with water and _____ in some food colouring.

5 _____ your plastic tube into the glass of water.

6 _____ the tube carefully and _____ the height that the food colouring moves up the tube.

7 _____ the same experiment with varying levels of water in the glass.

8 Record the results for the different amounts of water and finally _____ them all on a graph.

5c Now use the instructions above to write up the method as part of a lab report using past passive.

Method

A plastic sheet was wrapped around a knitting needle.

Reporting in speech

By the end of Part D you will be able to:

- use expressions to manage group dynamics
- start and finish seminars.

1 Using expressions to manage group dynamics

1a Work in small groups to brainstorm forms of water transport.

1b Answer the questions in groups.

1 Does your home town or the town you live in now rely on water for transport in any way? How?

2 What common items around the home do you think have relied on water transport at some time during their production?

3 What would be the consequences of not being able to transport goods by ship?

4 Have you ever been on a cruise holiday? What do you think might be the attraction of a cruise holiday?

1c List the possible benefits and disadvantages of shipping goods rather than using road or air transport.

1d Listen to five extracts from a seminar led by a teacher in which students are considering the importance and impact of water transportation. Identify the main topic of each extract from the list below (note: there is one extra topic which you do not need).

a factors influencing the popularity of shipping

b risks of shipping goods

c future trends in the transportation of goods

d environmental impact of shipping

e developments in ship technology

f economic significance of shipping

1e Work in pairs. Make a list of functions (that is, actions which speakers must be able to do) which are useful for managing group dynamics in a seminar.

Functions for managing group dynamics in a seminar

Invite others to speak

2.8

1f Here are nine extracts from the discussion in 1d. Listen and read. For each underlined phrase, say which of the following functions (A–E) they perform.

	1	2	3	4	5	6	7	8	9

A getting a conversation back onto the main theme

B inviting other students to speak

C offering turns to another student

D referring to a reading text or other information source

E requesting further information

1 <u>As it says in the reading text</u>, shipping traffic has never been higher.

2 If over 25,000 people are currently working at sea – <u>well, the reading doesn't say</u> how many people were employed directly at home, but I'm guessing it's at least four times as many as that.

3 <u>So, do you think</u> that sea transport is popular now because of environmental concerns over air transport?

4 Charlotte, <u>did you have any views on this</u>?

5 Charlotte, <u>did you find anything else</u> on the size of modern ships <u>when you were doing your research</u>?

6 That's interesting, but I <u>think it's going a little off topic</u>.

7 <u>So does anyone have any opinions on this</u>?

8 Sorry, <u>you go ahead</u>, Greg.

9 Sorry, Charlotte, <u>you had something you wanted to say</u>?

If a discussion is going well, students will be offering opinions, challenging the statements of others and possibly even asking questions of their own to elicit the views of others. However, sometimes participants in discussions need to encourage others to contribute, and may sometimes need to manage the turns so that everybody has an equal chance to speak, or make sure the discussion stays on topic. Below are some phrases which can help do this.

1g Match phrases 1–8 with the possible situation where you could use them (a–d).

1 Martin, have you found this to be true in your country?

2 OK, well, I think we have to move on to the next topic now.

3 OK, let's look at it another way.

4 I'd like to know what the others think about this.

5 Try to think of it from a personal perspective. Have you personally ever …

6 Magda, I wondered what you thought about this.

7 I'm sure some of the others in the group have an opinion on this.

8 OK, we have a lot to get through so let's leave that topic there and consider …

Managing people in a group discussion	
Possible situation	**Phrase(s)**
a One student is dominating the discussion too much.	4, 7
b One student is silent.	
c Nobody has an answer to a question.	
d The conversation is going on too long.	

> It is important to show you have been listening to others and that you respect their opinion, even if you disagree with them or would like to make a different point. Proficient speakers do this by acknowledging the other speaker's comment before commenting on or paraphrasing the other speaker's last point.

2.9

1h Listen to a short extract of three students, Yumi, Ahmed and Trang, discussing the importance of the cruise industry to tourism. Make notes on these questions. Then compare your notes in pairs.

1 Yumi speaks first – what is her main point?

2 How does Ahmed respond to Yumi?

3 How does Trang respond to Ahmed?

2.9

1i Listen to the extract again and complete the blanks with the exact words you hear each speaker say (contracted words fit one blank only).

Ahmed: Hmm, _____ _____, _____ show no signs of _____

_____ _____ _____. I think it's because …

Trang: _____, _____. _____ is probably ____ _____.

Maybe even the best thing about …

1j Work in pairs. For each mini-dialogue (1–3) below, think of a suitable way of commenting on or paraphrasing Student A's main point before Student B can continue with their own ideas. Write down Student B's possible response in the space provided.

1 Student A: I think that the popularity of cruise ships depends on the country you come from. Of the 12.8 million passengers who took a cruise in 2009, about 10.5 million of those were from North America.

Student B: _____. Cruises are not very popular with people in my country.

2 Student A: The Caribbean is still the most popular destination for people who go on cruises. Over 40% of all the cruises around the world stopped over in the Caribbean.

Student B: _____. The Caribbean is truly outstanding and not far for North Americans to travel to.

3 Student A: Ships need to be able to offer state-of-the-art facilities, which make most hotels look rather dull by comparison. They have surf pools, planetariums, ice rinks, golf simulators, and kitchens where celebrity chefs offer cookery classes. They even have billiard tables which are self-righting, so the balls don't fall off.

Student B: _____. It's possible to rent a villa on the ship, with your own private pool if you have enough money.

2 Starting and finishing seminars

2a Work in small groups. Cover the table in activity 2b, and make a list of what you think are the busiest five ports in the world in order of tonnage. Compare your ideas with other students. Justify your choices.

2b Look at the list of the top five busiest ports in the world in 2008. Work in pairs. Discuss these questions.

1 How many of the top five ports are in China?

2 Why do you think China features so heavily in the prominent shipping ports?

3 Discuss possible reasons why Singapore and Rotterdam are ranked highly in this list.

The world's busiest ports 2008	
Name	**Tonnes of goods shipped annually (millions)**
Singapore	515
Shanghai	508
Rotterdam	421
Tianjin	365
Ningbo	361

Source: American Association of Port Authorities, 2008

Beginning a seminar

2.10

2c Listen to the introduction to a seminar discussing the need to modernise a port. Write notes on these questions (you will need these notes later).

1 What is the definition of port industry?

2 What is the direct value of the port industry to the state of Louisiana?

3 What other companies may depend on the existence of a port?

It is the responsibility of the person leading the seminar to ensure that the participants are motivated. One way of maintaining motivation is through lively, conversational speech. It is easier to speak with more natural intonation if you speak to your audience using your notes to support you, rather than reading from a prepared script.

2d Work in pairs. Use your notes from 2c to practise giving an introduction to the seminar about Louisiana's ports. Use your notes only as an aid for your memory; concentrate on making eye contact with, and speaking directly to, your audience.

2e Read this introduction to a seminar on the possibilities of developing a marina in a tourist town. Write notes of the key points to use as prompts when giving the introduction.

Marina development in Poole

Yachting has developed considerably in the last 20 years. It continues to attract increasing investment and larger numbers of people. The marina facilities appeal to those coming down from London. However, they are generally not utilised by locals. The expansion of the marina is expected to improve the amenities in the surrounding areas and should attract considerable spending both on yachting equipment and related economic activity, such as restaurants and bars. Expansion is necessary to allow larger yachts to berth at the harbour, as the water at the site is currently not deep enough for larger vessels. This seminar aims to discuss whether further expansion of the marina is desirable.

Notes

2f Referring only to your notes, give the introduction to your classmates. Use your notes only as an aid to your memory; concentrate on speaking directly to your audience.

> When preparing for a seminar, you can use statements that you find in your preparatory reading as the basis for asking questions about the key issues of the seminar topic. For example, if you find the sentence 'The development benefits the local inhabitants in a variety of ways' in your reading, you could use this to ask the question 'In what ways does the development benefit the local inhabitants?' during the discussion.

2g Read the following extracts (1–6) from the preparatory reading for a seminar discussion. Then write questions for each one that could be used to raise some key issues about the marina development in 2e.

1 The development will threaten the wildlife in the nearby nature reserve.

_____

2 The current facilities are inadequate.

_____

3 The development will allow the town to host sporting events.

_____

4 A new marina will regenerate the area alongside the port.

_____

5 Visiting yachts inject a large amount of money into the town's economy.

_____

6 It is unclear who would fund this venture.

_____

Ending a seminar

As a seminar is an opportunity to learn from others, you will need to record and be able to recall what was said during the discussion. It is often the seminar leader's responsibility to summarise the main points at the end of the discussion. This provides time for those participating in the discussion to make a note of the main points.

2h Match the expressions (1–3) with their functions (a–c)

Summarising a seminar	
Expression	**Function**
1 It was generally agreed that ... There was a broad consensus that ...	**a** expressing individual views
2 Some felt that ... It was suggested that ...	**b** expressing agreement
3 It was impossible to reach a consensus on ... There was little common ground among the participants on the matter on ...	**c** expressing disagreement

2i Work in groups of three or four. Discuss these issues on the topic of hosting water sporting events. One person should take responsibility for each issue by providing a short introduction to it, keeping a record of the main points covered and summarising the main points of the discussion at the end of each issue.

1 To what extent do water sports attract international competition and large audiences?

2 Are there benefits in terms of tourism to hosting large water sports events?

3 How useful are the facilities for holding international water sports competitions to local people after the event?

4 Who should fund international water sport competitions? Why?

In this section you are going to hold a seminar discussion in small groups on this question:

Should the Panama Canal be extended?

3a Work in groups of three. Each student should choose one of the texts in **Appendix 10** (A, B or C) with information about the Panama Canal. Take notes on any information that might be relevant to the seminar.

3b In your groups, use your notes to share information with the other two students. As you listen, extend your notes with any new, relevant information.

3c Quickly read the other two texts to check the accuracy of your notes.

3d Work with students from another group and hold a seminar. One person should act as the seminar leader. Another will need to be prepared to summarise the discussion at the end.

4 Review and extension

Phrases for managing a discussion

4a Complete this discussion on the increase in shipping with suitable phrases.

> **Jacob:** OK, let's move on to the next question. Why do you think ships have become more popular in recent years, when there are clearly so many other alternatives available at the moment?
>
> **Sofia:** I think it's all ...
>
> **Daniel:** I think that ... **1)** _____
>
> **Sofia:** Thanks. Well, I think that it's all to do with the commercialisation of society. We buy more and more products and therefore there's been a general increase in the number of goods travelling round the planet.
>
> **Jacob:** Hmm, interesting.
>
> **Sofia:** **2)** _____
>
> **Daniel:** Yes, well, I agree with you there. I think that it is because of the sheer volume of goods being transported, but it also has to do with the general competitive nature of modern business. Companies have to compete on price, and that means that the cheapest method is the most important. And many developing countries have to offer poor labour standards because they can't afford to ...
>
> **Jacob:** **3)** _____. Does anyone else have any views on that? Gabby, **4)** _____?
>
> **Gabby:** I think it's mainly because access to airports is limited. There is a limited number of planes which can come through an airport on any given day, and most airports are already operating to maximum capacity simply transporting people and urgent goods. **5)** _____ in the reading text, the amount of goods which can be shipped is almost unlimited. New cranes can be installed on the dock side in a matter of months.
>
> **Jacob:** Thank you.

4b Listen to the conversation and compare your answers with what you hear.

2.11

Reporting in writing

By the end of Part E you will be able to:

- match sentence structure with purpose
- use the past passive to report procedures
- structure a technical (lab) report.

1 Matching sentence structure with purpose

1a Work in pairs. Ignoring the underlining for now, discuss the views expressed below (1–5). Do you agree/disagree? Why?

1 <u>There has been an increase</u> in the number of natural disasters in recent years.

2 <u>It is obvious that</u> natural disasters are caused by human activity.

3 <u>For many people living in developing countries</u>, access to water will be a major issue in the coming century.

4 <u>To better understand the situation</u>, considerably more investment needs to be made into researching water supplies before building further pipes and facilities.

5 <u>Following on from work in developing countries</u>, it may be worth researching whether there is a link between low water intake among children and poor concentration at schools in wealthier nations.

1b Match the underlined features of the five sentences in 1a with the correct grammatical descriptions below:

- infinitive phrase
- preposition phrase
- *It* + clause + *that* + clause ('impersonal *it*')
- present participle phrase
- *There* + a form of the verb *be* + noun phrase ('existential *there*')

> In academic writing, you should try to vary the way your sentences begin in order to make your writing more interesting. At the same time, you also need to manipulate complex sentence structures to be able to focus on the most important information.

There is + noun phrase / *It is* + noun phrase

1c Look at these sentences and relate each form to its meaning.

- *There is* a clear need for a wider canal through Panama to allow container ships to pass through.

- *It is* an issue which has not been well received by those living nearest to the proposed site for the expansion.

1 Use _____ + noun phrase – to say initially if something exists or not.

2 Use _____ + noun phrase – to refer to something which the writer has already shown to exist.

1d Complete these extracts using either *it* or *there*. Then compare your answers with a partner.

    1 _____ are many benefits associated with water transportation today. However, _____ is not a method of transport without risks these days.

    2 _____ has been a year-on-year increase in the number of attacks through piracy for the last three years. _____ is an issue which has forced local police teams to cooperate across international waters. However, _____ has been little success in preventing pirate attacks.

    3 _____ were more attacks in the Indian Ocean and the Gulf of Aden last year than worldwide in the previous year. _____ is a worrying trend and has led many companies to abandon plans to sail in the region.

Impersonal *it*

> Sentences sometimes begin with 'it' to comment on a fact or piece of evidence, using either an adjective or a noun.
>
> - Piracy is a threat to modern international economies. This is obvious.
>
>   **It is** obvious **that** piracy is a threat to modern international economies.
>
> - Piracy has increased worryingly in the Indian Ocean. This is not a surprise.
>
>   **It is** not a surprise **that** piracy has increased worryingly in the Indian Ocean.

1e Join these sentences in the same way.

    1 The International Transit Corridor is the safest way to travel through pirate waters. This is widely recognized.

    _____

    2 An international military presence in the area would help to reduce pirate attacks. This is agreed by most nations.

    _____

    3 Pirate activity has increased in the area. This is a fact.

    _____

    4 Victims should offer a robust and positive response to pirates if attacked. This is essential.

    _____

Participle and infinitive phrases

1f Look at these pairs of sample sentences and then answer the questions which follow.

    1a The team were keen to clearly establish the criteria because they knew the problems involved.

    1b Knowing the problems involved, the team were keen to clearly establish the criteria.

    2a The team will measure the time spent on collecting water from distant wells because they want to identify the effect of water collection on children's educational attainment.

2b To identify the effects of water collection on children's educational attainment, the team will measure the time spent collecting water from distant wells.

    1 What changes have been made to sentences 1b and 2b?

    2 Which sentence (1b or 2b) describes something that was known in the past?

    3 Which sentence (1b or 2b) describes an intended result?

1g Change these sentences so that they follow one of the two patterns in 1f.

    1 Statistics will be collected from two neighbourhoods because the researchers want to make a comparison between income groups.

    _____

    2 Water use was reduced by 32% because consumers took the advice offered by local councils.

    _____

    3 The team selected 25 households because they wanted to ensure that their view of the area was representative.

    _____

    4 The researchers will compare the results from the two neighbourhoods because they want to draw conclusions about how income affects water use habits.

    _____

Information ordering

> When writing in English, it is possible to change the emphasis within a sentence by rearranging the order in which the information is presented.

1h Identify the nature of the information the writer wants to emphasize in the sentences below (the time, the process, the cost, etc.).

    1 In the past, desalination has often been associated with unreasonably high costs in terms of capital and technology.

    2 Desalination has often been associated in the past with unreasonably high costs in terms of capital and technology.

    3 Unreasonably high costs in terms of capital and technology have often been associated with desalination in the past.

1i Change the word order in the sentences below to emphasize the idea in CAPITALS.

    1 In-depth surveys of the medical records will be carried out in the primary stage of the research with occupants of 25 households in each neighbourhood.

    THE TIME

    _____

    2 The inhabitants were interviewed in depth in an attempt to uncover details about health problems which may not have been available on public records.

    THE REASON

    _____

3 The team found that poorer neighbourhoods had many more disadvantages with regard to hygiene and water use.

THE FINDINGS

_____

2 Using the past passive to report procedures

2a Work in pairs. Discuss how paper is made.

2b Here are some instructions for making homemade paper (1–6). Using the passive voice and making any other necessary changes, rewrite the instructions as sentences from a lab report describing the procedure.

1 Mix the tree fibres with water.

The tree fibres were mixed with water. _____

2 Add chemicals to the fibre and water solution.

_____

3 Pour the mixture into a mould and stir.

_____

4 Drain any excess liquid from the mould.

_____

5 Turn the rough paper out onto a mat and put it through rollers.

_____

6 Hang the sheet for several days, then coat with gelatine.

_____

2c Often, the purpose of carrying out an action needs to be added. Add these reasons to the sentences above.

a to ensure that the ingredients were evenly distributed.

b to create an easier writing surface.

c to produce a flat interwoven sheet.

d to remove any dark colouration.

e to prepare it for rolling.

f to loosen the fibres.

2d Often, a science laboratory report needs to emphasize the purpose of carrying out an activity rather than the action itself. One way it can do this is by using the structure in the second sentence below. Underline and discuss the differences in word order and form between the two sentences.

The fibres were mixed with water to loosen them.

The fibres were loosened by mixing them with water.

2e Complete these sentences to emphasize the purpose, rather than the action.

    1 Chemicals were added to the fibre and water solution to remove any dark colouration from the paper.

       Dark colouration was removed from the paper …

    2 The mixture was poured into a mould to form the shape of the piece of paper.

       The piece of paper was shaped …

    3 The mixture was stirred to evenly distribute the ingredients.

       The ingredients were distributed evenly…

    4 The water was drained from the solution to create a loosely interwoven sheet.

       A loosely interwoven sheet was …

    5 The sheet was rolled to achieve a smoother, harder consistency.

       A smoother, harder consistency …

    6 The sheet was coated with gelatine to create a smoother writing surface.

       A …

2f The text in exercise 2g gives a sample academic description of the process of making paper. Match the verbs (1–7) with their definitions (a–g).

Verb	Definition
1 form	**a** take something away
2 drain	**b** add a thin layer of something
3 suspend	**c** give something a shape or structure
4 stabilise	**d** make something steady, not changing
5 turn out	**e** mix something in a liquid
6 remove	**f** carry water away
7 coat	**g** empty the contents of something

2g Put the verbs in brackets in the correct form (passive, infinitive or present participle).

Paper making

Paper **1)** _____ (form) by **2)** _____ (suspend) a dilute solution of fibres, such as those from timber, fabric or other sources, so that the water drains away leaving a randomly interwoven mat of fibres. The removal of water **3)** _____ usually _____ (aid) by **4)** _____ (press) the mat to **5)** _____ (extract) water at a greater rate.

Firstly, fibres **6)** _____ (suspend) in a solution of water and other chemicals to **7)** _____ (form) a pulp. Bleaching chemicals may **8)** _____ (add) at this stage. This **9)** _____ then _____ (pour) into a mould, and moved from side to side to **10)** _____ (ensure) that a uniform coating of fibres **11)** _____ (achieve). The fibres **12)** _____ (allow) to **13)** _____ (settle) and the water allowed to **14)** _____ (drain). When the fibres **15)** _____ (stabilise) but are still damp, they **16)** _____ (turn out) onto a sheet which **17)** _____ usually _____ (make) of fur or animal hair. This **18)** _____ then _____ (send) through a press, where the water **19)** _____ (squeeze out) to **20)** _____ (remove) excess water. The sheet can then **21)** _____ (remove) and hung out to dry. Papers **22)** _____ frequently _____ (roll) once they have dried to **23)** _____ (harden) the paper. Often, sheets **24)** _____ (coat) with a gelatine solution when they are dry to **25)** _____ (aid) the adherence of the ink to the paper.

2h Now close your book and summarise the process of making paper orally. Compare your ideas with a partner.

2i Look at these sentences. Underline any passive forms and circle any infinitives. Discuss any changes of tense and omissions you notice.

  a They found that the water in the lake contains high concentrations of nitrates.

    → The water in the lake was found to contain high concentrations of nitrates.

  b Scientists think the island appeared after a volcanic eruption.

    → The island is thought to have appeared after a volcanic eruption.

2j Now complete this table.

Passive + infinitive	
Change the verb of opinion or understanding to the passive form	Change the second verb to an infinitive form
Past understanding e.g. They found that the lake ... ->	Present event / state e.g. ... contains less fauna than other lakes. _____
Present understanding e.g. People think that the lake ... ->	Past event / state e.g. ... drained after an earthquake. _____

Note: There is a limited number of verbs of opinion or understanding which can be used in this construction. Some of the common ones are:

acknowledge, assume, believe, calculate, consider, discover, estimate, find, judge, know, prove, show, take (meaning to presume), think, understand

2k Change these sentences so that they follow the constructions in 2i/2j.

1 Early astronomers thought that the sun went round the earth.

_____

2 People believe that water is an infinite resource.

_____

3 Researchers found that groundwater sources are more reliable.

_____

4 The space probes discovered that Mars has only small amounts of water.

_____

5 They believe that acid rain is responsible for killing large areas of forest.

_____

3 Structuring a technical (lab) report

In this section you will look at aspects of language styles specific to scientific work.

3a Look at the page from a typical high school lab book. Complete the spaces 1–6 with these labels.

Date	Equipment	Conclusions	Method
	Results	Objective	

a

b

Elements and reactions

SOLUTIONS

Saturated solutions are achieved when enough solid material is added to a liquid medium to prevent the liquid dissolving any more.

For instance, copper sulphate makes a dilute solution when it is added to water. The solution becomes increasingly concentrated as greater quantities of copper sulphate are added, until finally the water reaches a point where it is unable to dissolve any more. This state is known as a saturated solution.

Identifying the solubility of a solute

c

1 _____: 1 July, 2010

d

2 _____: to measure the solubility of a solute

3 _____: electronic scales, distilled water, glass jars and sodium chloride (salt)

4 _____: Water was poured into the jar until a weight of 100g was obtained. Salt was then carefully measured and added at 5g intervals until a saturation point was created (i.e. no more salt would dissolve). The solubility of sodium chloride was then determined.

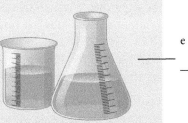

e _____

f _____

5 _____: Sodium chloride was found to have a solubility of 35g per 100g of water. After that point, the water was no longer able to absorb any more salt.

6 _____: It may be worth repeating this experiment with water at different temperatures to see if heat affects the solubility of substances.

3b Complete labels a–f with these descriptions.

i diagram

ii general theme of the topic under investigation

iii the writer's own experiment to test a hypothesis

iv general introduction

v the writer's thoughts about the experiment

vi a general description of a scientific law or principle

Title

3c Look at the title below from a biology report. Match the necessary parts of the title with an example from the title. Then complete the sentence below.

> Effects of variable water quality on the reproductive success of captive Japanese marsh shrimp (*Caridina multidentata*)

Titles	
Necessary parts of a title	**Example**
Factors to be manipulated	
Specific aspect of the subject being focused on	the reproductive success
Specific name of the subject involved in the experiment	

In general, these titles follow this pattern:

Effects of ………… on the ………… of …………(n.)…………

3d Use the pattern above to make titles for these experiments.

Example

The experiment was to test how quickly baby shrimp grow under different water conditions (use the word **rate** in your answer).

> Effects of variable water quality on the rate of growth of captive Japanese marsh shrimp (*Caridina multidentata*)

1 The experiment was to test if changes in the water temperature affected the shrimp's level of activity.

_____

2 The experiment was to test the effects of different food on stickleback (*Gasterosteus aculeatus*) size.

_____

3 The experiment was to test how long shrimp live under different water conditions (use the word **expectancy** in your answer).

_____

Introduction

3e Look at this introduction and complete the useful phrases in the table on p.100.

> ### The effects of variable concentrations of calcium fluoride on the jumping ability of frogs.
>
> Fluoride is a mineral that occurs naturally in most water supplies. Increased concentrations of fluoride have been artificially introduced to public water systems, mainly in English-speaking nations, since the 1940s. It is difficult to control its dosage accurately, however, and it was first reported that it may have negative effects on humans in the middle of the twentieth century (Colquhon, 1998). Further evidence has suggested a negative effect on animals dependent on the water system (Fagin, 1980).
>
> The present study was carried out in order to determine if the fluoridation of water supplies had any direct effects on jumping performance of frogs. It was hypothesized that the fluoridation of water would lead to decreased muscle mass and would therefore result in changes in jumping performance.
>
> We tested the effects of fluoridation on jumping performance by varying the concentrations in water supply to the frogs. Two different species were studied in order to determine whether the effects were similar in different frog populations.
>
> Adapted from:
>
> Biology Department of Union College. (2010). *The effects of jumpamine chloride on jumping performance in two species of frogs of the genus* Rana. *Retrieved from http://www.union.edu/academic_depts/biology/ Jumpamine.php*

Introductions	
Section	**Useful phrases**
Introduction of the subject involved in the experiment	X is a mineral ... It was 1) _____ that it may have ...
Introduction of the experiment	2) _____ if the fluoridation of water supplies ...
Statement of hypothesis	3) _____ that the fluoridation of water would lead to ...
Summary of the experiment	4) _____ of fluoridation on jumping performance by ... Two different species 5) _____ in order to determine whether ...

Materials and method

> The method section should briefly outline the method used in your experiment. Any detailed information which is contained in other documents, such as your lab manual, should be referenced with the relevant full citation. You do not need to copy these details out in your report.

3f Read these two extracts (A, B) from a methods section and match them with the descriptions on p.100.

Methods:

Part A

– 20 specimens of *Rana esculenta*, 10 for experimentation and 10 as the control group

– 20 specimens of *Rana arvalis*, 10 for experimentation and 10 as the control group

– A 10-gallon aquarium

– Fluoride in a 12mg/L solution of water

– Distilled water for the control group

Part B

Ten specimens of *Rana esculenta* were placed in 12mg/L solution of fluoride. Ten control frogs were given unfluoridated water. They were maintained at a temperature of 18 degrees C for ten days in two inches of water. On a daily basis, each frog was induced to jump three times by clapping behind the frog. The jump distance was the combined total of the three jumps. The procedure was repeated with the twenty specimens of *Rana arvalis*.

Methods		
Possible features	**Part**	**Key features**
Description of the experimental setup and all materials used.	( )	Bullet points or list form. Note form only.
Presentation of the above in narrative form.	( )	Full sentences. Grammatically correct and linked.

3g Look at the sample method below. Find examples of the following.

1 trivial information

2 a poorly identified variable

3 unnecessary repetition of information

> The frogs were kept in a small container before the experiment began. Our lab bench received frogs from treatment #1 and these were tested for jump length three times, so that there were three different sample jumps to measure on the floor chart. Bench #2 received frogs from treatment #2. These were also tested for jump length three times, resulting in three different sample jumps to measure.

3h If treatment #1 was a 5mg/litre solution of fluoride, and treatment #2 was distilled water, rewrite the methods section above so that it is more appropriate.

Results

> The results section should start with statements about what you found, not with a table or chart. You should make reference to any tables in your narrative before they appear.

3i Match the features (a–c) with the sections of the results below (1–3).

a brief description of the significant results in the table

b reference to the table

c one-sentence summary of the results

> ### Results:
>
> Species type influenced the effect of water fluoridation on jumping distance (see Figure 1)[1]. Fluoridation has a slight impact on *Rana esculenta*, with a more limited effect on *Rana arvalis*. The mean jump for *Rana esculenta* was 370mm for controls and 320mm for the fluoride-exposed group. The mean distance was somewhat shorter for the treated group[2].
>
> The mean jump for *Rana arvalis* was 390mm for the control group, and 370mm for the fluoride-exposed group. There was no significant difference in the mean results[3].

> Although the author points out significant data in the results, she does not draw any conclusions about the relationship between the two at this stage.

3j Look at the sentences below and join them to form a more coherent sentence, using the language of comparison.

Example

The mean jump of *Rana esculenta* after exposure to fluoride was 320mm. The mean jump of *Rana esculenta* in the control group was 370mm.

The mean jump of *Rana esculenta* after exposure to fluoride was somewhat shorter than the mean jump of those in the control group.

1 The average growth of *Oryza satavia* (rice) engineered with genes from *Ascophyllum nodosum* (bladder wrack seaweed) was 1.2cm per week. The average growth of *Oryza satavia* in the control group was 0.3 cm per week.

_____

2 The reproduction cycle of *Caridini multidentata* shrimp under the treated-water conditions was 26.8 weeks. The reproduction cycle of *Caridini multidentata* shrimp in the control group was 22.3 weeks.

_____

Discussion

> This is usually the most important part of any paper. You should present a clear conclusion based on the results of your experiment. It should contain any patterns that you have noticed, any relationships which appear meaningful, and a reference to how it supports your original hypothesis. If the experiment turned out differently from the way you expected, you should comment on this here as well. It is possible to reach the conclusion that no conclusion was drawn.

3k Look at this discussion section. Complete the table below with sample language from the discussion.

Fluoridation of water has a slight effect on the jumping distance of both species of frog. This supports our hypothesis that fluoridation would reduce jumping ability. However, there are differences between the species in how marked this effect is. For example, in *Rana arvalis*, little reduction in jumping performance between the test group and the sample group was observed. Such variability in the effects of pollution in different species of amphibians has been observed in previous studies (Ashton, 1998; Dexter & Johanssen, 2009).

The results are important for understanding the effect of fluoridation in water ecosystems. A decrease in jumping ability can be expected to decrease the frog's chances of survival. Moreover, this survival disadvantage impacts different species, suggesting imbalances of species in the wild can be expected.

The results have potentially serious implications for those countries which routinely practice fluoridation of water. It is recommended that experimentation on the effects of fluoridation be repeated on other aquatic species with a wider range of test subjects to increase the reliability of data produced.

Language for the discussion section	
Part	**Possible language**
Stating major conclusions	Fluoridation of water 1) _____ the jumping distance of ... This 2) _____ fluoridation would reduce jumping ability.
Expanding on results	3) _____ differences between the species ... For example, in Rana arvalis, 4) _____ in jumping performance _____ . Such variability in the effects of pollution in different species of amphibians 5) _____ .
Introducing new ideas	6) _____ for understanding the ... A decrease in jumping ability 7) _____ decrease the frog's chances of survival. The results 8) _____ for those countries which routinely ...
Improvements in the experimental design	9) _____ experimentation on the effects of fluoridation 10) _____

> **LESSON TASK** **4 Reporting science equipment**

4a Work in a small group. You are going to hold a mini-science fair, designing an experiment and presenting your proposal to the class. Choose one of these science projects.

Project A
Which citrus fruit (orange, lemon or grapefruit) contains the highest water content?

Project B
How does temperature affect the water consumption of mice?

Project C
Does access to scientific data on water shortages change people's water habits?

Project D
How do different amounts of water affect the growth of (a named plant)?

4b Write a specific title for your project here, in the form of a statement.

4c Write the methods section of your project below. Write the materials as a list, and also include a narrative description.

4d Create some results for your experiment (these can be based on what you expect to find). Write a results section, which should include a table, and refer to it.

4e Write your conclusions below.

4f Present your work to the others in the class, using the language of lab reports.

5 Review and extension

Passive form

5a Write the sentences below in past passive form.

   1 Place the liquid in the container.

   _____

   2 Heat the liquid to a temperature of 100 °C.

   _____

   3 Condense the steam in a cooling unit.

   _____

   4 Allow the liquid to drip into a collecting dish.

   _____

   5 Test the liquid with litmus paper.

   _____

   6 Record the results in the table.

   _____

Expressing purpose and method

5b Complete the sentences below with either an infinitive form or a *by* + *-ing* form.

   1 The liquid was frozen _____ (place) it in a cooling unit.

   2 The powder was weighed _____ (calculate) the exact ratio.

   3 The water was removed _____ (pass) it through an oven.

   4 The liquid was heated _____ (test) if it reacted differently.

   5 The experiment was repeated _____(see) if different species produced different results.

   6 The theory was tested _____ (introduce) fluoride into the water.

5c Change the sentences below to passive + infinitive constructions.

> **Builders found the body of a man preserved in the watery mud in Southern Ireland.**

1 At first, they thought the body belonged to a modern-day man, and the police were called.

_____

2 Following carbon dating, they now believe the man dates back to prehistoric times.

_____

3 After analyzing his bones, they discovered that the man was twenty years old when he died.

_____

4 They originally thought that the man died of natural causes.

_____

5 However, they now think he was murdered.

_____

6 They discovered that a mark on his throat was caused by a rope.

_____

7 They think that the man was involved in some sort of religious ceremony at the time.

_____

8 They believe that the preservation of the body for several thousand years was thanks to the boggy conditions.

_____

5d Complete this extract from a lab report with the appropriate form of the verbs in brackets.

> **Identifying the water content of various citrus fruits**
>
> Citrus fruits **1)** _____ (know) to contain high liquid ratios in comparison with other members of the fruit family. The experiment **2)** _____ (conduct) in order to determine which citrus fruits had the highest water content. **3)** _____ (hypothesize) that the larger fruits would have a higher water to weight ratio. The water content of three different fruits – a lemon, an orange and a grapefruit – **4)** _____ (test).
>
> **Method**
> – 1 kilo each of lemons, oranges and grapefruit
> – scales
> – juice extraction mechanism
> – distillation equipment

The fruits **5)** _____ (weigh) so that precisely one kilo of each fruit **6)** _____ (include) in the experiment. Then the fruit **7)** _____ (spin) at high speed to release the juice, which **8)** _____ (collect) in a jar. Then this juice **9)** _____ (heat) over a Bunsen burner attached to distillation equipment. The water which collected **10)** _____ (measure) and the results **11)** _____ (plot) on a graph.

Results

The water content of citrus fruit depended on the type. These results **12)** _____ (summarise) in Figure 1. It is clear from this figure that the grapefruit had the highest water content per kilo. The juice content was twice as high as the figures for both the orange and the lemon.

Unit 3 Progress

Unit overview

Part	This part will help you to …	By improving your ability to …
A	**Follow oral descriptions of processes**	• recognize and use time expressions to show sequence • understand the use of repetition, reformulation and rhetorical questions • use context to understand the meaning of new vocabulary.
B	**Follow written descriptions of processes and flow charts**	• use definite and indefinite articles • recognize and use conditionals in descriptions of a process • recognize and use prepositions with common verbs in academic writing.
C	**Understand writers' positions on a topic and develop and express your own position**	• recognize how writers use connotation to shape opinion • recognize and use vocabulary for describing research methods.
D	**Give an oral progress report, and explain events and their implications**	• use tenses to describe past actions and experiences • use tenses to describe future actions • use language to show a contrast between reality and expectation • use pausing to show attitude.
E	**Compare literature on a topic and write a progress report**	• understand the use of the first person in academic writing • recognize and use synonyms and parallel expressions to compare and contrast other writers' ideas.

Understanding spoken information

By the end of Part A you will be able to:

- recognize and use time expressions to show sequence
- understand the use of repetition, reformulation and rhetorical questions
- use context to understand the meaning of new vocabulary.

1 Recognizing and using time expressions to show sequence

3.1

1a Listen to five extracts (A–E) from two different process descriptions and match the extracts with these situations.

Situation	Extracts
An explanation of an industrial process	
A tutor's demonstration of a process in a lab	

3.1

1b Listen again. Complete the transcript with the time expressions you hear.

A

1) _____ you've disconnected the tube, pour the mixture from the test tube into the funnel. Make sure you get as much of the white product as possible into your funnel.

B

The first step in the mixing stage is to mix the corn starch and water, **2)** _____ which the active ingredient and lubricant are added. The mixture is blended together in a machine known as a Glen mixer, which removes air.

C

3) _____ the mixing is complete, the mixture is compressed into rough lumps known as 'slugs'. The next stage of the process is to remove more air, and any lumps, from the slugs.

D

4) _____ reconnect the rubber pipe and apply full suction for 30 seconds ... OK, that should do.

5) _____ we have these white crystals, you see? **6)** _____ break the suction by disconnecting the rubber tube from the flask.

E

This is done by filtering the mixture through a machine known as a Fitzpatrick Mill.

7) _____ all the remaining air has been expelled, and the mixture is smooth, the remaining lubricant is added ...

1c Which other time expressions can be used in a similar way to those above?

1d You are going to listen to a lecture describing a colour printing process. Work in pairs. What sequence of ideas do you expect to hear? Number the steps in the first column in chronological sequence in the second column. chronological sequence in the second column.

Step	Chronological sequence (my guess)	Actual chronological sequence
The paper is cut into pages.		
The image is transferred from the plate onto a rubber blanket.		
The document is written or the image created.	1	1
The ink is applied.		
The plate is mounted into the printing press.		
The paper is passed through an oven.	7	7
The document or image is transferred to a printing plate (one plate per colour: black, blue, red, yellow).		
The plates are dampened with water.	4	4
The paper is cooled.		

3.2

1e Listen to the lecture. Number the events in chronological sequence in the third column.

1f Listen again. Write the time expressions you hear below.

Time expressions

In the description of the printing process, the lecturer does not always mention the steps in chronological sequence, e.g. *Before the colours are applied, the plates are dampened with water.*

The time expression used (*Before*), its location in the sentence (at the start of the first step) and the verb tense used with it (present simple passive) can help to indicate the sequence of events.

1g Work in pairs. Read the five sentences from the extract below, describing the printing process. Answer these questions for each extract.

- Which two steps in the process are described and which comes first?
- Which verb tense is used in each step?
- Which step also includes a time expression?

1 After the journalist has finished their article ... , it must be transferred onto a printing plate.

2 When the image has been transferred onto the plate, the plate is mounted into the printing press.

3 The images are transferred onto the paper only after they have first been transferred onto a rubber blanket.

4 Before the pages can be cut ... , the ink must be set to prevent smudging.

5 Once the ink has been set ... , the pages are cut and bound.

The present perfect indicates that an action is complete. In a sentence presenting two steps in a process, the present perfect can be used with a time expression to indicate the first step. The present simple can then be used to indicate the second step. The time expressions 'before' and 'after' make the order clear and so the present simple can be used for both steps.

1h Work in new pairs. Use the steps (a–c) involved in preparing for a lab session to help you complete the text with suitable time expressions.

Preparing for a lab session

a Read the lab manual
b Check the meaning of any new vocabulary, in particular lab equipment
c Prepare your logbook by answering pre-lab questions

1) _____ a lab session, you should read the lab manual and check the meaning of any new vocabulary, especially lab equipment. 2) _____ you have read the lab manual, you should prepare your logbook by answering any pre-lab questions.

> With *after*, it is possible to change the order of the two clauses without changing the meaning.
>
> **Example**
>
> **After** *you've disconnected the tube, pour the mixture from the test tube into the funnel.*
>
> *Pour the mixture from the test tube into the funnel* **after** *you've disconnected the tube.*

1i Is it possible to do this with the other time expressions? Discuss with your partner.

1j Complete the steps taken from descriptions of two different processes with suitable time and sequencing expressions from the box below. (Some words can be used more than once.)

prior to	now	after	before	once	when	following

Using the university careers service

We recommend that you show a draft CV to one of our advisers **1)** _____ you send it to any companies.

2) _____ you've used the diagnostic computer programs, you might find it useful to speak to a careers adviser.

3) _____ your appointment with a careers adviser, we add you to our database for your chosen career path.

4) We recommend that you only start to apply for jobs _____ you have attended our CV writing and interview training sessions. This puts you in the best position to succeed.

Taking a patient's blood pressure

5) _____ taking the patient's blood pressure, ensure that they have been resting for several minutes.

6) Ensure that the patient is sitting comfortably, with their arm rested on the table at this height. _____ , put on the band and start the machine.

7) _____ taking the first set of readings, rest the patient for a minute or two and then repeat the readings a second time.

3.3

1k Listen to the processes in 1j and compare the original with your answers. Did you use the same, or different, time expressions? If you have used a different expression, has the meaning of the sentence changed?

1l Work alone. Use the steps (a–d) involved in requesting an inter-library loan to write a short description of the process. Use appropriate time expressions and verb tenses to show the sequence of events.

Requesting an inter-library loan

a Ensure that no copies of the requested item are available in the library.

b Check the location of the nearest available items.

c Complete the inter-library loan request form, either on paper or on the library computers.

d Receive emails from the library to inform you of when your requested item will arrive and to ask you to collect your requested item.

1m Compare your answers with another pair. Do you agree or disagree? If you disagree, how do any differences affect the meaning?

2 Understanding the use of repetition, reformulation and rhetorical questions

3.4

2a Listen to two extracts where a lecturer describes a process. What kind of process is being described?

2b Listen to the two extracts again. Complete these extracts as you listen.

> **1**
> The first stage of the process is weighing each ingredient so that the proportions are correct. They're weighed separately, and after that **1)** _____ mixed together. The first
> **2)** _____ in the **3)** _____ stage is to mix the corn starch and water ...

> **2**
> After this, it is ready to be compressed into individual tablets. When the **4)** _____ have been **5)** _____, they must be tested for quality. The **6)** _____ establish whether the tablet is hard enough ...

2c Work in pairs. Read these descriptions of repetition and reformulation, then find examples of each in the extracts above.

> • Repetition means reusing the same word more than once.
> • Reformulation means expressing an idea again using different words or word forms.

2d Identify the words which are being repeated or reformulated in the extracts in 2b. How does this repetition and reformulation help you to follow the process?

2e Work in pairs. Choose a word or phrase from the box to complete the extract below.

the tablets	aspirin tablets	the containers	they

> **3**
> Assuming that **7)** _____ pass the testing stage, **8)** _____ go to an assembly line to be packaged, either into foil blister packs or plastic bottles, which are then individually sealed with great care. Finally, **9)** _____ are labelled with information for consumers, and a batch number and expiry date are added. At this stage, the tablets are ready to be shipped. And that's how **10)** _____ are made.

2f Now listen to the extract. Check that your answers in 2e were correct.

3.5

> Rhetorical questions are also often found in descriptions of processes. The
> question is used to engage the listener's attention and help the listener to focus
> on the next step, predicting what they will hear. Because of this, rhetorical
> questions in processes often not only prompt *yes* and *no* responses, but also raise
> the question of *how, why, what* and so on.

2g Listen to four examples from the description of the printing process in 1d. Do the
questions prompt a *yes* or *no* response, or do they predict what the speaker is likely
to say next?

3.6

2h You are going to listen to part of a lecture about changing trends in magazine
readership. Before you listen, look at the rhetorical questions below (1–3) and
predict how repetition or reformulation might be used in answering them by
completing them with a word from the box.

reason	bad	explanation	circulation	answer

1 So what's the cause of this fall in sales? Well, the most likely _____ for the
decline is the growth of the Internet, which has damaged magazine _____
as readers turn to free content online.

2 However, is the picture entirely bleak for advertisers? Perhaps it's not as
_____ as marketers fear, because there is one part of the market in which
sales have shown impressive growth in recent years.

3 But is this the only _____? Why, for instance, don't readers choose to
get their health and fitness advice online rather than from a magazine? The
_____ may lie in the nature of the publications themselves.

2i Listen and check your answers.

3.7

3   Using context to understand the meaning of new vocabulary

> Descriptions of industrial or technical processes often contain specialist
> vocabulary. At times, this vocabulary will be defined, or explained through
> reformulation, as you have seen in previous units. You may also be able to work
> out the meaning of a new word through examining how it is formed, e.g. by
> looking at prefixes or suffixes.
>
> Often, however, a word's broad meaning can be deduced from context, simply by
> looking at the words around it and guessing at the meaning.

3a Listen to two extracts from the lecture on how aspirin is produced. Choose the
broad meaning of each word from the options given.

3.8

Extract 1

To **disintegrate** means

a to break into small pieces.

b to cause unwanted side-effects.

c to taste unpleasant.

Extract 2

A **blister pack** is

a a plastic bottle used for storing medicine.

b a liquid medicine used for pain relief.

c a foil or plastic container for tablets.

> Context can be helpful in many ways: the following factors may all help you to work out a word's meaning.
>
> - Background knowledge
> - Description
> - Comparison (e.g. synonyms) / contrast (e.g. antonyms)
> - Pictures
> - Examples

3b Work in pairs. Discuss what helped you deduce the meaning of **disintegrate** and **blister pack**.

3.9

3c Work out the meaning of the following vocabulary from its context by listening to the extracts. Which factors described (*background knowledge, description on p.113* etc.) helped you?

- to filter
- to expel
- ailment
- papyrus scrolls
- needles
- herbal

▶ LESSON TASK   **4 Describing a process**

4a Divide into two groups: Group A and Group B. Look at the corresponding process for your group (**Appendix 11**) and, as a group, write a description of it using time expressions, rhetorical questions, repetition and reformulation.

4b Now, work with one student from the other group. Listen to their description of the process and take notes on the steps. Stop and ask questions if you need to.

4c Show your partner your notes. Ask your partner to check if you have understood the process correctly.

4d Consider your partner's description (listen again if necessary). Did you hear:

- time expressions?
- rhetorical questions?
- repetition and/or reformulation?

4e Could your partner have made the process clearer?

5 Review and extension

5a Have you ever wondered how new novels are published? In what order would you expect these steps to occur? Label them 1–5.

		Steps	Order
A		The sales team assess who might be interested in buying the book.	
B		The writer sends the work to the publishing house.	
C		The publishing house sends the work to reviewers and booksellers.	
D		The work is edited.	
E		Publishing house readers evaluate the work.	

5b Listen to the lecture on how new novels are published and check your answers.

3.10

5c Listen to a short extract from the lecture again. Write the two rhetorical questions you hear.

1

2

3.11

5d You heard this vocabulary in the lecture in 5b. Can you work out the meaning of each word from its context? Write your definitions below (listen again if necessary) and then check in your dictionary. Were you correct?

Vocabulary	Definition
1 manuscript	
2 marketability	

3 commissioning editors	
4 a rejection slip	
5 a hardback	
6 royalty rates	
7 provisional	
8 dust jacket	
9 typeface	
10 proofread	

Understanding written information

By the end of Part B you will be able to:

- use definite and indefinite articles
- recognize and use conditionals in descriptions of a process
- recognize and use prepositions with common verbs in academic writing.

1 Using definite and indefinite articles

1a Cover the text in 1b with a piece of paper. What process do you think pharmaceutical companies go through in order to develop new medicines? Discuss your ideas in a small group and draw a rough flow chart below.

1b Skim read the sentences taken from a description of the drug development and approval process. Were your ideas in 1a correct?

A The discovery stage

The first stage is the discovery stage, where, for example, genetic research may identify a particular gene which appears to have a role in a specific disease.

B The target validation stage

Following the discovery of a potential treatment target, researchers must attempt to demonstrate that the target does play a role in a particular illness, and that a particular drug may have a particular effect.

C The screening stage

Various drug compounds are created and tested to discover whether they might have a significant effect on the disease that the drug is targeted against. Many compounds are rejected, but a few compounds which do seem to have an effect are usually identified.

D Full-scale development

Once screened, researchers may decide to take the drug to the next stage of the process: full-scale development, where the safety of the drug is extensively tested.

E Clinical trials

Extensive trials are carried out on human volunteers and on actual patients in order to assess the effect of the drug on the human body, and its efficacy in treating the disease.

F Registration

The pharmaceutical company which has developed the drug must submit an application to a regulatory agency (which works closely with the government) to have the drug recognized as being safe and effective for human use.

1c Now add one of these sentences to each of the sentences in 1b. What helps you match them?

1 _____

Several versions of the drug are tested on organisms with the illness to see how they react. If the researchers can show a clear link between the target and the illness, then the drug validation is successful.

2 _____

The gene then becomes a potential target for treatment with a suitable new drug.

3 _____

If the regulatory agency deems the drug safe and effective (this may not happen, even if the drug has passed its clinical trials), the manufacturing company may then manufacture and market the drug.

4 _____

The compounds are then taken to a further stage of testing, where their effect on the target illness is evaluated. This stage can take years to complete.

5 _____

Approximately 90% of drugs fail during the clinical trial stage. The volunteers often experience unwanted side effects, or the drug is simply found to be ineffective.

6 _____

This testing is the lengthiest and the most expensive period in the creation of a new drug.

1d Use of the definite article (*the*) and indefinite article (*a* or *an*) is one grammatical feature which helps tie a text together. Read again the sentences in 1b and 1c. Circle the definite articles and underline the indefinite articles.

1e What do you notice about the way the articles are used in the description of a process? Answer these questions.

    1 Which article is used the first time something is mentioned?

    2 Which article is used to refer to something which has already been mentioned? Is it used with all types of nouns?

1f There are other rules for the use of the definite and indefinite article. Work in pairs. Read these sentences and choose the best option.

    1 The definite article is used when a noun is *clearly* / *not clearly* defined (e.g. _the human body_).

    2 The definite article *is used* / *is not used* with superlative forms.

    3 The indefinite article is used where there is *only one* / *more than one* of something (e.g. _a disease_).

    4 The *definite* / *indefinite* article is normally used with ordinals ('first', 'second', etc.).

1g Find an example of each rule in the sentences in 1b and 1c.

1h The Wellco pharmaceutical company has developed a new shampoo treatment for dandruff. Complete the summary report of the product development process with the correct articles.

Wellco has traditionally produced drugs to alleviate minor ailments and conditions, such as tablets and medicines for **1)** _____ common cold, coughs and allergies. In 2005, the company decided to diversify, adding **2)** _____ skin and body-care product range. **3)** _____ new anti-dandruff shampoo, Flakeze, is **4)** _____ first product in this range. **5)** _____ specialised laboratory was built and **6)** _____ new team was taken on in order to research **7)** _____ best active ingredients. Several small amounts of shampoo were then produced, and **8)** _____ agency was then used to carry out consumer tests to determine **9)** _____ ideal consistency, colour and smell. Following **10)** _____ agency's report, a prototype was made, which was first tested on animals and humans before going into large-scale production. Meanwhile, after **11)** _____ product had passed its initial safety tests, **12)** _____ packaging design company had been contracted to develop **13)** _____ bottle and **14)** _____ label design. Finally, Flakeze was marketed, first in the local area and then nationally. Future plans are in place to extend production to Wellco's bases in other parts of the world.

1i Compare your answers in groups. If you have different answers, explain why you chose what you did. How is your choice supported by the rules?

2 Recognizing and using conditionals in descriptions of a process

The continuation of a process usually depends on one step being completed before the next can begin. Often, a step has more than one possible outcome.

Example

If the researchers show a clear link between the target and a particular illness, *then the drug validation is successful.*

- Outcome 1: Researchers *can* show a link between the target and a particular illness. The drug validation is successful.

- Outcome 2: Researchers *can't* show a link between the target and a particular illness. The drug validation isn't successful.

2a Look at some more sentences from the description of the general medicine and development process. What are the two possible outcomes of the underlined step in each?

1 If the target validation is not successful, researchers *have* to return to the discovery process.

2 If the potential drug passes its clinical trials, it *enters* the next stage of the process, known as registration.

3 If the drug is successful at the registration stage, it *is* then suitable for large-scale manufacture and marketing.

2b What tense is the verb in the first step (underlined) in the sentences in 2a?

2c What tense is the verb in the second step (*in italics*) in the sentences in 2a?

2d This structure is known as the zero conditional. When is it used? Work in pairs. Complete the table.

Steps
Structure:
Reasons for use:

2e Wellco contracted the company Paxpress to design the bottle for *Flakeze*. Paxpress always follows the same process in packaging design. Work in pairs. Look at this flow chart and write two sentences to describe any stages in the process that have more than one possible outcome.

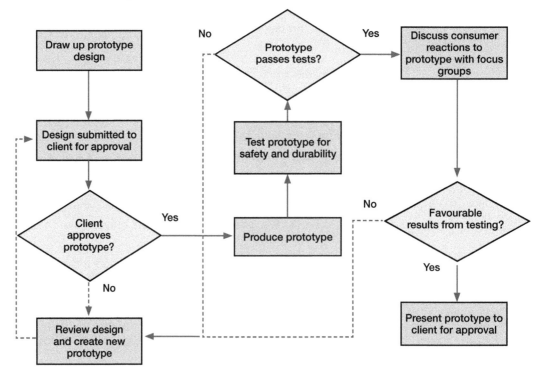

2f Work in pairs. Complete the sentences from Paxpress's brochure with *if* or a verb from the flow chart in 2e.

> Our design process is a tried and tested means of getting the best design for your product. Following an initial consultation with the client, our creative team draw up a prototype design. This design is then taken back to the client for initial approval. **1)** If the client **2)** approves the design, our packaging engineers **3)** _____ a prototype product. From here, our team are fully responsible for testing the product. Firstly, we test the prototype for safety and durability. **4)** _____ the product **5)** _____ these tests, we **6)** _____ consumers' reactions to it through focus groups, and then, **7)** _____ test results **8)** _____ favourable, we **9)** _____ the prototype to our client for approval. However, we change the product design and develop a new prototype **10)** _____ the product does not **11)** _____ any of our tests.

2g Read the sentences (a–c) from the next stage of *Flakeze's* production. They focus on the process of designing an advertising billboard. Then, answer the questions (1–4).

> a If Wellco's team approves a design, the advertising agency will go forward and create a complete final design for the billboard.
>
> b If Wellco doesn't approve the final design, the advertising agency will need to develop another design.
>
> c Wellco will instruct the advertising agency to begin creating the billboard if final approval is given.

1 What verb tense shows the first event in each sentence? What verb tense shows the second event in each sentence?

2 What do you notice about the order of the steps and the punctuation used in sentence c? How is this different from sentences a and b?

3 When the first event happens, is the second event possible or impossible?

4 Do the sentences generally refer to actions that happened in the past, actions that are always true or actions that might happen in the future?

2h The structure on 2g is known as the first conditional. When is it used? Work in pairs. Complete this table.

Structure:
Reasons for use:

2i The flow chart on p.122 shows the guidelines Wellco is planning to use to test its new anti-hair-loss shampoo *Natural Results*. Work in small groups. Write conditional sentences which show how this process will work.

Example
If negative reactions are observed during lab tests, the product formula will be reviewed.

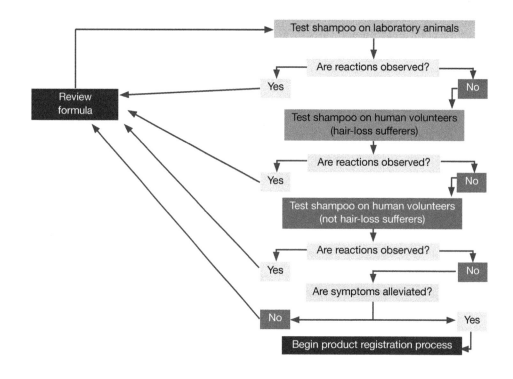

3 Recognizing and using prepositions with common verbs in academic writing

3a Wellco's new shampoo, *Natural Effects*, relies on plant ingredients to help treat a medical condition. Work in pairs. Discuss these questions.

1 Do you believe natural products can be effective in treating medical conditions?

2 Have you ever tried any natural or alternative remedies (complementary medicine)? Did they work?

3b Read sentences a–h from a text about conventional and complementary medicine use. The verbs in bold are followed by a preposition.

1 Circle the prepositions.

2 Can any of them be replaced by a different preposition?

3 What follows the prepositions?

a Conventional medicine – sometimes labelled 'scientific', 'modern', or even 'Western' medicine – is that **based** on empirical research and development of medicines and therapeutic techniques designed to treat specific illnesses or conditions in a patient.

b It has been estimated that 80% of all people in developing countries **rely** on traditional medicines for their healthcare.

c Every year in the UK, an estimated £1.6 billion is **spent** on non-conventional medical treatments.

d It would give a false picture to portray traditional medicine use in the developing world as **stemming** solely from poverty.

e More economically well-off members of society, particularly in cities, may often be better able to access and **pay** for conventional Western medicines.

f Some claim that patients who **opt** for traditional remedies are wasting money.

g There are concerns that there are no standard methods or training for traditional medicine, which can **lead** to inconsistent application.

The prepositions in these verb + preposition + noun (or gerund) patterns are known as *dependent prepositions*. There are a great many of these in English and, unfortunately, there are few consistent rules about which preposition goes with which verb. Some verbs have only one preposition, e.g. *stem* is always followed by *from*. However, other verbs may be followed by more than one preposition based on the meaning.

3c What is the difference between these pairs of verbs and prepositions?

1 to care about / to care for

2 to argue with / to argue for

3 to dream of / to dream about

3d Work in pairs. Below are some English verbs which commonly go with dependent prepositions. Which preposition goes with each group?

Group 1
• to consist _____ something
• to think _____ somebody/something
• to approve _____ somebody/something

Group 2
• to depend _____ somebody/something
• to insist _____ something
• to concentrate _____ something

Group 3
• to stare _____ something
• to aim _____ something
• to laugh _____ somebody/something

Group 4
• to commit _____ something
• to refer _____ somebody/something

Group 5
• to succeed _____ something
• to engage _____ something
• to specialise _____ something

Group 6
• to be discouraged _____ (doing) something
• to be exempted _____ something
• to suffer _____ something

Group 7
• to account _____ something
• to hope _____ something
• to prepare _____ something

Group 8
• to agree _____ somebody
• to dispense _____ somebody/something
• to continue _____ something

Group 9
• to complain _____ something
• to talk _____ something
• to learn _____ something

3e Complete sentences 1–6 using a suitable preposition and an idea of your own. Then discuss your ideas in pairs.

1 Students are advised to leave plenty of time to prepare …

2 Third-year students are expected to specialise …

3 The Student Union runs a counselling service where students can come to talk …

4 Participants in the experiment were asked to stare …

5 Students are encouraged to seek help if they have worries that prevent them from concentrating …

6 Students should be aware that they are strongly discouraged …

> **LESSON TASK** **4 Timed error correction**

Sara Abboud is an international student on a Master's course in Complementary Medicine. For her dissertation, she is going to look into the effects of hypnosis on people suffering from insomnia.

4a Work in groups. Discuss these questions.

1 What types of complaint can hypnosis be used to treat?

2 What other cures for insomnia do you know of?

3 How successful do you expect hypnosis might be in treating insomnia?

4b Sara has written the following summary of the process she will follow in her research. Unfortunately, she has made a number of errors in this summary with:

1 use of articles

2 use of conditional structures

3 dependent prepositions.

Work in pairs. Your teacher will set you a time limit to complete these two tasks.

1 Identify Sara's errors by circling or underlining them and writing 1, 2, or 3 depending on the error type.

2 Correct Sara's errors.

Primary research will be conducted from February to May 2011. A research will depend in volunteers from the University's students (aged 18–25) and staff (aged 40–60). Naturally, only those who suffer in insomnia will be selected to participate.

Prospective participants will be interviewed from their medical history to assess the severity of their insomnia and ensure they are suitable candidates. Interview questions will be based around Bell-Hausmann's 2007 research. If there will be any signs that hypnotherapy will be dangerous to them, or if they have already been referred in another specialist to control their insomnia, they will be rejected. Ideally, final selection of participants will consist in about ten male and ten female participants from each age group.

For a first month, all participants will be asked to keep a sleep diary, noting a times when they have difficulty sleeping, anything this might stem on (e.g. if they have been drinking or studying late), as well as total number of hours they estimate they have slept each night. Participants will of course be instructed not to change their normal routines during an experiment. However, they are withdrawn from experiment if for any reason their insomnia improves during this first month.

In March, the participants will be divided into two groups. A first group (A) will simply be responsible on keeping sleep diary as before. Group B will also continue on sleep diary, but will also begin the two-month course of hypnotherapy, initially attending bi-weekly hypnotherapy sessions, which will later be reduced at weekly sessions. If participant will miss more than two sessions, he or she is withdrawn on a study. The first session will aim to determine possible causes of their insomnia, and following sessions will concentrate with improving their sleep.

In the final fortnight, no participants will receive hypnotherapy but will be asked to continue with a sleep diary. This final stage aims to learn more on the lasting effects of hypnotherapy.

5 Review and extension

The zero article

> The **zero article** is where a noun or noun phrase is not accompanied by a definite or indefinite article.
>
> **Examples**
>
> The drug was developed by a company in ~~the~~ New York. (incorrect)
>
> The drug was developed by a company in New York. (correct)

5a Read sentences a–d about a new drug and circle the nouns which have zero articles.

> **a** The drug was developed by a company in Japan, at its headquarters in Yokohama.
>
> **b** The drug was tested on women.
>
> **c** Testing new drugs can give patients hope.
>
> **d** The tablet should be taken with water.

5b Now read four reasons for using the zero article. Match each reason with the best sentence or sentences from 5a which illustrate the use.

1 For plural and uncountable nouns (unless specifying a particular one):

Example 1:_____

Example 2:_____

2 When speaking about something in general:

Example:_____

3 With the names of countries and places*:

Example:_____

4 Where a pronoun is used before the noun:

Example:_____

*Note: there are some countries which require the definite article, e.g. *The United Kingdom*

Dependent prepositions

5c Look at the list of verbs below, which are all common in academic writing. Find out what prepositions are commonly used with them.

1	derive	**6**	impact
2	proceed	**7**	interact
3	respond	**8**	contrast
4	occur	**9**	impose
5	assist	**10**	emerge

Understanding the language used in describing a process

5d Find a short text on the Internet which describes a process in your area of study. Identify the following.

    1 The writer's use of articles (zero article, definite and indefinite articles)

    2 The writer's use of conditionals

    3 Any verbs with dependent prepositions

Part C Investigating

By the end of Part C you will be able to:

- recognize how writers use connotation to shape opinion
- recognize and use vocabulary for describing research methods.

1 Recognizing how writers use connotation to shape opinion

> Though academic writing often appears to be objective, a closer analysis of the language used may reveal ways in which the author is attempting to influence the reader's opinion. Choosing words for their connotations is one way of influencing a reader's interpretation of a text. A **connotation** is a psychological and emotional interpretation of a word. For example, *clever* and *cunning* share a similar meaning ('intelligent') but have different connotations: *clever* is usually associated with positive impressions, whereas *cunning* has a number of negative associations.

1a Compare the underlined words in sentences 1 and 2. Which dictionary definition (**a** or **b**) applies to them?

a lacking in knowledge of a subject or issue

b very simple in design

> 1 Until relatively recently, inhabitants of the area relied on <u>basic</u> natural remedies and were largely <u>unaware</u> of modern medicine.
>
> 2 Until relatively recently, inhabitants of the area relied on <u>primitive</u> natural remedies and were largely <u>ignorant</u> of modern medicine.

1b Which of the two examples in 1a do you think conveys a more negative view of the society in question?

1c Work in pairs. Read the pairs of sentences below. In each pair, one sentence is neutral and one has either a positive or a negative connotation. Tick (✓) the neutral or 'objective' sentences, put a + next to those whose connotation is positive, and a – next to those whose connotation is negative.

1a Recently, there have been calls to improve regulations regarding the sale of natural remedies, following suggestions that those under the age of 18 are too immature to evaluate potential side effects.

 b Recently, there have been calls to improve regulations regarding the sale of natural remedies, following suggestions that those under the age of 18 are too young to evaluate potential side effects.

2a One doctor recently attacked complementary medicine, declaring 'it is pathetic that families are led to false hope by the notion that alternatives may succeed where modern medicine has failed'.

 b One doctor recently criticised complementary medicine, noting 'it is sad that many families are led to false hope by the idea that alternatives may succeed where modern medicine has failed'.

3a Initial tests suggest that this may indeed be a miracle cure.

 b Initial tests suggest that this may indeed be an effective remedy.

1d You are going to read an extract from a text about crystal therapy (the use of crystals and stones to attempt to treat physical illness). Work in pairs. Discuss these questions.

1 How do you think crystals might be used as a form of therapy?

2 What do you think crystals might be used to treat?

3 Do you believe crystals could be a successful alternative remedy?

4 Would you try using crystals to treat a medical condition?

1e Ignoring the underlined words for now, read the extract and check if it mentions any of your ideas.

Crystal therapy

Crystals have long been used around the world to improve physical, emotional and spiritual well-being. Anecdotal evidence clearly demonstrates a variety of health benefits from this unconventional source of healing.

Certified crystal therapists report astonishing results from the use of different crystals. Perhaps the greatest success comes from using crystals to heal psychological rather than physiological conditions. Rose quartz is one of the more popular crystals, proven to be effective in enhancing positive emotions and having a calming effect which can cure insomnia. Other crystals with similar benefits are ruby, which can treat anxiety, and iolite, which enables sufferers from eating disorders to manage their weight.

However, experienced crystal therapists confirm that crystals can also be effective in healing physiological conditions. Indeed, it seems that the side-effects of routinely prescribed conventional medicines are suffered needlessly, as they can be avoided through use of crystals. Consumption of aspirin, ibuprofen and paracetamol may be superseded by use of malachite, and many of those who take daily medication to lower their blood pressure may see equally effective results through use of crystals such as emerald or carnelian. Even conditions as debilitating as epilepsy (treated with onyx) may be cured.

Unfortunately, government funding into such cures is severely restricted, as it seems that wealthy pharmaceutical companies continue to dictate policy regarding medical research ...

Source: Gouldwood, J. (2007). Seeking Alternative Funding for Crystal Therapy Research. *Canadian Journal of Traditional Medicine*, 4(1), 16–22.

1f Work in pairs. Read the extract in 1e more carefully and answer these following questions for each underlined word.

1 Does the word have a more positive or a more negative connotation (e.g. *well-being – positive*)?

2 Can you think of an alternative word with a similar meaning which has a neutral connotation (e.g. *well-being – health*)?

3 How might the writer's use of the word affect a reader's interpretation (e.g. *well-being may suggest that crystals are more than just healthy*)?

1g What is the overall effect of these connotations on the reader with regard to impressions of:

- crystal therapy?
- other types of medicine?
- the government?
- pharmaceutical companies?

From what you know, are these fair or reasonable impressions?

1h You are now going to compare two texts which make claims about the reasons for the rising popularity of complementary medicine. Are the writers of Text A and Text B for or against complementary medicine?

A

A great deal has been written recently about the growing popularity of alternative medical treatments – those that eschew rigorous scientific testing in favour of vague explanations based on 'traditional' knowledge. In fact, the supposed popularity of complementary and alternative medicine (CAM) is itself illusory: the data indicates that the numbers of people who choose to use these therapies are, in fact, tiny.

Only very small numbers of the population in England, and presumably the entire UK and beyond, actually use individual CAM treatments.

According to Thomas et al. (2001), this is only about 10% of the population for all types of CAM treatments. For both sexes its use is mainly found in the 45–54 age group, which suggests that small numbers of people turn to CAM in desperation after years of unsuccessfully trying conventional treatments. Despite claims that demand for CAM is widespread (see for instance Fulder, 1988; Thomas et al., 2001), the figures actually indicate only a very small number of people are actually willing to trust their health to this confused assortment of New Age rubbish.

B

CAM treatments enjoy widespread popularity in the UK. As early as 1988 Fulder observed a growing appetite for access to alternative treatments. As the data in Table 2 above indicates, people interested in receiving CAM in England can choose from a wide menu of alternative treatments, so it is unsurprising that as many as 10% of the population use CAM treatments annually. With an estimated 47% of the English population likely to turn to CAM treatments at some point in the course of their lives (Thomas et al., 2001, p.5), it is perhaps fair to say that the medical system in England (if not the UK as a whole), is one which fairly balances both scientific, modern, medical therapies with non-conventional approaches to treatment.

1i Look at the annotated version of the first sentence of Text A. Match an explanation (1–4) with each circled word or phrase.

A great deal has been written recently about the growing popularity of alternative medical treatments – those that eschew rigorous scientific testing in favour of vague explanations based on 'traditional' knowledge.

1 This word has a negative connotation, usually meaning to avoid something considered harmful. The writer implies that those who use CAM treatments think that modern medicine is harmful.

2 The use of inverted commas often gives a negative connotation to a word. The writer suggests that this kind of knowledge is questionable, possibly superstitious.

3 This has negative connotations. The writer implies that the explanations are not well argued.

4 Very positive connotation. The writer suggests that this kind of research is of high value.

1j Work in two groups, A and B. Group A should annotate the remaining part of Text A and Group B should annotate Text B in 1h. Identify words or phrases whose meaning tries to create a particular impression on the reader. Discuss what the writer is trying to create. Finally, share your ideas with a student who looked at the other text.

2 Recognizing and using vocabulary for describing research methods

A great deal of specialised vocabulary is used to describe the research process. You already saw some of this (related to scientific research) in Part C of Unit 2 of this book.

2a Work in pairs. Can you remember the meaning of these words? Try to define each item in the box.

Vocabulary	Definition
1 correlation	
2 hypothesis	
3 implication	
4 material	
5 observe	
6 placebo	
7 population	
8 reliable	
9 sample	
10 validity	
11 variables	

In addition to scientific research, there are a great number of business, social and educational research methods. Many of the steps involved in these and scientific methods cross over, so a lot of the same vocabulary is used.

Understanding such vocabulary is essential when reading about a topic, as much of the reading you do may be based on other writers' accounts of their research.

2b Read the text and decide on the most appropriate title from the following (1–3). Ignore the highlighted words.

  1 Variety of research methods in academia

  2 The importance of reading other writers' accounts of their research

  3 The problems of validity of research data

Uncertainty is a fact of life in academic research. When academic writers make claims, they inevitably do so knowing that the claims themselves are based only on evidence which might be true. This uncertainty comes from a variety of different sources. Firstly, most claims are based on research data, and this data is only as strong as the methods that were used to collect it, so a study which used a flawed method may well produce data which is inaccurate or distorted. Even a study in which the method is sound may be limited by other factors such as the number of people interviewed or measurements taken. If, for instance, you want to find out what proportion of the UK population have tried Chinese medicine, you cannot realistically interview all of them, so you must rely on a sample which you hope is representative of the population as a whole. This immediately means that you can't be sure that the results are perfectly accurate.

Uncertainty can also creep in when you analyze data. It may be that you accidentally misinterpret data as suggesting something that is not, in fact, the case. You cannot be certain that your own interpretation, or that of others, is entirely accurate; you can only try to make sure that it is as accurate as possible. Writers can also run into trouble when using data or claims from other authors to support their own work. The writers and researchers whose work you are using may themselves have used data which is inconclusive, or they may in turn have interpreted the data incorrectly. It is also, unfortunately, the case that some sources of information deliberately misrepresent the data that they use in order to persuade their readers to accept their claims. As a consequence, academic writing tends to be viewed with suspicion if it makes claims which are overly certain, or does not appear to acknowledge the possibility that the viewpoint it puts forward may be inaccurate. The best academic writing instead carefully indicates how certain the author is about the information they are using, and the claims they base on it.

2c Now use the highlighted words to complete this vocabulary record.

Vocabulary for describing research

- A <u>study</u> = a piece of research

Research methods / steps:

- To take _____
- To _____ people

Collocations with 'claim'

- To _____ a claim

- To _____ or reject a claim

- To _____ a claim on something

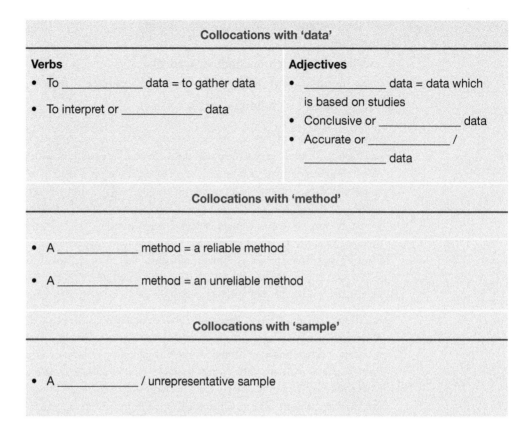

Collocations with 'data'

Verbs	Adjectives
• To _____ data = to gather data	• _____ data = data which is based on studies
• To interpret or _____ data	• Conclusive or _____ data
	• Accurate or _____ / _____ data

Collocations with 'method'

• A _____ method = a reliable method

• A _____ method = an unreliable method

Collocations with 'sample'

• A _____ / unrepresentative sample

2d Work in pairs. Can you add any more words to the table in 2c from words about research that you have learned in Unit 2?

2e Look at some students' summaries of research methods they have read about (**Appendix 12**). Add any extra or new words to the vocabulary record in 2c.

> **LESSON TASK**   **3   Using vocabulary to describe research methods**

3a Work in small groups. Discuss these questions.

1 What do you understand by the word *superfoods*?

2 Can you give any examples of superfoods? What effects are they said to have?

3 How might you test the value of a superfood through research?

3b Work in two groups, A and B. You will read a summary of recent research into superfoods. Read your allocated text (**Appendix 13**) and do the following.

1 Check if your allocated text mentions any of your ideas from 3a.

2 Identify the research methods used.

3 Draft a poster presentation which would show and explain the research process.

4 Review and extension

Recognizing connotation

4a Annotate this text about the medical system in India by identifying words or phrases whose meaning has a particular effect on the reader. Decide if the word has a positive or negative connotation. What overall impression is the writer trying to create?

> Like many other nations, India's medical system is based on the modern 'scientific' approach to healthcare (sometimes known as the 'Western' system). The modern Western medical system tends to rely on treating patients with high-tech equipment and expensive drugs manufactured by multinational pharmaceutical companies. Consequently, it is limited to those who can afford to pay. Many ordinary Indians cannot afford to do this. A further issue with modern medicine in India is the awareness that it is not effective in every situation. However, as it is the dominant system promoted by the government, many Indians feel forced to use it because they have no cheaper or more effective option.

4b Select a text you are currently reading as part of your studies which includes some opinion. Select and copy two or three paragraphs and annotate the text by identifying words or phrases with positive or negative connotations.

4c Add the vocabulary for describing research methods from today's class to your personal vocabulary logbook.

4d Find a short article detailing some research in your own field. How many words or collocations from this lesson can you find in it? Can you find any examples of words which have connotations which might be influencing the reader's opinion? Add any new vocabulary to your vocabulary logbook.

Reporting in speech

By the end of Part D you will be able to:

- use tenses to describe past actions and experiences
- use tenses to describe future actions
- use language to show a contrast between reality and expectation
- use pausing to show attitude.

1 Using tenses to describe past actions and experiences

> A progress report is a clear and concise summary of how a piece of work is progressing. This is common in academic study, as students often summarise their progress with a particular essay or project to their class tutor or academic supervisor. Progress reports are also found in the workplace, e.g. a report to a manager on a project which is being conducted, and may be in written or oral form.

1a Work in small groups. Discuss these questions.

1 Have you ever given a progress report?

2 If so, when and why did you give the progress report? At what stage of the project were you? What information did your report contain?

> A progress report is a clear and concise summary of how a piece of work is progressing. This is common in academic study, as students often summarise their progress with a particular essay or project to their class tutor or academic supervisor. Progress reports are also found in the workplace, e.g. a report to a manager on a project which is being conducted, and may be written or oral reports.

Progress report

Past (project start)   Current status   Future (project end)

1b You are going to listen to a student giving a progress report to their academic supervisor on a research project they are working on. In what order would you expect the student to complete the research steps below? Label them 1–6.

_____ decide on a data collection method

_____ gather data

_____ plan the methods section

_____ recruit participants

_____ write the literature review

_____ write up the report

3.12

1c Listen and check your answers.

1d Listen again. This time, focus on whether the step is complete (write *finished*), is currently being done (write *current*) or remains to be done (write *future*). Write your answers next to the steps in the table on p.135.

Step	Finished/Current/Future	Tense
1		
2		
3		
4		
5		
6		

1e Listen again and write what tenses are used for each step. Check your answers with a partner. Do you have the same information? Did you identify the same tenses? Why do you think these tenses were used?

Describing finished steps

3.13

1f Listen to two students, Debbie and James, discussing their progress in their research projects with their academic supervisor. Whose research project seems to be going less well? Why?

1g Listen again. Complete the dialogue by writing the exact words you hear.

Supervisor: Thanks for coming, both of you. Your research schedules both show that you should have finished your data collection by the end of this week. How are you getting on?

Debbie: I'm on schedule with my data collection. You may remember I 1) _____ / _____ / _____ to do the experiment individually, which would have taken a lot of time. However, when I 2) _____ the method two weeks ago, I 3) _____ to do it in groups, which has made it much more realistic. I've recruited as many participants as I need and I'm meeting them in small groups this week to conduct the experiment. I 4) _____ / _____ three groups so far and it's going very well.

Supervisor: Good, I'm glad you found a way to conduct the experiment more effectively. How about you, James?

James: I set up my email questionnaire on time, ten days ago, but I must admit that I 5) _____ /_____ some problems in getting responses. I 6) _____ / _____ the link to over three hundred students but the response rate so far is just 9% ...

Supervisor: That is low. Have you thought of any solutions?

James: Yes, in fact I wondered whether I might change the data collection method. I 7) _____ /_____ that an online questionnaire would be the easiest for students to complete, as they could do it at any time. I'm afraid most of them 8) _____ /_____ it even easier to ignore, though! I still want to use the questionnaire I designed, but I would like to administer them myself, perhaps in the library or in the student union café ...

1h Check your answers in pairs. Discuss these questions.

    1 What tense is used in each gap?

    2 Do you know why these tenses are used?

1i The following time references were used by Debbie and James:

two weeks ago   so far   ten days ago

Which tense or tenses can they be used with? Why?

1j Study these three actions which James talks about. What tense is each action?

- I **set up** my email questionnaire on time, ten days ago.
- **I've** actually **had** some problems in getting responses.
- I **had imagined** that an online questionnaire would be the easiest for students to complete.

1k When do the actions 'happen' in relation to each other? Write them on this timeline:

Ten days ago   Now

⟵─────────────┴───────────────────────⟶

1l Work in pairs. Look at these progress report statements, which were made by a student doing a similar research project. Can you improve the use of verb tenses in each statement?

    1 I finished the literature review on 5 February, but it has taken me longer than I expected.

    2 I've finished trialling the questionnaires three weeks ago, but I found there was a problem with the questionnaire.

    3 Now, I almost finished my data collection – I've got 150 of my 200 questionnaires back.

    4 I've planned to collect everything by yesterday afternoon, but I need a bit more time.

1m You are now going to role-play the progress report meeting in pairs. Decide who will be the student and who will be the supervisor. Complete the prompts below for the role you will play.

> ### Student
>
> **Today's date is 10 March**
>
> I finished the literature review …
>
> I had originally completed the methods section on … but I found …
>
> I therefore redesigned …
>
> I've recruited …
>
> I've almost collected …

Supervisor

Today's date is 10 March

OK, the research schedule says that you were due to finish your …

Have you finished the … ?

You were due to … by …

When you finish, change roles. Complete your new prompts. Consider changing details this time. Do you need to change any verb tenses you use?

2 Using tenses to describe future actions

> In Audio 3.13 you heard Debbie and James use these ways of referring to the future:
>
> • *When **I do have** the right number of participants* (= present simple)
>
> • *It **should go** quite quickly* (= **should** + base form)
>
> • *After the data gathering **is complete*** (= present simple) ***I'll still have** two months to finish* (= *will* + base form)

3.14

2a Listen to a continuation of Debbie and James's conversation with their supervisor. Answer these questions.

  1 What problems have the two students had?

  2 Are both students still confident that they will be able to finish on time?

3.14

2b Listen again and match the speaker with the tasks which are mentioned (A–D).

  1 James

  2 Debbie

  A Update sections of literature review with fresh information

  B Change data collection method

  C Read more sources

  D Reduce time for analysing and interpreting data

2c Work in pairs. The expressions below can all be used to show future meaning. Use the expressions in the table to help you predict which words or phrases can be used in the gaps in the transcript on p.138.

Way of referring to the future	Example(s)
Time adverb + present simple	**When I complete** the surveys …
should + base form	I **should finish** ahead of schedule.
will + base form	I **will recruit** participants for the survey via email.
Going to + base form	I'm **going to finish** sooner than I expected.

Present continuous	I'm **finishing** the literature review on Friday.
Future perfect	The respondents **will have sent** their questionnaires back by Monday.
Future continuous	I **will be visiting** the library tomorrow.

James: ... Yes, in fact I wondered whether I might change the data collection method. I had imagined that an online questionnaire would be the easiest for students to complete, as they could do it at any time. I'm afraid most of them have found it even easier to ignore, though! I still want to use the questionnaire I designed, but I would like to administer them myself, perhaps in the library or in the student union café.

Supervisor: Yes, I think that if you administer the questionnaires in the café or library, that 1)_____ work, though it will take more time on your behalf. When 2)_____ you be able to do it?

James: It will take more time, but at least I'll be sure to get the responses I need to get the data analysis done on time. Fortunately I have a bit of time this week: the school where I usually do voluntary work is closed for half term. I'm 3) _____ go to the café and library tomorrow and I'll go again on Friday if I need to.

Supervisor: Yeah, that sounds like a sensible suggestion. You really can't afford to let your data collection over-run, or you 4) _____ find it very hard to analyze and interpret the data!

James: I know, although I've actually been taking a short SPSS course at the library, which 5)_____ next week. I'm feeling much more confident about my data analysis now, and I think that I 6) _____ be able to analyze it in six days rather than the nine days I originally planned.

Supervisor: Excellent – that 7) _____ leave you a bit of time for any unexpected surprises! How about you, Debbie, are all of the other parts of your research going well?

Debbie: Well, as you know, I had some problems with my literature review: three of the key sources I needed were not available. Fortunately two of these have now arrived through inter-library loans, so 8) _____ updating those sections of my literature review today and tomorrow. When the final source 9) _____ on Friday I'll be able to read and incorporate that. I should 10)_____ it all finished by next week.

Supervisor: Good, that will mean you're on track to analyze the data and write up your findings on time too. Well, it sounds as though both of you are getting along OK ... Shall we meet up again in two weeks to check your progress? You should 11) _____ finished your data analysis by then and be writing up your final projects ...

2d Listen to Audio 3.14 again to check your answers.

2e Check the transcript again and circle any more examples of expressions with future meaning that you can find.

2f Work in pairs. Discuss the difference in meaning between these two phrases.

1 I'm finishing on Friday.

2 I should finish on Friday.

2g Work in pairs. Look at the examples in 2c again and discuss which ways of referring to the future a speaker can use to appear more certain that something will happen, and to suggest less certainty.

2h Now look at this research schedule and the accompanying notes. Imagine that these are your notes and that today is 16 October. Work in pairs. Discuss how you could report the progress using different ways of referring to the future. Plan your progress report below.

Research schedule		
Step	**Intended finish date**	**Notes on 16 October**
Read literature and make notes	20 October	*Already finished except one final source, arriving through inter-library loan on 17 October.*
Write first draft of literature review	15 November	*Already started writing – may finish early.*
Read about interview methods and design interview	31 October	*On schedule. Time set aside for reading next week. Hope to complete interview design following this, depends on the literature on interviews. May need more time?*
Conduct interviews	20 November	*Interview dates scheduled in London for 15–18 November.*
Analyze data	End November	*On schedule – depends on data collection (fixed).*
Write up first draft	12 December	*Driving theory test date: 10 December. Might need a few more days to finish writing up?*

Progress report
The final source for my literature review is arriving tomorrow. I should finish reading and making notes on time ...

2i Present your progress report orally to another pair. How similar were your ideas? If you used different tenses, were both versions acceptable?

3 Using language to show a contrast between reality and expectation

> When describing your progress in a particular project, you may not be at the stage you had expected in your original plan. Many things may happen during the course of your work which could put you ahead of or behind schedule, or which might simply alter the sequence of events you planned to follow.
>
> Using discourse markers can help you deliver your progress report by signalling whether the reality is different, or similar, to what you expected.

3.15

3a Listen to Angus giving a progress report. Where is Angus doing his work experience placement?

1 a medical research laboratory

2 an advertising agency

3 a public library

3.16

3b Listen to the discourse markers Angus uses in his replies to five questions from his line manager. Complete the dialogue with the exact words you hear.

1

Line Manager: So, Angus, how's it going? Did you manage to file the report on the project we finished yesterday?

Angus: Umm ... I didn't, **1)** _____. I know you said it was important but, erm, I just couldn't work out the filing system.

2

Line Manager: OK, hopefully they're in a safe place for now then, are they?

Angus: **2)** _____. I've put them in the document safe and I've scanned a copy into the client file.

3

Line manager: Good. How about the new project – I don't suppose you've had much time to find anything yet, have you?

Angus: I have, **3)** _____. I've got the last two years' sales figures from the clients and I've costed the billboards that you were wondering about.

4

Line Manager: Excellent. Were the billboard costs as high as we thought?

Angus: No. **4)** _____, I thought they were very reasonable ...

5

Line Manager: Did you ask the company to send written confirmation of those rates?

Angus: Well, erm, **5)** _____, but, er, I did get a contact name and number for the representative I spoke to ...

3c   Which of the discourse markers in 3b show a difference between expectation and reality, and which show that the situation is as expected?

3d   Work in small groups. Can you think of any more discourse markers?

3e   You are doing some work experience in a firm of solicitors. Your supervisor has asked you to do these tasks. Decide whether or not you have done them.

    1   File the Sanchez and the Wallis case files from yesterday.

    2   Send the Gordons' initial contract paperwork by first-class post.

    3   Arrange for a courier to take signed contract paperwork to Hanson Ltd.

    4   Update the appointments book for next week by checking recent emails and phone messages.

    5   Reply to any emails or phone messages requesting house purchase information packs.

3f   Write your answers to these questions according to what you decided in 3e. Introduce your answers with a suitable discourse marker.

    1   Have you filed the Sanchez and the Wallis case files?

    _____

    2   What about the contract paperwork for the Gordons? Have you sent it yet?

    _____

    3   OK. Did you arrange for a courier to take the paperwork to Hanson Ltd?

    _____

    4   And have you updated the appointments book?

    _____

    5   What about emails and phone messages concerning the house purchase information packs? Have you replied to any?

    _____

3g   Work in pairs. Take turns to ask each other the questions in 3f.

4   Using pausing to show attitude

Attitude may be expressed directly in academic English, for example through use of discourse markers to show opinion, and through your choice of adjectives and adverbs. However, meaning is also carried by the way in which you say things. Correct pronunciation is therefore important in conveying the correct message to your listener.

Language for Study 1 looked at the way in which pausing is used during lectures to give the audience more time to digest key points. Pauses may signal the end of a point, the introduction of a new point, or may be used around new or technical vocabulary. Pauses may also be used for these purposes in discussions. In addition, the position of pauses in a sentence can reflect the speaker's attitude.

4a   Work in pairs. Some pauses are silent, and others are filled with sounds or 'filler' expressions. What sounds and expressions do you know? Write them in the table on p.142.

Notes
erm, er, let me see,

4b Listen again to the conversation between Angus and his line manager (Audio 3.15). Answer these questions.

1 When do you hear more pauses? Why do you think this is?

    a When something positive is conveyed?

    b When something negative is conveyed?

2 At what points in the sentence do you hear most pauses?

3 What other sounds or 'filler' words indicating pauses did you hear? Add them to your notes in 4a.

4c Where would you expect the speakers to pause in the following interactions from progress reports at work? Draw a line (/) where you expect to hear a pause *because something negative is about to be conveyed*.

1

Project Manager:	Right, Stewart, I understand you've costed the job. Was it close to the £5 million we expected?
Stewart:	Actually, it was quite a lot more. Meeting the £5 million target would be very difficult. We'd have to compromise quite a lot on quality. You don't want to do that, do you?
Project Manager:	Absolutely not! But perhaps we can save on labour costs if we put back the finish date ...

2

Line Manager:	Anna, how are you getting on with the new poster campaign? Have you contacted the graphic design agency yet?
Anna:	Yes, I have, but in truth I think we should consider this new design agency too. The last posters we commissioned were rather unoriginal, I thought.

3

Department Supervisor:	Ashraf, I had a phone call from the paper supplier this morning. Did you put in the order last week?
Ashraf:	I'm afraid I didn't. Actually, I don't recall any order. Did you ask me to do it?
Department Supervisor:	In truth, I don't remember. I thought I had asked you but maybe I asked Joseph instead. In fact, thinking about it, yes, I think I did ask Joseph. Sorry, Ashraf! I'll check with him.

3.17

4d Listen and check your answers. Take a different coloured pen and draw a line (/) where you hear pauses because something negative is about to be conveyed.

4e Work in pairs. Repeat the task from 3g. This time, add pauses at appropriate points to show whether you are conveying something positive or negative.

> **LESSON TASK** 5 **Improving your speaking and discussion skills**

5a Work in pairs. Discuss these questions.

 1 How do you define 'good academic speaking skills'?

 2 How long have you been studying academic English?

 3 Consider how much your speaking skills have improved at this point, and your expectations before you started studying academic English. Has your improvement matched your expectations?

5b Work in pairs. Read the list of techniques for improving your academic speaking skills. Can you add any ideas to the list?

 • Using academic English websites for practice and advice

 • Using conversational English websites for practice and advice

 • Watching online presentations to get ideas about good speaking skills

 • Watching online discussions and seminars to get ideas about good speaking skills

 • Practising discussions or presentations with friends

 • Using pronunciation practice software

 • Joining a discussion group or university club

 • Watching video recordings of yourself during presentations

 • Reading study skills handbooks to get advice and tips

5c Rank the techniques that you have tried in order from 1–5, where 1 = most useful and 5 = least useful.

5d Work in pairs. You are going to give each other progress reports on the steps you have already taken to improve your academic speaking skills, and on any steps which you plan to take in the future.

Student A: Use the table on p.144 to plan what you will say in your progress report. As you make your plan, consider:

 • Correct use of verb tenses

 • Discourse markers to show whether the reality meets expectations

 • How you might show your attitude using pausing and intonation.

Student B: Plan questions to ask your partner. Use these key words to help you develop questions.

Example

Key word – reasons

Question – What were your reasons for starting to study academic English in the first place?

Key words:

1 reasons	**3** current progress	**5** discoveries	**7** goals
2 expectations	**4** difficulties	**6** plans	

Key information for report	Notes
Background information (e.g. how long you have been studying, why you are studying, etc.)	
Before starting the course, your expectations of how much you would have progressed by now	
Your actual progress so far	
Problems encountered	
How you plan to improve in future	

5e After you have practised giving your report, swap roles. **Student B** should give a progress report while **Student A** makes questions to find out more.

6 Review and extension

Time reference and tenses

6a Identify the mistakes in the underlined parts of these sentences. Rewrite them so that they are grammatically correct.

  1 I will write the first draft <u>after I completed the research</u>.

  2 <u>Somebody already borrowed</u> the book by the time I got to the library.

  3 <u>I have finished</u> the research two weeks ago.

  4 <u>I have planned to do the experiment</u> in June, but then I had to postpone it until July.

  5 So far <u>I had no problems</u>.

  6 <u>I should finished</u> last week, but it took longer than I expected.

  7 The <u>project went well</u> lately.

6b Write sentences about your own academic work using the time expressions below.

so far	frequently	over the last (two weeks)	at Easter
sometimes	last month	lately	in 2009
for some time now	recently	last June	up 'til now

Expressing future plans

Another way of expressing future meaning is to combine an auxiliary verb with the base form of the main verb.

Way of referring to the future	Example
plan to + base form	I **plan to complete** my research by next week
be due to + base form	I **am due to visit** London on the 17th
expect to + base form	I **expect to finish** by Friday
intend to + base form	I **intend to interview** 60 people
hope to + base form	I **hope to finish** before August

6c Discuss which ways of referring to the future a speaker can use to appear more certain, and to suggest less certainty.

6d Write sentences to explain your future plans on these topics. Use an auxiliary verb and base verb.

1 After graduating from university

2 An academic deadline

3 Your expected achievements at university

Reporting in writing

By the end of Part E you will be able to:

- understand the use of the first person in academic writing
- recognize and use synonyms and parallel expressions to compare and contrast other writers' ideas.

1 Understanding the use of the first person in academic writing

> As you have seen, grammatical structures such as the passive voice are used to distance the writer from their work and make it seem more objective.
>
> However, when researching you will find that some authors present their ideas in a more subjective way. This is particularly true when writers are presenting and developing an argument where research data might be quite limited.

1a You are going to look at some extracts from texts which discuss whether progress is largely positive or negative for humankind. Before you read, work in small groups and discuss this question:

How has progress in the following areas affected humankind over the past 100 years? Decide whether the changes have been positive or negative. Give reasons for your answers. You may want to focus on these areas:

- *Economic wealth*
- *Healthcare*
- *Information technology*
- *Society*
- *Transport*

1b Look at these extracts and answer the questions which follow each one.

> **A**
> Technological developments have undoubtedly brought great potential to enhance quality of life. However, we hardly seem better off if we consider the accompanying risks: environmental collapse, warfare and potential nuclear meltdown.

1 Is the author's position on technological progress positive, negative or neutral?

2 How do you know?

> **B**
> The use of fossil fuels did indeed bring a revolution in industry, transport and in enabling leisure time and activities, from travel to domestic appliances to games consoles. However, anybody who thinks that this progress is positive for humankind is severely misguided: in pursuing such short-term gains we have, and continue to, severely jeopardise the planet for our future generations.

3 Does the author believe that technological progress is largely positive or negative?

4 How do you know?

C

There has certainly been some tragic loss of lives as a result of this technological progress, but we can hardly deny the fact that we live longer, eat better, enjoy better health and work less than at any point in our past.

5 Does the author believe that technological progress is largely positive or negative?

6 How do you know?

D

Those who claim that economic progress has enslaved the West to work, debt and misery should consider the luxury that allows this view to be held. Our grandparents' generation, even less those before them, worked very hard to own very little. The same is true of the millions of people born into economically developing nations over the world. The notion that our choice to work, for example, sixty hours per week to pay for a five-bedroom house, amounts to suffering belittles those who are less fortunate and should shame us.

7 Does the author believe that economic progress is largely positive or negative?

8 How do you know?

1c Work in pairs. Look at the extracts in 1b again. Underline any uses of the first person and discuss why the writer has used it.

1d Skim read the extract below from a text about progress, and answer these questions.

    1 Does paragraph A present arguments broadly in favour of or against the view that progress is positive for humankind?

    2 Does paragraph B present arguments broadly in favour of or against the view that progress is positive for humankind?

    3 Does the author believe progress is broadly positive or negative? What helped you decide this?

A There is a common belief in the linearity of social progress, that 'progress' in human affairs is inevitable. This belief tends to confuse social progress – improvements in the condition of human life – with simple technological development: where there are technological developments, it is argued, there naturally follow improvements in the conditions of life. This benign view of the world, which has its foundations in the writings of Enlightenment scholars such as Voltaire and Locke, trusts in reason, rationality and the knowledge developed from scientific inquiry.

B However, many authors challenge this optimistic view of progress, arguing that technical and material progress do not automatically lead to improvements in the quality of life which is experienced by many millions of people in the world. Certain events suggest precisely the opposite: technology might have advanced, but human behaviour is unchanged. This mix of technological advances with unchanged human needs and behaviours has led to severe problems and risks: the world wars of the 20th century; the more modern threats of nuclear conflict and environmental degradation; these are constant reminders of the danger of putting our faith in technological progress alone. There are difficulties, too, in equating progress with economic development. Many developing countries find that high GDP growth rate has not necessarily reduced socio-economic deprivation for large sectors of their populations. While it is undeniable that scientific, technological and economic developments have brought very real benefits to millions, if not billions, of people around the world in the course of human history, we should be cautious about equating technical and economic development with real advances in social progress.

Source: Kirkup, 2007, p.15

1e Now read the text in 1d again and underline the phrases used to refer to other sources in an impersonal way. The first one has been done for you.

2 Recognizing and using synonyms and parallel expressions to compare and contrast other writers' ideas

2a Work in pairs. To what extent do you agree with the following statement from an essay question?

Progress is by definition positive. Economic, technical and social advances have only benefited humankind.

2b A student is defining the term *progress* for the essay in 2a. Look at the student's sources, notes and finished text. Underline the parts of the sources she took her notes from.

Sources

> More recently, the United Nations' annual Human Development Report measures progress not in terms of industrial output or economic growth alone, but instead considers it from the point of view of the quality of life that people can enjoy; in this view, progress is determined by the percentage of people that receive education, enjoy long and healthy lives [...] and have political and social freedoms.

Source: Jones, 2008, p.21

> There is a common belief in the linearity of social progress, that 'progress' in human affairs is inevitable. This belief tends to confuse social progress – improvements in the condition of human life – with simple technological development: where there are technological developments, it is argued, there naturally follow improvements in the conditions of life. This benign view of the world, which has its foundations in the writings of Enlightenment scholars such as Voltaire and Locke, trusts in reason, rationality, and the knowledge developed from scientific enquiry.

Source: Kirkup, 2007, p.15

> A belief in reason and scientific progress which has its roots in the Enlightenment view that scientific enquiry could lead to material and social betterment.

Source: Goyal, 2010, p.237

> The most basic aims of any program for human development are to enhance well-being for the greatest number of people – to help people to 'live a long and healthy life, to be educated and to enjoy a decent standard of living' (United Nations, 1990, p.8).

Source: Cohen, 2009, p.11.

Notes

Prog. ← Enlightenment: sci. enquiry (Goyal, 2010; Kirkup, 2007) & reason (Kirkup, 2007

Def?

• UN: standard of life (in Cohen, 2009; Jones, 2008)

• Not only tech. dev. – also social dev. (Jones, 2008; Kirkup, 2007)

Extract from student's essay

> Stemming from Enlightenment ideals of reason and scientific enquiry (Goyal, 2010; Kirkup, 2007), progress is seen today not only as a sum of technological and economic advances, but as encompassing the social changes that have come about because of these. As such, it can be used to gauge quality of life (UN, 1990, cited in Cohen, 2009).

2c Identify synonyms and parallel expressions for these words and phrases in any of the source texts and the student's essay.

1 advance

2 measure

3 quality of life

4 stemming from

2d The information about the UN is contained in two sources (Jones, 2008 and Cohen, 2009), yet the student has only referred to Cohen. Both of the following ways of acknowledging the information are acceptable. Work in pairs. Discuss the advantages and disadvantages of each method. Explain which one you would prefer.

1 As such, it can be used to gauge quality of life (Jones, 2008; UN, 1990, cited in Cohen, 2009).

2 As such, it can be used to gauge quality of life (UN, 1990, cited in Cohen, 2009).

2e Later in the essay, the student wants to discuss whether increasing GDP is a positive or negative development. Look at the student's sources, notes and finished text.

1 Underline the parts of the sources that she took her notes from.

2 What synonyms and parallel expressions for these terms can you find?

  a increase in GDP

  b economic downfall

  c existence of poverty

3 Has the student organized her notes by source or by idea?

4 How has paying attention to, and using, synonyms and parallel expressions helped her to do this?

Sources

There are difficulties, too, in equating progress with economic development. Many developing countries find that high GDP growth rate has not necessarily reduced socio-economic deprivation for large sectors of their populations. While it is undeniable that scientific, technological and economic developments have brought very real benefits to millions, if not billions, of people around the world in the course of human history, we should be cautious about equating technical and economic development with real advances in social progress.

Source: Kirkup, 2007, p.15

Another dearly held view of those who believe in the idea of constant progress is that economic development will automatically lead to social improvement, but disastrous falls in the stock market, such as the Wall Street Crash of 1929, or the more recent stock market troubles of 2008, demonstrated that the trend of financial development is not always up. Furthermore, the continued and intractable existence of poverty should give us pause before we make claims about the powers of the economy to improve people's lives.

Source: Goyal, 2010, p.237

Though poverty still clearly exists, the trend is towards an improvement of GDP throughout the world, affording more people the possibility, or at least the hope, of improvements in their quality of life. Where technical and economic progress goes, so too does social progress.

Source: Maxwell, 2010, p.18

Notes

GDP ↑(Maxwell, 2010; Kirkup, 2007)
   ↑(potential) enhanced standard of life (soc. prog.) (Maxwell, 2010)
   BUT does it?
   • Goyal: downturns, e.g. 1929, 2008
   • Poverty still present (Goyal, 2010; Kirkup, 2007)

Extract from student's essay

Views surrounding economic progress are complex. While GDP does seem to be increasing worldwide (Maxwell, 2010; Kirkup, 2007), Goyal (2010) rightly points out that there have recently been considerable economic downturns. In addition, although it may be true that economic advances bring the potential for an enhanced standard of life (Maxwell, 2010), to what extent this potential is realised remains questionable. Poverty is still clearly prevalent in both developing and developed nations (Goyal, 2010; Kirkup, 2007).

2f You are going to write the same essay. Two of the points you have decided to include are:

1 technological advances have led to warfare

2 technological and social advances have led to a better educated and more socially proactive population.

You have selected the following sources, which mention these two points.

1 Underline the parts which support point **1**.

- Look for the exact words or for synonyms and parallel expressions to the terms *technology, advances, lead to, warfare*.
- Decide if the source supports your point.

2 Circle the parts which support point **2**.

- Look for the exact words or for synonyms and parallel expressions to the terms *technological, social, advances, better educated, socially proactive*.
- Decide if the source supports your point.

Sources

The industrial revolution in Britain gave birth to a generation of wealthy, socially conscious philanthropists, who considered it a duty to improve the lot of the people who worked for them. This sense of social responsibility to those less fortunate has now become deeply embedded in the idea of good government at both the national and international levels. It is no exaggeration to say that technological and economic developments over the course of the last few centuries have brought greater democracy and freedom to many millions around the world. .

Source: Cohen, 2009, p.11

The development of the Internet has facilitated a genuine revolution in free expression and enabled untold numbers of people to access educational resources and directly influence politics in their societies [...]. However, [...] it is unrealistic to imagine that, through the development of modern science and technology, people will cease to behave in irrational or inhumane ways.

Source: Davis, 2010, p.309

[...] advances in technology can strongly support irrational or inhumane behaviour and ideas – think of the developments in weaponry and communications technology which have facilitated wars in the modern world (and made the technology of war that much easier to get hold of).

Source: Davis, 2010, p.309

The entire course of the twentieth century has proven that technological development does not lead to improvements in people's lives, and often affects them for the worse: think of the devastation of the two world wars or man-made environmental catastrophes, from the US Dustbowl through the meltdown at the Chernobyl nuclear reactor, to the massive damage caused by oil spills, whether accidental, as in the case of the recent oil leak in the Gulf of Mexico, or deliberate, such as the deliberate firing of oil wells in the aftermath of the Persian Gulf War.

Source: Goyal, 2010, p.237

In an intellectual current running from ancient Greece until the Enlightenment in the 18th century, we find the idea that human development is development towards greater levels of knowledge, rationality, and culture.

Source: Jones, 2008, p.21

This mix of technological advances with unchanged human needs and behaviours has led to severe problems, and risks: the world wars of the 20th century; the more modern threats of nuclear conflict and environmental degradation; these are constant reminders of the danger of putting our faith in technological progress alone.

Source: Kirkup, 2007, p.15

We cannot overlook that fact that our technology is implicated in certain tragic episodes in our history; the devastation of most modern wars is only possible with the industrial production of weaponry, for instance.[...] Nevertheless, we should not look at isolated disasters and say that they are the sum of human experience. The trend is ever upwards.

Source: Maxwell, 2010, p.18

Where technological and economic progress goes, so too does social progress. Improvements in medicine or information technology, for instance, are not merely technical developments: they also create very real improvements in human social conditions, and where people are healthier, richer, and empowered by education, they in turn can contribute to greater progress for the generations that follow them.

Source: Maxwell, 2010, p.18

2g Use the sources to write notes either on point **1** or on point **2**. You will use these notes to write a sentence or a short paragraph. Keep your notes brief by organising them by idea. Don't forget to include any in-text citations necessary in your notes.

Notes

2h Write a sentence or a short paragraph below to support either point **1** or point **2**. Don't forget to include any in-text citations necessary in your paragraph.

2i Swap your paragraphs with a partner. Read your partner's paragraph and compare it with the original source texts. Answer these questions.

1 How accurate is your partner's presentation of the other sources' ideas?

2 Has your partner correctly acknowledged the sources?

3 How well has your partner compared differing sources on the topic?

> **LESSON TASK**   **3**   **Taking notes to compare sources**

3a You are writing an essay entitled *Complementary and Alternative Medicine (CAM) has no place in modern society. The only treatments which are proven safe and effective are the drug therapies and surgical interventions of Western medicine. Discuss.*

As part of this essay, you have found some information about different treatments for rheumatoid arthritis, a common disease in which the body's immune system attacks its joints, leading to swollen, painful and deformed joints, particularly in the hands and feet. Before you read, work in pairs. Discuss these questions.

1 How might arthritis affect the life of a sufferer?

2 There is no cure for rheumatoid arthritis, but symptoms can be greatly relieved. How would you expect rheumatoid arthritis to be treated? Using:

   a conventional Western medicine?

   b CAM?

3b Work in two groups, A and B. Individually, read the appropriate text for your group in **Appendix 14** and write notes on:

- treatments for rheumatoid arthritis
- the safety of these treatments.

Write your notes in your own words and add any necessary in-text citations so that you know which source the information came from.

Notes

3c Compare your notes as a group. Make sure that all members of your group have identified all of the relevant information in the text.

3d Change groups so you are working in pairs: one student from group A and one from group B. Compare and contrast the ideas in your notes. To what extent do the two sources agree on the following topics?

1 Treatment   4 Diet and lifestyle

2 Complementary medicine   5 Side effects

3 'Modern' medicine

3e Write a paragraph below to express your own position about the treatment of arthritis in relation to the original essay question.

Complementary and Alternative Medicine (CAM) has no place in modern society. The only treatments which are proven safe and effective are the drug therapies and surgical interventions of Western medicine. Discuss.

- Support your points with reference to the sources that you took notes on.
- Make sure that you represent the original writers' positions accurately.

3f Compare your paragraph with a partner. Give each other feedback on:

1 organization

2 conciseness

4 Review and extension

Self-mention in academic writing

> Although academic writers try to make their work appear more objective and impersonal, especially by removing any self-mention through pronouns in the text, there are variations in the use of personal pronouns between different academic disciplines.

4a Tables 1 and 2 summarise the results of a study about the use of personal pronouns for self-mention. The study calculated how often expert writers use personal pronouns in research papers, and compared this with the number of personal pronouns used by non-English-speaking student writers in their essays. Compare the information in the two tables and answer these questions.

1 In which discipline are personal pronouns used most?

2 Are the ways that expert writers and students use personal pronouns similar?

Table 1: Average frequency of writer pronouns per research paper

Discipline	Singular pronouns (*I, Me, My*)
Marketing	1.6
Philosophy	33.0
Applied Linguistics	17.2
Sociology	11.7
Physics	0.0
Biology	0.0
Electronic Engineering	0.0
Mechanical Engineering	0.0
Average	7.9

Source: Hyland, K. (2002). Options of identity in academic writing. *ELT Journal, 56*(4), 351–358. [Excerpt from p.353]

Table 2: Personal reference in student essays

Field	Singular pronouns (*I, Me, My*)
Science and engineering courses	7.7
Business and professional courses	9.2
Average	8.6

Source: Hyland, K. (2002). Options of identity in academic writing. *ELT Journal, 56*(4), 351–358. [Excerpt from p.354]

4b Find one of your own essays or reports. Read through and underline any personal pronouns (*I, me* or *my*) that you have used. Write the total number of personal pronouns you have used in the second column of this table.

Pronoun	My own writing	A paper from my discipline
I		
Me		
My		

4c Find a research article from the discipline that you are studying. Read through and calculate the total number of pronouns *I, me* or *my*. Enter them in the third column of the table in 4b.

4d How do your results compare with the data in 4a?

4e Look again at your own writing. Decide which of the personal pronouns you have used are necessary and which could be replaced. Try to think of ways to replace the personal pronouns and keep the same meaning.

Synonyms and parallel expressions

4f Read the text below, then complete the table with information about the words in bold which are common in academic writing.

There is a strong belief, in Europe and the industrialised nations which have their philosophical roots in the Enlightenment, that 'progress', increasing modernization and technological development, will lead **inevitably** to a safer, more **rational**, humane and **ethical** world. We believe that technology and modernization will make people everywhere more moderate and understanding, and **consequently** better able to control the dangers of our world – war, poverty, natural disasters, illness, and so on.

It is certainly true that science and technology have made many real **contributions** to the well-being of people around the world. Who could argue, for instance, that reductions in poverty or improvements in healthcare were anything but positive results of technological development? It is estimated, for instance, that over 200 million lives have been saved by penicillin since its first use as a medicine in the 1940s. The development of the Internet has **facilitated** a genuine revolution in free expression and **enabled** untold numbers of people to access educational resources, and directly influence politics in their societies. Arguably, the ease of communication that the Internet offers has profoundly influenced our understanding of other cultures, and our own responsibilities as members of a truly global community.

Word	Word class	Synonyms	Antonyms
inevitably	adverb	naturally	surprisingly
rational			
ethical			
consequently			
contribution			
facilitate			
enable			

Language review

4g Choose one specific point from a report or essay you are currently researching for and/or writing as part of your studies.

Identify any parallel expressions and synonyms which helped you to identify the sources' relevance to your topic.

Unit 4 Art, creativity and design

Unit overview

Part	This part will help you to ...	By improving your ability to ...
A	**Understand lectures more effectively**	• recognize speaker attitude • understand signposting expressions to improve comprehension • understand the relationship between parts of a talk.
B	**Read intensively**	• understand register variations in academic and non-academic vocabulary • understand the use of affixes in academic vocabulary • understand nominalisation.
C	**Report on research**	• recognize key research terminology • understand the language features of research reports • write about research limitations.
D	**Gather research data and discuss findings**	• describe and comment on research findings • form indirect questions • use appropriate pronunciation and language when agreeing and disagreeing.
E	**Write abstracts and understand academic essay titles**	• recognize and use the structure and grammar of abstracts • write an abstract using concise language.

Understanding spoken information

By the end of Part A you will be able to:

- recognize speaker attitude
- understand signposting expressions to improve comprehension
- understand the relationship between parts of a talk.

1 Recognizing speaker attitude

1a Work in pairs. Look at the photos of products below. Which products do you associate with these words?

| luxury | ordinary | attractive | practical |

1b A study is conducted to discover how consumers feel about the appearance of human models used in advertising. 300 volunteers are shown two versions of an advertisement for a supermarket: the first version uses a 'highly attractive model' (HAM); the second version uses a 'normally attractive model' (NAM). The volunteers were asked this question:

Which model do you trust more?

Read the results of the study, then make a note of your answers to the questions which follow.

	Trust HAM more (%)	Trust NAM more (%)	Unsure (%)
Male volunteers	40	53	7
Female volunteers	48	49	3

1 What does the data suggest about the difference between men's and women's feelings towards HAMs?

2 How likely is it that the appearance of the model can have an effect on the success of an advert?

3 Do you agree with this statement: 'Consumers definitely prefer adverts featuring NAMs'? Use the data in the table to justify your answer.

1c Work in pairs. Read your answers to your partner. As you listen to your partner, make a note of the following points.

1 What is your partner's opinion or attitude on each point?

2 How does your partner express their opinion?

The following forms of language can be used to express an opinion or attitude toward the topic.

- reporting verbs (*claim, imply, suggest*, etc.)
- modal adjectives (*likely, possible, improbable*, etc.)
- modal verbs (*can, may, might*, etc.)
- attitude adjectives (*fundamental, important, significant*, etc.)

Examples

*The data **suggests** that consumers respond to a believable model.*

*It is **likely** that consumers respond to believable models.*

*Consumers **may** respond best to models who resemble them.*

*The appearance of a human model is a **significant** element in successful advertising.*

1d Work in pairs. Read 10 sentences from a lecture about advertising and decide whether the speaker believes the topic:

a is certain to be true/untrue.

b is possible or likely but not completely certain to be true/untrue.

c is important or relevant.

Write **a**, **b** or **c** next to each sentence in the space provided. Then underline the word or phrase that helps you to recognize the speaker's attitude.

1 _b_ The findings suggest there may be differences between product types.

2 ___ It is impossible to determine whether this is the case.

3 ___ Ratings of trustworthiness might be related to model attractiveness.

4 ___ The model's physical attractiveness should be influential in the effectiveness of the advert.

5 ___ The certainty of these results is questionable.

6 ___ This finding could be explained by the argument that consumers trust adverts in which the models more closely resemble themselves.

7 ___ The lack of a clear link between attractiveness and perceived trustworthiness in this study may be unimportant.

8 ___ While the link is not conclusive, it seems probable that there is some relation between them.

9 ___ There is a fundamental relationship between consumer value judgements and their identification with the models used in adverts.

10 ___ It is certain that a relationship between the two exists.

1e Make a note of each type of expression used in 1d in the appropriate column.

Reporting verbs	Modal adjectives	Modal verbs	Attitude adjectives
suggest	probable	may	unimportant

> The speaker can use a variety of ways to indicate the same attitude to the information. For instance, the first three sentences below all suggest a similar attitude.
>
> There **may** be a relationship between perceived trustworthiness and the model's looks.
>
> There is a **possible** relationship between perceived trustworthiness and the model's looks.
>
> The evidence **suggests** a relationship between perceived trustworthiness and the model's looks.

1f Compare these pairs of phrases. Do you think each pair expresses similar or different attitudes to the information?

1   **a**   It is <u>possible</u> that there is a relationship between model attractiveness and the effectiveness of an advert.

    b   It is <u>probable</u> that there is a relationship between model attractiveness and the effectiveness of an advert.

2   **a**   It seems <u>likely</u> that there is a strong link between the attractiveness of the model and the extent to which consumers trust the advert.

    b   The link between the attractiveness of the model and the extent to which consumers trust the advert is <u>significant</u>.

3   **a**   There is a <u>potential</u> difference between product types in this regard.

    b   The difference between product types in this regard is <u>certain</u>.

4   **a**   It is <u>unlikely</u> that consumers are affected by the appearance of the model used.

    b   Whether consumers are affected by the model's appearance is quite <u>uncertain</u>.

5   **a**   Bower's findings <u>indicate</u> that negative comparisons with HAMs can actually reduce the effectiveness of an advert.

    b   It is <u>possible</u> that negative comparisons with HAMs can actually reduce the effectiveness of an advert (Bower, 2001).

4.1

1g Listen to an excerpt from a lecture about the attractiveness of human models used in advertising. Decide which of the statements most closely describes the claim the speaker makes.

1 There is no relation between the attractiveness of a human model and the success of an advert.

2 There is a strong link between the attractiveness of a model and the success of an advert.

3 The relationship between model attractiveness and the success of an advert is unclear.

1h Work in pairs. Discuss what types of attitude words could be used to complete the transcript of the lecture, then listen again and write the words the speaker uses in the blanks.

There is a great deal of research interest in the match between human models and product types in advertising, for obvious reasons: it is the 'science' of advertising, if you like, to discover the elements that make an advert most appealing, most effective – in other words, that will sell a lot of product. Now, common sense might tell us that the people you want in your adverts are the most highly attractive ones – the ones who will stop consumers in their tracks with their sheer beauty and draw attention to the product. What many of the studies _____ **(1)**, however, is that this common sense idea may not always be the case. What the evidence tends to suggest, in fact, is that people _____**(2)** respond better to adverts where the model's attractiveness seems to match the product type. In 2001 Bower and Landreth conducted a study which _____**(3)** that consumers trusted highly attractive models less in adverts for ordinary products. What Bower and Landreth's findings _____**(4)** was that an advert may be more effective if the consumer can believe that the person in the advert is the type of person who would use that product. This contradicts an earlier finding by Michael Kamins in 1990, which _____**(5)** that in products related to attractiveness – clothing, jewellery and cosmetics and so on – more highly attractive models were more effective, but that in products which were unrelated to attractiveness, food, furniture polish, and so on, there was no difference between using a highly attractive model and an 'ordinary'-looking one. So what does this tell us? Well, there is some evidence that seems to suggest that attractiveness is _____**(6)** to be a factor which should be considered when designing commercials, but quite what the relationship is between the beauty of the model and the effectiveness of the advert is as yet_____**(7)**.

1i What is the speaker's attitude about each of these points?

1 the way people respond to adverts in which the model's attractiveness matches the product type

2 the certainty of Bower and Landreth's findings

3 the certainty of Kamins's findings

4 the extent to which model attractiveness overall affects the success of adverts

1j Read the claims below about the use of models in advertising. Then discuss with a partner whether you agree with them.

Claim	Speaker's attitude and attitude expressions used
There are things which most people would agree are beautiful.	
A sense of what is beautiful is of interest to people working in the creative industries.	
Notions of what a 'beautiful' person is vary between different cultures.	

4.2

1k Listen to excerpts from a lecture in which the speaker makes these claims. Pay attention to the attitude expressions that the speaker uses. What is their attitude to the information they are giving? Make notes in the second column of the table.

1l Work in pairs. Check your answers with a partner, then discuss whether you share the same attitude as the speaker.

2 Understanding signposting expressions to improve comprehension

In *Language for Study* level 1 you were introduced to signposting expressions that speakers use to order information and show how ideas are developing in their talk. Speakers also use signposting expressions to signal what they are doing in different parts of their talk.

1 Digression
The speaker moves away from the main subject that they are talking about and temporarily talks about something different.

2 Emphasis
The speaker indicates that something is particularly important.

3 Definition
The speaker explains the meaning of a word, phrase or concept.

Recognizing expressions such as these can help you to understand a long lecture more easily.

2a Work in pairs. Match the types of signposting from p.162 (1–3) with the examples below.

a <u>By</u> 'normally attractive model' <u>I mean</u> someone who looks about average, like you or me.

b <u>The fundamental point is</u> that luxury products are more closely associated with glamour and, therefore, good looks.

c There may be room for future research on so-called 'problem-associated products', <u>which refer</u> to those products associated with solving a problem, say acne cream, tissues or cold medicine.

d One study by Kahle and Homer in 1985 found that razor blade adverts that featured attractive celebrities were more successful than those which didn't. Actually, <u>that reminds me</u> of a story I heard from a colleague of mine …

e Kamins found that it may be important to match up the model with the type of product in order to make consumers trust that the model has some expertise on the subject. <u>Incidentally</u>, have any of you seen that shampoo advert with the Hollywood actress pretending to be a scientist?

f <u>Crucially</u>, for products in which attractiveness is irrelevant – vacuum-cleaners, for instance, or power tools – there was no relationship between model attractiveness and consumer trust. <u>Which reminds me</u>, don't forget to submit your essays on consumer trust on Wednesday.

g These types of adverts had higher credibility – <u>which is to say</u>, consumers tended to believe the claims made by the adverts.

h The findings suggest that there is a relationship between perceived trustworthiness and attractiveness. However, <u>I'd like to emphasize that</u> the nature of this relationship is still not clear.

2b Read each of these excerpts from a lecture and decide what type of signposting is being used in each case.

1 There is room for future research on the extent to which product type is associated with the attractiveness of the models used to advertise them, certainly. But, the essential thing is, there is definitely a link between the two things.

2 … this suggests a preference for normally attractive models. By the way, there is also some debate about whether the 'highly attractive'–'normally attractive' distinction is based on reasonable assumptions of what the consumers themselves look like.

3 So today I want to talk about 'affect', which in this field refers to the psychological impact of a particular image, and the positive or negative emotions associated with it.

2c Listen to three short excerpts from a lecture in which the speaker digresses, and answer these questions.

4.3

1 What is the speaker's main focus in each excerpt?

2 What does the speaker talk about during the digression?

2d Compare your answers with a partner.

2e You are researching the most effective way to advertise a single product in different cultures. You want to find out what research suggests about how people in different cultures respond to different types of advertising models.

In small groups, discuss what you think are the most likely answers to these questions.

1 Do people in different cultures share similar ideas about what an 'attractive' model is?

2 Do people in different cultures expect the same thing from adverts?

3 If an advert filmed in one country, and intended for consumers there, was broadcast in a different country, how effective would the advert be?

4.4

2f Listen to a different lecturer speaking about this topic. How many times does the speaker digress?

2g Listen again. Take notes in the space below only on the information which is relevant to answer the questions in 2e.

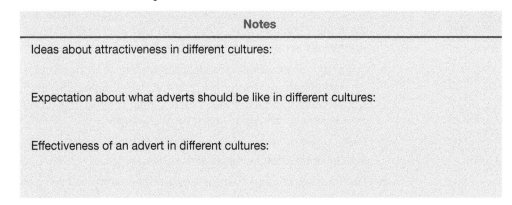

Notes
Ideas about attractiveness in different cultures:
Expectation about what adverts should be like in different cultures:
Effectiveness of an advert in different cultures:

2h Compare your notes with a partner. Add any information that you missed.

3 Understanding the relationship between parts of a talk

In *Language for Study* level 1 you learned how coordinating conjunctions such as *and*, *so* and *but* are used to show logical relations between ideas in a talk. Speakers can use a number of additional techniques to show logical relations between ideas. This might include expressions for:

1 Giving additional information
This shows the importance of perceived appearance. Furthermore, consumers have been shown to show a strong preference for products displayed in a believable context.

2 Giving contrasting information
A study by Hamm in 1996 indicated that Americans tended to estimate 'beauty' more by bodily shape. In contrast to this, a study by Kono in 2004 suggested that many Japanese tended to judge 'beauty' from facial features.

3 Giving similar information
Kono's research has been reproduced in a number of East Asian countries of different linguistic and cultural backgrounds. Similarly to Kono, these studies tend to find a definition of 'beauty' in terms of facial rather than bodily characteristics.

3a Read these words and phrases for showing logical relations between ideas, and decide what type of relationship each one shows: additional information (A), contrasting information (C) or similar information (S).

	A, C or S		A, C or S
An additional point		A further point	
Besides		As well as	
Another point		Another thing to bear in mind	
Further		Although	
A similar point		Furthermore	
In addition		Moreover	
In much the same way		However	
Similarly		On the other hand	
Apart from		Whereas	
Additionally		Rather	
We can add		Nevertheless	
Despite		Alternatively	
In a similar way		Not only … but also	

3b Work in pairs. Read the short excerpts from a lecture about advertising. Each excerpt contains two ideas. Discuss what kind of relationship the two ideas have (e.g. addition, contrast or similarity) and what kind of expression can be used to link them.

1 The feeling of 'beauty' is a mysterious effect of the arrangement and combination of different things – colours, shapes, forms and so on. It's not found in any single element; _____, it's a feeling that we get from just the right combination of those elements.

2 Research evidence suggests that there are certain things which most people would agree are beautiful; _____, there is still a great deal of debate about the extent to which notions of beauty are common between people.

3 Now, the sense of what is beautiful is of interest, clearly, to people involved in a range of creative industries. Product designers, for instance, are guided _____ by their own sense of beauty, _____ by a feeling for what other people, consumers, for instance, might agree is beautiful.

3c Listen to the excerpts and fill in the blanks in the transcript in 3b.

4.5

4a Divide into two groups. Each group should choose one of the studies below. Each study investigates the effect of using 'highly attractive models' (HAMs) or 'normally attractive models' (NAMs) in advertising. Read the information from the study and discuss your attitude to it. Each member of the group should prepare notes that you can use to help you give a speech presenting your ideas to your classmates.

Make notes about:

a the aim of the study

b the method of the study

c the results of the study

d your attitude about what the results of the study reveal.

Study 1

Aim: To investigate whether consumers trust adverts more depending on the attractiveness of the models used.

Method: 250 female students were shown pairs of adverts for a range of products. One of the adverts featured an HA model; the other advert featured an NA model.

Findings:

	% Rating HAM as more trustworthy	% Rating NAM as more trustworthy	% Not sure
Coffee advert	43	51	6
Soap advert	53	47	0
Make-up advert	58	40	2
Insurance advert	46	49	5

Study 2

Aim: To investigate the relationship between product type, model attractiveness and consumer trust.

Method: Thirty individuals of mixed ages and genders were shown pairs of adverts for four different products. One of the adverts featured an HA model; the other advert featured an NA model. Participants were asked to say which advert and model they trusted more.

Findings:

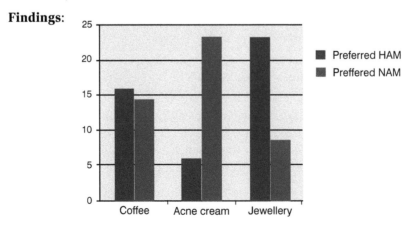

4b Work in pairs, with one member from each of the two groups in 4a. Take turns delivering a short speech about each study to your partner. As you listen, decide what the speaker's attitude is to the information that they are presenting.

5 Review and extension

Using adverbs with modals to show attitude

5a The words below can be used to modify the modal adjectives that you looked at in 1c.

Example

It is **highly likely** that the attractiveness of the model used can influence the success of an advert.

Decide which of these adverbs show *very strong certainty* (V), *strong certainty* (S), and *moderate certainty* (M).

	'V, S or M'			'V, S or M'
1 extremely		4 quite		
2 fairly		6 very		
3 reasonably		5 highly		

5b Look back at the data from the two studies in 4a. Make sentences using adverbs and epistemic adjectives to give your opinion on these questions.

1 How likely is it that the attractiveness of a model can affect consumers' opinions about adverts?

2 How likely are women to trust a coffee advert featuring a NAM?

3 How likely are people to trust an advert for acne cream featuring

    a A HAM?

    b A NAM?

5c Listen to a speaker give their opinions on the questions in 4a. To what extent do you agree with their ideas?

4.6

Using signposting

5d Read the excerpts from a lecture and decide which of the underlined words or phrases in each pair is more appropriate.

1 The creation of adverts presents a considerable challenge to marketers and advertisers. <u>One crucial aspect of this is / What I mean by that is</u> the appearance of the model used.

2 One study found that attractive celebrities are considered more believable in adverts than unattractive ones. <u>Moreover / Nevertheless</u>, this is true no matter what product they are advertising.

3 Consumers give higher ratings of trust to models who they believe appear to be experts. <u>Another point I'd like to make is / However, it's important to remember</u> that this may not be related to attractiveness alone.

4 Let's think about the 'product–model match-up'. <u>What that means is / By the way</u> the model must seem to be well suited to the product they are advertising.

5 One researcher found the attractiveness of the model made no difference when advertising products where attractiveness isn't relevant, such as tools or car insurance. <u>However / Furthermore</u>, he suggested that using overly attractive models for products like these might actually decrease people's trust in them.

4.7

5e Listen to the excerpts and check your answers.

Understanding written information

By the end of Part B you will be able to:

- understand register variations in academic and non-academic vocabulary
- understand the use of affixes in academic vocabulary
- understand nominalisation.

1 Understanding register variations in academic and non-academic vocabulary

The vocabulary of English is formed from a mixture of words of quite different origin. Many shorter words are originally Anglo-Saxon (sometimes called 'Old English'). Alongside these, there are also many words with identical meanings which originated from Greek, Latin or French.

Example

*Perspective is a **way** of representing a three-dimensional object on a flat surface.* (Anglo-Saxon)

*Perspective is a **method** of representing a three-dimensional object on a flat surface.* (originally from Greek *meta*, meaning 'after', and *hodos*, meaning 'way')

Words of Greek, Latin or French origin are often considered more scholarly and formal, and tend to be used more in academic writing.

1a Read this excerpt from a student essay. Answer the questions.

1 According to the writer, how did Renaissance art differ from the art of the medieval period which had preceded it?

2 Which country is often associated most closely with the Renaissance?

The Renaissance marked the **period** in fifteenth- and sixteenth-century Europe which saw a transformation in artistic styles. The **term** Renaissance itself literally means 'rebirth' or 'revival', and it was indeed a period in which artistic interest in the natural and realistic arts of classical Greece and Rome was revived. The Renaissance, however, was more than simply a revival of interest in the art of antiquity, but was also a break from the non-realistic style of painting in medieval Christian Europe. Whereas artists and craftsmen in the medieval period, which preceded the Renaissance, had created more stylised and less lifelike images, Renaissance art was characterised by so-called 'truth to nature': artists of the period strove to **observe** things as they actually were, and **imitate** real life; they were concerned to **represent** proportion and perspective accurately in the images they **created**. Thus while medieval art can often look two-dimensional and unrealistic, the art of the fifteenth and sixteenth centuries more often **resembles** real figures and scenes, as though the aim of the artist was to create a convincing illusion of reality.

The nation most often associated with the Renaissance is Italy, which is unsurprising given the large number of classical Roman ruins available as sources of inspiration to artists in the country. However, the creation of innovative, lifelike art also **occurred** elsewhere throughout Europe around this time.

1b Discuss your answers with a partner.

1c Work in pairs. The words in bold in 1a are more formal. Match them with their less formal synonyms.

1	see	5	make
2	happen	6	word
3	look like	7	copy
4	show	8	time

1d Here are some more formal words. Work in pairs. Check any words you don't understand in a dictionary. Then match the more formal words in (1–10) with their less formal synonyms (a–j).

French / Graeco-Latin words	Anglo-Saxon words / phrases
1 assist	a feeling
2 attain	b way
3 response	c reach
4 depart (from)	d help
5 obtain	e spread
6 distribute	f answer
7 consume	g move away from
8 technique	h need
9 require	i get
10 attitude	j use

1e Read the extract below from a textbook about art history. According to the writer, how did the art created in Italy differ from that created in Northern Europe during the Renaissance? Discuss with a partner.

Europe **made** beautiful, and realistic, art in the fifteenth and sixteenth centuries. This **time** is known as the Renaissance, or 'revival', because it **moved away** from the less lifelike art of the Middle Ages (the period between the Classical Age of ancient Greece and Rome, and the Renaissance) and revived the more true-to-life art of classical times. Classical art was thought to be more 'real' than art in the Middle Ages because it aimed to capture a genuine image of the human form: people **looked like** real people. Renaissance artists revived this reality, or 'truth', in their art, with classical writing on proportion, and contemporary Italian scientific discoveries about perspective, helping to make this possible. Mathematics **helped** artists in the recreation of nature's beauty in sculpture, architecture and paintings: human beings could be **shown** with accurate proportions; landscapes could be recreated on flat walls as though a window had been opened to the world. Meanwhile, art in Northern Europe was less affected by Renaissance teachings. While some art continued to be created in a flat, less true-to-life, manner, Jan van Eyck (1390?–1441), of the Netherlands, did try to make his paintings realistic. He copied minute detail such as individual hairs in an animal's fur and strands in a tapestry to make his images seem true to life, but did not try to recreate the world only by using the Italian **ways** of perspective or proportion. Jan van Eyck did make his painting beautiful and realistic through making his art colourful and detailed, with his art no less effective in terms of beauty and reality than his Italian counterparts'.

1f Work in pairs. In the text in 1e the words and phrases in bold could be replaced by more formal expressions. Replace them with more formal equivalents from 1a and 1d.

1g Work in pairs. Read the two extracts below and decide if each word in bold is formal or less formal. Try to make the language more academic in tone by exchanging any informal words for more formal ones where appropriate. Use a dictionary or thesaurus to help you find more formal alternatives where necessary.

> **1**
>
> 'Contrapposto' is a classical **technique** used in the visual arts to make the human form **appear** more lifelike, or dynamic. In sculpture and drawings of the human body, the weight of the subject is taken on one foot, with the arms and shoulders twisting away to create movement. During the Middle Ages this technique was never used, with artists unconcerned about **making** true-to-life impressions of human beings. This technique was **revived** in Renaissance Italy, and can be seen in the work of fifteenth- and sixteenth-century artists from **across** Europe.

> **2**
>
> The **period** of European history between the fifth and fifteenth centuries is still, largely, **known** as the 'Middle' or 'Dark' Ages. Both are negative terms that were coined in Italy in the fifteenth century to **say** that classical learning had been lost with the destruction of the Roman Empire in the fifth century, but was being **brought back** in the classical Renaissance of the fifteenth century. These derogatory **terms** still affect the way many people judge the art of this **period**.

2 Understanding the use of affixes in academic vocabulary

Academic vocabulary contains a large number of complex words. Complex vocabulary is often formed by combining a word *root* with one or more *affixes*.

Affixes can be either *prefixes* (which come before the root word) or *suffixes* (which come after the root word). The word 'unacceptable' is formed in this way:

Prefix	Root	Suffix
un	accept	able

Most prefixes change the meaning of the word, e.g. ***un*** + *acceptable* gives the word a negative meaning.

Most suffixes change the word class, e.g. *accept* + ***able*** = *acceptable*, changing the word from a verb to an adjective.

The root can be an independent word, e.g. *re* + ***create***. However, some roots can only appear with an affix, e.g. *re* + ***vert***; *de* + ***tract***. This is because the meaning of the root has changed or no longer exists in modern English.

Understanding what affixes mean, and how they affect the word root, cannot help you to understand the exact meaning of an unknown word while you are reading, but it can help you to get some idea of the general meaning of a new word, and therefore help you to understand a text without having to check so many words in a dictionary.

Prefixes

2a Work in pairs. Use the example sentences below to decide the meaning of each prefix. Make a note of these in the table. Note that, as described on p.171, in some cases the root no longer exists in modern English.

1 This style of art gradually **dis**appeared during the fourteenth century.

2 This suggests there was some **dis**satisfaction with the less true-to-life art of the medieval period.

3 During this period, artists **re**vived the more true-to-life art of classical times.

4 Mathematics helped artists in the **re**creation of nature's beauty in sculpture, architecture and paintings.

5 He has been criticised for **over**using bright colours in his work.

6 The art of the medieval period was **under**valued for generations.

7 It is so common as to be quite **un**important.

8 Art experts and restorers will need to work carefully to **un**bend the frame without damaging the piece.

9 Older paintings are easily damaged if **mis**handled.

10 Her works, though popular, are widely **mis**understood.

11 Despite being unknown during his lifetime, his work is now widely considered to **out**sell that of other artists from the time.

12 Experts from across Europe are **co**operating to investigate the discovery.

13 The two **co**-authors of the article have defended their claim about the image.

14 The two volunteer groups were **sub**divided into three teams each.

15 The report should be completed with clear headings and **sub**headings.

16 It is **im**probable that the work was created much earlier than 1900.

17 Despite claims that it was painted in 1604, this is in fact **in**correct; it was probably painted around 1620.

18 Though he has described himself as **non**-political, in fact many of his paintings carry a clearly political message.

Prefix	Meaning(s)
dis-	*opposite of the root word*
re-	
over-	
under-	
un-	
mis-	
out-	
co-	
sub-	
im/in-	
non-	

2b Read the sentences below and decide which of the two prefixes in brackets is most suitable.

1 This eighteenth-century painting (mis/re)creates the Battle of Bosworth Field, which took place in 1485.

2 (Dis/Re)colouration – the loss or change of original colour from paint – is common in very old works.

3 Though a popular painting, it was in fact created by an (un/re)named artist whose identity remains a mystery.

4 This method was forgotten during the medieval period, but was (un/re)introduced during the Renaissance.

5 Critics complain that his last work was (mis/over)priced, selling for about three times more than it was actually worth given its poor quality.

6 The image, which for many years was (mis/re)taken for the Roman philosopher Seneca, is now believed to represent the Greek poet Hesiod.

7 Despite being dismissed by critics, her art (out/co)sells all others on display at the gallery.

8 By the time of her death, the work was still (un/in)complete.

9 A new exhibition of art from the Silk Road will be (non/co)-funded by three museums in Europe and one in China.

10 A new study using MRI compares the brain activity of an artist with that of a (non/in)-artist.

11 Despite a knowledge of perspective, artists of the Northern Renaissance still produced images of objects that were (im/non)possible.

12 Fifteenth-century Northern European artists have tended to be unfairly presented as a less-important (sub/mis)group of the Renaissance.

Suffixes

2c Work in pairs. Discuss the meaning of each of the words in the table, then complete the table by changing the word forms, using the suffixes in the box.

-ise	-en	-ate	-fy/ify	-tion	-ity	-ness	-ous	-al

Noun	Adjective	Verb
critic		
	bright	
optimum		
		recreate
	real	
	ugly	
fame		
danger		

2d Work in pairs. Choose the best form of each word to complete the sentences.

1 Some scholars have tended to unfairly (critic) _____criticise_____ art and architecture of the Middle Ages over the years.

2 Area lamps are frequently used to (bright) _____ dark corners of rooms.

3 Computers would be designed into the workspace in order to (optimum) _____ work performance.

4 Mathematics assisted artists in the (recreate) _____ of nature's beauty in sculpture.

5 Italian artists of the Renaissance were using different techniques to attain beauty and (real) _____ in their art.

6 This is a quality known as 'affect' – the feeling that an individual has when they feel pleasure or unease, or sense beauty or (ugly)_____.

7 Brunelleschi (1377–1446) is (fame) _____ for both his invention and use of classical Roman techniques in his architecture.

2e Work in small groups. You are going to read an extract from a journal article about the relationship between the design features of rooms and the moods of people who work or study in them. Before you read, discuss the effect that each of these features might have on an occupant's mood and ability to study or work successfully.

A lighting   D colour schemes

B arrangement of furniture   E decorations

C design of furniture   F plants

2f Read this extract from a journal article about room and building design. What type of word (e.g. noun, verb, etc.) do you think belongs in each blank?

Ergonomics research has been employed extensively to 1) _____ optimal environmental conditions for individuals at work. It is well understood that human task performance and mood can be 2) _____ by the design of the work or study environment. For instance, there is evidence that students studying in rooms with green plants tend to get higher scores than those where greenery is absent, while on the other hand, test subjects tend to report lower moods in rooms where the colour scheme is 3)_____. It has also been suggested that there is a significant 4)_____ between room design and individual levels of 5)_____. It is worthwhile, therefore, to try to 6)_____ which aspects of room design are most closely associated with improvements in the psychological state and task performance of their occupants.

There are a number of environmental features such as odour, building materials, decoration, proportionality, noise and so on which may be 7)_____ in mood and performance. However, one key feature of room design is the level and type of lighting available: the 8)_____ of a room has been shown to positively affect mood and work performance in a number of studies; students have been found to score lower on simple reasoning tests taken in 9)_____ rooms, while research with undergraduates indicates that poor lighting can 10)_____ feelings of tension.

2g Work in pairs. Choose words from the box below to complete the blanks in the extract in 2f.

windowless	heighten	brightness	identify	optimised
investigate	monotonous	implicated	creativity	interaction

3 Understanding nominalisation

> Nominalisation – expressing complex ideas with noun phrases rather than verb phrases – is very common in academic English. Nominalisation is the process of converting a clause into a noun phrase; doing this makes it possible to present the information from two or more clauses in one sentence. While this is more efficient, it can also make the ideas in academic texts more difficult to understand for someone who is not familiar with academic writing.

3a Read two short versions of the same text below. Which one do you think is more typical of academic writing, and which seems more typical of a spoken lecture?

> **1** During the Renaissance, artists produced 'beautiful' and 'realistic' art. Some artists in Italy used classical ideas about proportion and new techniques of perspective to help them with this, whereas some artists in the Netherlands preferred to make their art realistic mainly by copying details observed from real life.
>
> **2** The Renaissance period's production of 'beautiful' and 'realistic' art was achieved in Italy through the use of classical ideas about proportion and new techniques of perspective, whereas in the Netherlands this realism was achieved through the copying of details observed from real life.

3b Read two extracts from the texts above. How is the word 'produce' used differently in the two sentences?

1 During the Renaissance, artists produced 'beautiful' and 'realistic' art.

2 The Renaissance period's production of 'beautiful' and 'realistic' art was achieved …

> Nominalisation can be achieved in several ways:
>
> **1 Exchanging verbs for noun phrases**
>
> *Example*
>
> *Italian artists **used** new techniques – Italian artists' **use** of new techniques*
>
> *Roman Italy **dominated** the world – Roman Italy's **domination** of the world*
>
> **2 Exchanging adjectives for nouns**
>
> *Example*
>
> *Renaissance art is more **realistic** – The **realism** of Renaissance art / Renaissance art's **realism***
>
> *This is an **important** event – The **importance** of this event / This event's **importance***

3c Nominalise these sentences to change them into clauses.

    1 German tribes destroyed Rome.   *Rome's destruction by German tribes*

    2 The flying buttress was unpopular.

    3 Medieval architects were inventive.

    4 The German artist Albrecht Durer toured Italy.

    5 They imitate classical models.

Nominalisation can be used to combine ideas from two sentences into a single sentence.

Example

Italian artists produced beautiful and realistic art. The artists achieved this by using classical ideas about proportion.

⬇

Italian artists' production of beautiful and realistic art was achieved by using classical ideas about proportion.

3d Use nominalisation to create a single sentence from the following sets of sentences.

    1 The Roman architect Vitruvius showed the connection between human proportions and geometry. Vitruvius's ideas inspired Italian artists such as Leonardo da Vinci to use mathematical calculations when drawing people.

    2 Fifteenth-century artists relied on classical teachings about proportion. These teachings influenced their art.

    3 Roman Italy had dominated the world. However, Rome's dominance was gradually destroyed by German tribes including the 'Goths' and 'Vandals'.

    4 Italian Renaissance writers used negative language to discuss the art of the Middle Ages. This has influenced the way people have viewed the art of the period.

> **LESSON TASK** **4 Reading texts with high-frequency academic vocabulary**

4a Use the information you have learned about art in this unit to help you discuss these questions in small groups.

    1 Which countries are particularly associated with the Renaissance?

    2 What innovations in painting were developed during this period?

4b Read the text on p.177 and answer the questions. (At this stage, do not use a dictionary to help you with unknown words.)

    1 What are the author's opinions about the two questions in 4a?

    2 Why are the artistic innovations of the Renaissance important?

The art historian Ernst Gombrich (1976) famously divided the **achievements** of visual arts in the Renaissance into two categories: the development of **perspective**, and the way that light reacted with various types of surface material. The first **phenomenon** is often **linked** with the Italian Renaissance, whereas the second is more **distinctly** associated with the Northern European painters, **specifically** artists in the Netherlands. There has tended to be an academic **focus** on Italy as the '**dominant paradigm**' of the Renaissance (Silver, 2006), with the **innovations** of the Northern European artists being somewhat overshadowed by those of their Italian counterparts. This **bias persisted** until relatively recently thanks in large part to the claims of influential scholars such as Gombrich and Panofsky. However, recent research has somewhat **reversed** this imbalance in the view of the achievements of the Northern and Italian Renaissance traditions.

So-called 'single-point' perspective is **significant** because it is a highly effective method of **simulating convincing** illusions of three-dimensional relationships between objects created on a flat, two-dimensional surface. **Hence**, it has **acquired** a reputation among art historians and laypeople alike as symbolising the highest achievement in **complexity** in fifteenth-century art.

Though the Italian Filippo Brunelleschi (1377–1446) is **acknowledged** as the pioneer of the use of single-point perspective in art, the first to write down **instructions** for artists on the use of perspective was in fact Leon Battista Alberti (1404–72). Alberti had developed an interest in ancient Greek and Roman **texts** while studying law at the University of Bologna, and this interest may well have informed his later interest in the application of classical theories to art. Alberti wrote his first work, *On Painting*, in both Latin and Italian language **versions**, though his work was not **published** until the following century. However, the evidence indicates that painters were already **responding** to the ideas in his text well before this date.

Alberti's **theories** of perspective and proportion in art are **derived** from investigations of optics and geometry found in the writings of Ancient Greek philosophers such as Euclid and Aristotle. Beginning with a **brief** outline of the basics of geometry before discussing vision and **proportion** in more detail, Alberti's text **establishes** a **framework** for the use of perspective in paintings.

4c Compare your answers with the other members of your group.

4d In the text above, the words in bold are some of the most frequently used in academic English. Understanding frequently occurring words such as these can improve your reading comprehension and speed. Scan the words in bold and make a note of any words that you do not understand. Then answer these questions for each unknown word:

1 What class of word is it (e.g. noun, adjective, etc.)?

2 What does the sentence around it mean?

4e Work in pairs. Try to guess what any unknown words might mean from their context before you check in a dictionary.

4f Enter any new words into your vocabulary logbook.

5 Review and extension

Academic vocabulary

5a Read the sentences 1–10 below and decide whether the underlined word is suitably formal or not. Then replace the underlined words with their more suitable academic equivalents, as in the example below.

Example

Interest in visual arts has been ~~brought back~~ *revived* in recent years.

1 The charging of an admission fee has not <u>stopped</u> visitors from coming to the museum.

2 People interviewed said that they couldn't understand specialised artistic <u>words</u>.

3 The museum will display a collection of statues from the medieval <u>time</u>.

4 This has been painted using a <u>way</u> known as chiaroscuro.

5 It is likely that the painting was <u>made</u> in the early seventeenth century.

6 The effect of contrapposto is to make the subject <u>look</u> more life-like.

7 This effect <u>happens</u> when oil paints are mixed with sand or sawdust.

8 Museums and art galleries across the country are currently struggling to <u>get</u> funding.

9 The results of the research <u>show</u> that appreciation varies according to the amount of time spent considering a painting.

10 Three of the volunteers claimed that they had a negative <u>feeling</u> towards art in general.

Affixes

5b Identify the prefixes and suffixes in the underlined words in these sentences. Then make notes on the following questions.

• What are the meanings of the prefixes in these words?

• Which suffixes indicate: a noun? a verb? an adjective?

1 Toyne (1996) has observed the <u>interaction</u> between gallery visitors and artworks.

2 Visitors were asked to rate their <u>pre- and post-visit</u> attitudes towards the exhibition.

3 Viewers of paintings are said to <u>transfer</u> their own personal meaning onto the paintings they view.

4 Yves Klein produced a series of <u>monochrome</u> works during the 1950s.

5 Sculptor Carl Smith was considered by many to be a <u>pseudo-intellectual</u>.

6 The <u>surface</u> of the canvas is quite rough.

7 A high <u>percentage</u> of visitors to the gallery are American.

8 Toyne (2001) rejects the <u>supremacy</u> of Renaissance art.

9 The <u>workmanship</u> is of the highest quality.

10 <u>Postmodernist</u> criticism has contributed greatly to the development of contemporary western art.

Part **C** Investigating

By the end of Part C you will be able to:

- recognize key research terminology
- understand the language features of research reports
- write about research limitations.

1   Recognizing key research terminology

1a   Work in small groups. Discuss these questions.

1   Have you ever done any primary research?

2   If so, what were the aims of the research?

3   What methods did you use to gather the information?

4   What results did you find?

5   Were there any limitations in your research?

> Understanding key research terminology helps you to understand other people's studies as well as to design and write up your own research. In this section, research terminology is divided into three categories:
>
> **1** qualities of research method and results
>
> **2** objects of study
>
> **3** researcher's actions.

1b   Work in pairs. Match the words in the boxes with the definitions in the tables that follow. Use a dictionary to help you. Some definitions have more than one word.

1

> reliability   validity   ~~representative~~   random   limitations   generalisable   findings
> observation   confounding factors

Qualities of research method and results	Definition
	a measure of how likely the conclusions of a study are to be truthful
representative	a sample population which is typical of all the other members of the population from which it is drawn
	the quality of a study which gives the same results each time it is repeated
	happening by chance; without choosing or doing something deliberately
	the recording of facts or information
	the quality of conclusions from a study which can be applied to other situations
	unexpected factors which may affect the results of a study in a way that makes the findings less certain

	aspects of a study which prevent the conclusions from being applied to other situations, or reduce the certainty about the conclusions
	the results of a study

2

variable~~variable~~ sample   sample size   respondent   population   control   (test) subject
participant   volunteer   phenomenon

Objects of study	Definition
variable	a quantity or condition which can be affected by another thing; the relationships between two or more of these are often the objects of a study
	an object or individual which is not changed, so that its condition can be compared with objects or individuals that are deliberately changed as part of the study
	a group of people or things chosen from a larger group, and tested or researched in order to reach conclusions about the larger group
	something that exists or happens and which can be felt or experienced.
	members of a sample group
	the number of objects or individuals included in a study
	individuals who are interviewed or tested as part of a study

3

~~carry out~~   conduct   generalise   evaluate   observe   control a variable

Researcher's actions	Definition
carry out	to do or complete a task (especially something that you had planned to do)
	to judge the quality, value or importance of something
	to take a measurement or record data
	to apply the conclusions of a study on a small group to the larger group from which they originated / to apply the conclusions in other situations which are similar to the ones studied
	to reduce the chance that an unexpected factor may affect the results of an experiment

1c Work in pairs. You are going to read one description of an ergonomics research project each, either A or B only. Read about your project and make separate notes on what the researchers discovered, using these headings.

- Aims
- Subjects
- Findings
- Variables
- Methods

A

It is widely understood that a poor posture while typing is responsible for back and shoulder problems in office workers. Researchers attempted to investigate how effectively a new ergonomic chair and table design can help to improve posture and reduce back pain.

Participants:

50 'heavy' computer users (25 male; 25 female) aged between 19 and 64.

All suffer from back pain.

Method:

Participants were randomly divided into two groups: Group A (25 people) used the new design of chair and table; Group B (25 people) was a control group and continued to use ordinary equipment.

The researchers tested the design by asking participants in both groups to record their back pain and hours of computer use over a period of six months.

Findings:

Table 1: Average hours spent on the computer per day and per session

	Group A		Group B	
	Male	Female	Male	Female
Per day	8.1	6.7	7.9	8.0
Per session	2.5	2.8	1.5	2.2

Table 2: Respondents reporting instances of back pain during the study period

	Group A (%)	Group B (%)
Male	14	28
Female	13	26

Table 3: Average frequency of back pain episodes during the period of the study

	Group A		Group B	
	Male	Female	Male	Female
Frequency	3	2	4	3

1 – infrequent (less than once a month); **5** – persistent (every time the participant worked at the desk)

B

Researchers noted that heavy computer users can suffer repetitive strain injury (RSI) in their hands as a consequence of typing on a keyboard too much. A new ergonomic keyboard is designed which it is hoped will reduce RSI in heavy computer users.

Participants:

Ten 'heavy' computer users. All 10 participants have a history of RSI.

Method:

The participants used the new keyboards for a period of three months. They were asked to keep a record of incidents of RSI and hours spent typing each day.

Findings:

Table 1: Hours spent typing per day and per session

	Male	Female
Per day	4.3	4.9
Per session	1.2	1.1

Only three of the test subjects reported problems with RSI during the period of the test.

1d Using the vocabulary from 1b to help you, prepare to explain this research to your partner by adding to your notes. Then take turns to describe your research projects.

2 Understanding the language features of research reports

2a Work in pairs. Discuss these questions.

a When you are typing, do you prefer to support your forearms somehow?

b Does supporting your forearms make a difference to your sitting posture?

c Which is more comfortable: working at a computer screen or reading a book which is flat on a desk?

d How would you define a 'good' posture for working at a desk?

e Have you ever seen or used a desk or chair which has been specially designed to improve posture?

There is variation between disciplines and individual writers, but the *methods, results* and *discussion* sections of a research report tend to have distinct patterns in:

1 the verb tenses used

2 the extent to which the researchers mention their own ideas

3 the use of modal verbs (e.g. *may, might, could*)

4 the use of modal adjectives meaning *definite, probable* or *possible* (e.g. *likely, possible, certain*).

2b Work in small groups. Discuss what you think the differences may be between *methods, results* and *discussion* sections, in terms of the factors mentioned above.

Methods section

2c Read an example methods section from a study investigating posture while working at a desk. Identify the features mentioned above, and check your answers to 2b.

2 Methods

2.1 Study design

The independent variables in this study were display height and desk type. Three levels of display height were investigated: (1) high, where the top of the computer display screen was set at the participant's eye height; (2) mid, where the bottom of the computer display was set at desk height; (3) book, which was a piece of paper laid flat on a desk. The second factor, desk type, had two levels: (1) 'traditional' straight desk set at 3 cm below participant's elbow height with forearms unsupported; and (2) 'horseshoe' partly wrapped-around curved desk set at 3 cm above elbow height, enabling full forearm support.

2.2 Participants

Eighteen males and eighteen females aged between 18 and 25 years were recruited by notices in local universities and community newspapers and through personal contacts. This age range was specified to ensure that the skeletal condition of each participant was mature but not affected by ageing. These participants had no history of significant chronic disorders in the neck and upper limb, no current neck and/or upper limb pain and no diagnosed conditions in their bones, muscles, tendons and so on (musculoskeletal system). Participants were of average height. All participants were using computers at least two times per week for a total of at least two hours per week. Level of typing skill was measured using a standardised typing test (TypeMaster Pro, TypingMaster Inc., Helsinki, Finland).

2.3 Variables

Highly visible markers were placed at key points on the participants' bodies. Markers were also placed on the desk and display. The positions of the markers were recorded by seven cameras, and their positions in the 2nd and 3rd, 5th and 6th, and 9th and 10th minutes were determined after the experiment was complete. Angles of change in the gaze (eye to visual target), head and neck, trunk, shoulder, arm and wrist were calculated from the position of the markers.

2.4 Procedure

Participants completed a general history knowledge task in each condition which required reading from an electronic (with navigation by mouse) or paper encyclopedia and completing an activity sheet using either keyboard/mouse or pen-and-paper input. The order of the task was randomly allocated to task condition. The study was conducted in a climate- and lighting-controlled laboratory. Upon arrival at the laboratory, participants signed written informed consent, were fitted with reflective markers and were instructed in the task.

A standard office chair was adjusted to the participant's height. A specially designed desk was adjusted to height and shape. An adjustable height display arm was used to adjust the computer screen so that the top of the display was set level with the participant's eye height / bottom of display at desk height or turned away from the participant during paper conditions. The same keyboard and mouse were used in all computer conditions.

The natural range of movement for each participant was then measured. Finally, participants sat in a relaxed 'usual' posture looking at an eye-height visual target. Participants performed each task for ten minutes. Between tasks, participants moved away from the desk area while the desk and display were adjusted. Participants worked for ten minutes in each condition followed by five-minute breaks. The study was approved by the Human Research Ethics Committee of Curtin University of Technology.

In a methods section, the writer describes the key actions that were carried out during the research.

1 Reference to the researcher's actions, frequently written in the past tense, passive voice: *Eighteen males and eighteen females aged between 18 and 25 years* **were recruited** *by notices in local universities and community newspapers and through personal contacts.*

2 Reference to the actions of test subjects, frequently written in the past simple tense: *Participants* **completed** *a general history knowledge task.*

2d Work in pairs. Correct the tense and voice errors in this extract.

> In Experiment 1, we examine the effect of the arrangement and height of a work chair and desk on participants' ratings of comfort. We have selected three different types of desk-and-chair combination. We will ask participants to carry out an essay-writing task by hand. In addition, the participants must type the essay on a computer keyboard set at a fixed distance from the edge of the table.

> Words and phrases which show the writer's opinion (e.g. modal verbs such as *may, might,* etc; attitude adjectives such as *important, useful,* etc.; and modal adjectives such as *likely, possible,* etc.) tend to be avoided in methods sections.

2e The extract from a methods section below contains words and phrases which show the writer's opinion. Read the extract and make notes about how to improve it.

> Sixteen participants were recruited to join the study. Each participant was paid £20 for their involvement, as we thought this was likely to attract more people to volunteer. However, the low number of recruits suggests that this payment may have been too low. The participants were randomly assigned to one of the desk-and-chair arrangements. The mean age of the female volunteers was 21.1 years; the mean age of the male volunteers was 23.9 years, however, so it is possible that the results may be affected by this age difference. That said, it is not a very significant gap in ages, so this may not have affected the study. The reason for the difference in ages is unclear.

Results section

2f Read the results section from the study investigating posture while working at a desk and check your answers to 2b.

> ## 3 Results
>
> Table 5 shows the spinal angles in the different study conditions. Table 7 shows the upper limb angles in the different conditions. Significant effects of display and desk were found on spinal and arm postures.
>
> Compared with the mid display, the high display resulted in 15" less head change in the angle of the head (flexion), 6" less neck flexion, with a 23" less gaze angle. There were no upper limb differences between high and mid displays. There were even larger differences in head and neck postures between book and high display. Compared with the mid display, the book display resulted in marked increases in head (20") and neck (18") flexion associated with a 39" lower gaze angle. The book display also results in more bending of the spine, characterised by bending of the head (2" to the right) and neck (3" to the left), 5" more head rotation to the left and 2" more trunk rotation to the left than both electronic displays. The mid display postures lay between high and book postures.
>
> The curved desk resulted in spinal postures essentially similar to the straight desk except for 2" less head flexion. In contrast, the curved desk resulted in quite different arm postures, characterised by straighter wrists and raised shoulders.

In the results section the writer summarises the key findings of the study.

1 Both present and past tense can be used in this section.

Examples (a) *Table 5 **shows** the spinal angles in the different study conditions.*

(b) *The book display also **results** in more bending of the spine.*

(c) *There **were** no upper limb differences between high and mid displays.*

The past tense can be used to indicate specific results that are unique to the study. It gives a more objective feel to the claims, reporting only what was observed in the research. The present tense can be used to describe findings which are more generally applicable.

2 Words and phrases which show the writer's opinion (e.g. modal verbs such as *may*, *might*, etc; attitude adjectives such as *important*, *useful*, etc.; and adjectives such as *likely*, *possible*, etc.) may appear in results sections.

Example

Significant *effects of display and desk were found on spinal and arm postures.*

However, the aim is for the results section to be an objective description of findings, so the writer's opinion is not strongly emphasized in this section.

2g Work in pairs. Read the extract from a results section of a study investigating a new design of computer mouse. What did the researchers discover?

> As Table 1 shows, pressure on the wrist while holding the mouse in a resting position was higher in the standard-design mouse (A) than in the ergonomically designed one (B). During the dragging and clicking task, pressure on the user's wrists rose significantly in mouse type A, while there was only a slight increase in wrist pressure in type B. In the participant response evaluation, users rated Mouse A as significantly less comfortable than Mouse B. There were two reasons for this: firstly, Mouse A required more pressure to move, and the more traditional shape of the mouse meant that users had to grip it more tightly with their fingers when moving it.

2h The extract presents a more objective view of the results by using the past tense. Which verbs could be changed to the present simple to suggest that some of the results of the study could be more generally applied?

2i Work in pairs. Choose one of the studies outlined in 1c, then write a suitable description of the results.

Discussion section

2j Read the discussion section from the study investigating posture while working at a desk and check your answers to 2b.

4 Discussion

This data is the most comprehensive description of head and arm postures during information technology use. No prior studies have compared computer and paper information technology.

The high display had no important effects on upper limb posture, but resulted in substantially less change in the angle of the head and neck than the mid display, as was expected. However, as we have argued (Burgess-Limerick et al., 2000), whilst less head angling of the head has been recommended, it is possible that the physical impact on deep muscles may be increased, though the impact on the muscles has yet to be estimated.

The book display had a substantial effect on the changing angle of the head and neck (flexion), as expected. Whilst a number of studies have reported postures during reading and writing with paper (e.g. Bridger, 1988; Freudenthal et al., 1991), we were unable to find any other study comparing adult postures during computer and paper use. Bridger (1988) reported marked head/neck flexion when writing on paper placed on a flat desk which was reduced slightly with a sloping desk surface. Freudenthal et al. (1991) reported similar findings for reading and writing on a flat surface and slightly inclined desk surface. The actual head and neck flexion values from both studies are difficult to compare with our findings due to their angle definitions.

The increased head and neck flexion when working with paper suggests a higher level of physical stress. Interestingly, the possibility that working with paper could be a greater physical risk than computer work has not been widely accepted.

An important new finding was the increased curving of the spine in the book condition compared to the computer conditions. This is often considered a risk factor and there is some evidence to support this belief. For example, Hunting et al. (1981) and Faucet and Rempel (1994) found increased symptoms with increased head rotation in studies of office workers. Our research clearly shows the increased spinal curving associated with the use of paper information technology, adding to the potential increased risk associated with greater head and neck flexion.

The curved desk had minimal effect on spinal posture. The 2" less head flexion was probably due to the slightly higher and further away visual target when participants were looking at the book or the keyboard in the curved conditions. This is reflected in the 3" less gaze angle and in greater curved versus straight differences during active keying (when non-touch-typists were looking at the keyboard frequently). The findings suggest that the effect of desk design on head posture may be of little practical importance.

The clear implication of these results is that display and desk design can affect working postures. However, these results are insufficient to determine the best display and desk design. The relationship between posture and musculoskeletal disorder risk is fuzzy and a number of factors are involved. Factors involved in physical risk include: increased resistance with increased angulation away from a vertical position, increased pressure/tension at more extreme postures, and also from repetition and monotony. The mean posture results presented here give an insight into the risks associated with gravity and posture extremes, but measures of variation in posture are also needed.

In the discussion section, the writer explains and considers reasons for the findings in the study, draws conclusions based on the findings, and attempts to make generalisations if appropriate. The writer may also discuss the limitations of the research (limitations are discussed further in section 3 of this unit).

1 Present tense is more commonly used to describe generalised findings:

*Display and desk design **can affect** working postures.*

2 Modal verbs, adjectives and attitude adjectives are used to express the writer's claims:

*… the effect of desk design on head posture **may** be of little practical importance.*

*… it is **possible** that the physical impact on deep muscles may be increased.*

*The book display had a **substantial** effect on the changing angle of the head and neck.*

*An **important** new finding was the increased curving of the spine in the book condition compared to the computer conditions.*

3 Reporting verbs + *that* clauses are used to introduce ideas:

*The findings **suggest that** the effect of desk design on head posture may be of little practical importance.*

4 Recommendations for possible uses of the information, or future research:

e.g. *The mean posture results presented here give an insight into the risks associated with gravity and posture extremes, but measures of variation in posture **are also needed**.*

2k Work in pairs. The writer of the discussion section below makes very strong claims about the results of their research. Read the text and make notes on what the writer should do to make the claims more cautious.

> The design of effective workstations for study is a considerable challenge. However, based on our research into ergonomic chair and desk arrangements, it is obvious that the new design of chair improves posture. This must mean that back pain is reduced for users of this design of chair. Moreover, the results prove that people using the new chair design are able to work for longer periods during the day, and for a greater length of time during each session. This is probably because the ergonomic design is more comfortable than the traditional one.
>
> Stress caused by poor seating causes students to perform poorly and impacts grades, particularly for final-year students who develop poor sitting habits during the lengthy period of their studies. When students are given the opportunity to use properly designed furniture in their study spaces, they produce work of a much higher quality. More attention must be paid to the type of workspaces provided in university libraries and student accommodation.

2l Compare your ideas with another pair of students.

3 Writing about research limitations

3a Work in small groups. Discuss these questions, then read the information in the box below and check your answers.

1 What is a limitation in a research study?

2 How can limitations affect a study?

3 In which section of a research report should the writer mention limitations?

> The purpose of most research is to identify rules which can apply generally to the nature of the physical universe, ideas, society or the individual. However, as no research can account for every possible variable, there will always be limitations on the claims a researcher makes.
>
> A good researcher should try to reduce these limitations as much as possible, but it is necessary to acknowledge any limitations which you know might affect the accuracy of your methods, or the generalisability of your results.
>
> There are several different places in a report in which limitations are usually mentioned: in the methods section, in the discussion, or the conclusion. They may even be included in a separate section of their own, depending on the size of the report.

3b Read these excerpts from the ergonomics research reports. Underline the parts of the texts which describe

- what the limitation is
- the effect the limitation has on the generalisability of the findings.

> There are several limitations to this study. First, the desk at which the participants worked was not a conventional workstation. This may have affected the ease with which the mouse could be used, with a consequent impact on wrist pressure and the users' comfort ratings.
>
> Second, the time spent on each task was very brief (only two minutes). However, data from other studies suggests that pressure on the wrist is stable for longer periods than this. Third, the size of the sample was small. A larger sample size would have helped to reduce the risks of accidental error. Fourth, only healthy participants were included in the study. It may be that individuals with a history of physical problems in the wrist, or Carpal Tunnel Syndrome, would respond differently to the two designs of mouse. Therefore, further research with individuals suffering from disorders of the wrist or hand is required before these findings can be generalised to these populations.

> Interpretation of these results must be made relative to the limitations of this study. First, the sample size was smaller than expected due to difficulties with recruitment. This means that it is difficult to generalise about the findings. Also, it emerged during the experiment that the amount of time for which the participants were observed (two minutes) may have been too short. Consequently, it is not possible to state that the new design is clearly better than the existing one. Thus, more research is needed to confirm the findings indicated here.

> It is not certain that the limitations affect the study in the way that the researcher suggests – it is only a possibility, therefore cautious language should be used when describing the effects of limitations. This can be done in two ways:
>
> **1** using modal verbs (e.g. *may, might, could*)
>
> **2** using modal adjectives followed by a *that* clause (e.g. *it is possible that; it is likely that*).

3c Underline all the examples of cautious language in the texts in 3b. Discuss why you think the writer has used this kind of language for the limitations section of the report.

3d Look at this phrase used in the text and discuss the questions.

> This may have affected the ease with which the mouse …

1 Does this refer to a present or past situation?

2 What different verb forms can you identify?

3e Circle all the other similar verb forms in the text in 3b.

> To describe the possible effects that the method had on the study, we use past modal forms.
>
> ***Example***
>
> *This may have affected the ease with which the mouse could be used.*
>
> To describe possible improvements on the research method / suggestions for changes in future research, both past and present modal forms are possible.
>
> ***Examples***
>
> *Past: A larger sample size would have helped to reduce the risks.*
>
> *Present: A larger sample size would help to reduce the error.*

3f Complete the extract from a research paper below using a modal verb from the box and changing the form of the verbs in brackets (1–7) if necessary. More than one answer may be possible.

> | may | may have | could have | might have |
> | --- | --- | --- | --- |

> An important limitation of this study was the short duration of each test condition. When participants have worked with a different desk and display for several weeks, they **1)** _____ (develop) different postures. Therefore our results **2)** _____ (not be) relevant to normal working conditions. The computing tasks we asked participants to do **3)** _____ (not involve) a full active use of the keyboard, since only written texts were produced. Asking participants to use the number keys to process statistics **4)** _____ (produce) slightly different results in this area. Similarly, the book tasks involved book page turning, but not tasks actually writing in the book. Asking participants to underline sentences or make notes **5)** _____ (give) a more complete picture of the posture changes.
>
> The method of analysis used **6)** _____ (obscure) significant differences in posture and muscle activity. In addition, the postural effects of desk and display designs reported here were for young adults, but results for different age groups **7)** _____ (differ) from these considerably.

3g Work in pairs. Discuss the difference between using a past and present modal form to express possible improvements in research methods.

3h Work in pairs. Read the research proposal on p.190 and discuss the questions below with a partner.

1 What is the aim of the study?

2 What limitations might there be in the research design?

3 What effect might the limitations have on the study?

> This study aims to investigate how easy it is for left-handed people to manage at home, such as using cooking equipment, bathroom facilities and opening doors. An experimental home is set up, containing a variety of different equipment. Three volunteer families are asked to live in the home for one week each. The researchers use video cameras in the home to monitor the family members and find out which items they tend to use most often, which they have difficulty with, and which they tend to avoid.
>
> The three groups of people, each with one left-handed person:
>
> **Family 1**
> Two middle-aged adults (husband and wife) with two elderly parents
>
> **Family 2**
> Two adults in their 60s
>
> **Family 3**
> Two young adults with two children aged between three months and nine years old.

3h Work in pairs. Imagine you have finished this research. Write a paragraph describing any limitations you see in the research design. You should include

- the limitations that appeared during the research
- any possible solutions for future research
- modal verbs referring to present and past time.

> **LESSON TASK**   **4 Discussing research designs**

4a Read the description of a proposed research project into the design of a new office workspace design. What is the aim of the research?

> The main aim of the study is to try to evaluate user responses to a new office workspace design. It is intended that an experimental office will be built which has been designed on ergonomic principles. These would include newly designed furniture (in particular work desks and chairs) and an arrangement of the desk space so that the person sitting at the desk can complete a number of tasks without having to move around excessively. The research would investigate users' views on the extent to which the new office design is more comfortable and efficient than traditional designs.

4b Work in small groups. Discuss the study and decide on the methodology you would use to be able to gather the data required. You need to consider

- the type and number of subjects you would use
- what data you would need to gather
- the procedure for data collection
- how you would analyze the data.

One of the group should take notes.

4c When you are ready, present your research design to the rest of the class.

4d As you listen to other groups present their design, take notes of any possible limitations you find in their design and give feedback with how these limitations might be addressed.

5 Review and extension

Research terminology

5a The passages below are excerpts from a study investigating the design of a new ergonomic computer keyboard. Complete each passage by choosing the best word from the box. You may need to change the form of some words.

respondents	reliability	generalise	sample size	randomly	control group
findings	representative	limitations	evaluate	validity	variables
quantitative	qualitative	population	confounding factors	participants	conduct

A

This study was conducted to 1)_____ the design of a new ergonomic keyboard and the extent to which it prevented users from getting repetitive strain injury (RSI) when typing.

Ten 2)_____ were recruited by advertising in the university. They were 3) _____ assigned to two groups, one using the new ergonomic keyboard, and a control group using a traditional keyboard.

B

The independent 4) _____ were type of keyboard and hours spent typing. The dependent variable was the number of instances of RSI. 5) _____ data was gathered on the number of hours spent typing each day, and the number of instances of RSI. Average scores were calculated for hours spent typing and instances of RSI, and these are reported in the 6) _____. Additionally, a questionnaire was used as a 7) _____ assessment to determine how comfortable the volunteers felt the new keyboard design was.

C

8) _____ using the new ergonomic keyboard had fewer instances of RSI than the 9) _____ using the traditional keyboard. Furthermore, 30% of the participants indicated they would use the new ergonomic keyboard in future.

D

There are several 10) _____ to this study. First, the 11) _____ was relatively small, and the participants were only in the 18–26 age group, therefore it may be difficult to 12) _____ the findings to the wider 13) _____. Furthermore, we had to find a simple method of data collection in order to encourage the participants to regularly record results during the three-month period of the study. For this reason we chose to ask the respondents to complete daily diaries with estimates of the time spent studying, and self-assessment of instances of RSI – therefore we were unable to measure these quantities directly. This might have reduced both the 14) _____ and 15) _____ of the study.

E

The degree to which the findings are 16) _____ of the broader population are uncertain. There are other possible 17) _____ which may affect the validity of the study: the number of hours spent working at the keyboard may indicate different amounts of time actually spent typing; the posture of the respondents may also have affected their use of the keyboard. Furthermore, it is possible that the effect of the keyboard would be different for individuals who can touch type. Further research should be 18) _____ to determine whether these variables have an effect on the usability of the new keyboard.

The language of research reports

5b Find a report or journal article online which describes a piece of research in your own field of study. The text should have clearly marked *method*, *results* and *discussion* sections. Read the text and complete these activities.

1 Identify the author's aim and main findings.

2 Compare the language used in the method, results and discussion sections of the report with the guidelines given in this unit. How closely does it match the guidelines given in the information boxes in this part of the unit?

3 Identify any sections where the author discusses limitations. Underline the expressions used to describe the limitations and their consequences.

Writing about limitations

5c The first column of the table below contains some limitations of a piece of research; the second column contains possible consequences of these limitations. Write sentences using modal verbs or modal adjectives to express the limitations and their consequences. For example:

Small sample size / Samples don't represent population.

*The sample size in this study is small, therefore the samples **may not** represent the population.*

*The sample size in this study is small, therefore **it is possible that** the samples do not represent the population.*

Limitation	Possible consequence
test subjects all male university students	Results don't apply to female university students.
results taken from short questionnaire	Results don't reveal the effects of long-term computer use.
study only done on one occasion	Repeat studies would give different results.

Reporting in speech

By the end of Part D you will be able to:

- describe and comment on research findings
- form indirect questions
- use appropriate pronunciation and language when agreeing and disagreeing.

1 Describing and commenting on research findings

1a Work in small groups. Discuss these questions.

1 In your opinion, what are the characteristic features of a 'modern' room, compared to a 'traditional' room?

2 What kind of room do you find it easy to study in? Why?

3 What kinds of features would you say make a room more suitable for creative work?

4.8

4.9

1b Listen to a speaker give a report on what makes a room 'creative'. Does the speaker have similar ideas to your group?

1c Listen to five short extracts (1–5) from the report and match each one with a function A–E. Then listen again and make a note of any words or phrases the speaker uses to indicate the function.

Function	Extract	Word(s) or phrase(s)
A to introduce what the visual shows		
B to summarise the main points		
C to draw attention to a visual aid		
D to give an overview of results		
E to highlight some interesting points		

1d Read this extract from the lecture. Underline the phrases used to refer to the visual aid.

> So if we look at Figure 1 here on the screen, we can see the percentage of respondents who gave a 'high' rating – that's either a four or a five on the scale – to each of the elements. Now obviously there's a preference there for natural furnishings, wood and so on, and to some extent lighting is important as well.

1e Speakers do not just describe findings, but also comment on them. Read the extract below and answer these questions about the underlined phrases, a and b.

1 Which phrase is **describing** what was done?

2 Which phrase **comments** on the findings?

> So, we gathered fifteen images of different rooms from a variety of different sources. They were all workspaces, to an extent, but laid out in different ways, and as you can see from the table here, [a] <u>we had them grouped into four main categories</u>: 'modern', 'traditional', 'peaceful' and 'energetic', depending on the type of decorations and furniture and so on. I've got the images here if you want to have a look at them in a moment. So, what does this tell us about the ratings? [b] <u>What we see, of course, is that most of the answers tend to cluster around the middle of the scale, which was to be expected</u>.

1f Work in pairs. Read this extract from a lecture and predict which phrase could be used to complete each blank.

If we look at	possibility	suggests
had higher	possible	we find that

> However, an interesting point, I think, is that people seemed to rate the more 'conventional' rooms as being better for creativity – the ones with a standard modern or traditional look. They both _____ **1)** ratings at the top end of the scale than the energetic and peaceful rooms, which were the ones with more overtly 'creative' features like unconventional furnishings and decorations.
>
> If you notice here in Table 1, if we combine the strongly positive ratings of 4 and 5, we get scores of around 100 for the traditional and modern rooms, but only around 72 for the peaceful and energetic rooms. That's reversed _____ **2)** the bottom end of the scale: combining ratings 1 and 2, _____ **3)** significantly more people rate the energetic and peaceful rooms as being poor for creativity compared to the traditional and modern ones. Now of course this was quite a limited study, and there are a number of _____ **4)** reasons why this may be so, but the fact that we also have more people giving lower scores to these two unconventional rooms _____ **5)** something interesting that's going on. One _____ **6)** is that people tend to feel more creative in, or give a higher rating to, the rooms that they're more comfortable in – more familiar with, if you like.

1g Listen and check your answers.

1h Work in pairs. Identify the highlighted phrases in 1f which are *descriptions* and those which are *comments*. Write the phrases in the table below.

Description	Comment

1i You are going to describe and comment on a graph, using language you have identified in the activities above. First, work in pairs. Discuss these questions.

  1 Do you think it is important to have a lot of light in a house?

  2 How satisfactory is the amount of light (natural or artificial) in your accommodation?

1j Look at the graph below, then make a note of how you might describe the graph and then comment on it.

Description	Comment

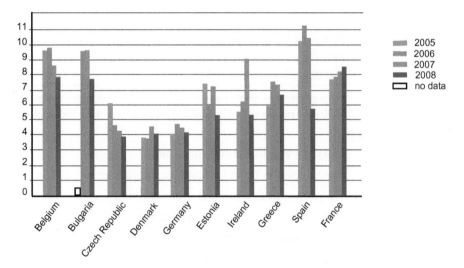

Share of total population considering their dwelling as too dark %

1k Work in pairs. Use your notes to describe and comment on the graph in 1k to your partner.

1l Prepare a brief presentation on the graphic with your partner. When you are ready, join another pair. Take turns giving your presentations and asking the other pair questions about their own presentation. After the presentations are complete, give feedback to the other pair on their presentation. Give feedback on how well the speaker described and commented on the findings. What could they do to improve?

2 Forming indirect questions

2a You have been given this topic to research:

Investigate how people feel about different room designs and which ones they feel will encourage most creativity in the people working in them.

You have decided, as part of your research, to give people a questionnaire to complete. Work in groups. Think of some questions you might ask.

> Indirect questions are usually considered to be more polite. They can be formed by adding a preparatory phrase to the front of a direct question and changing its syntax.
>
> | Question type | Questions in present or past simple |
> | --- | --- |
> | **Direct Wh-questions** | *Why **do** you prefer this room?* |
> | **Indirect Wh-questions**
 Could you tell me / Do you know + subject + verb (delete auxiliary verb *do*) | *Could you tell me why **do** you prefer this room?* |
> | **Direct Yes/No questions** | ***Do** you like this room?* |
> | **Indirect Yes/No questions** *Could you tell me / Do you know* + *if / whether* + subject + verb (delete auxiliary verb *do*) | *Could you tell me if / whether **do** you like this room?* |

2b Work in pairs. Change these direct questions into indirect ones. Use *Could you tell me … ?*

  a What do you like about this room?

  b How does this room compare to the first one?

  c Do you think this room is more relaxing?

  d What would this room be like to work in?

  e How would you describe this room?

  f What do you think of the lighting?

2c Look back at the questions you wrote in 2a. Change any direct questions to indirect ones, then compare your ideas with the other members of your group.

2d Read a description of a piece of research that a student has done on p.198. What is the aim of the research?

A student wanted to discover the effect of different study spaces on the ability to concentrate. Two desks were set up.

Desk 1: The first desk was set facing a large window. The window provided a lot of natural light. The view from the window was a busy street, with trees and a small park across the road. There were no decorations in the room.

Desk 2: The second desk was set in a room without any windows. Light was provided by a desk lamp. There were no other decorations in the room.

Ten volunteers, randomly assigned to two groups, completed a reading task sitting at one of the two desks. Afterwards, students were asked to complete a short test about the text they read.

Results were gathered in two ways:

1 test scores

2 A questionnaire given to each volunteer, asking how easy they found it to concentrate on the tasks. Scores were given from 1 (very difficult to concentrate) to 5 (very easy to concentrate).

Results

Test

Desk	A (window)	B (no window)
Average test score	82%	78%
Average rating in questionnaire	4	3

2e You are attending a presentation of the researcher's findings in 2d. You want to know more about the three points below. Form indirect questions to ask about them.

1 who the volunteers were

2 what the researcher thinks these results show

3 why the desk at the window received higher ratings

2f Compare your ideas with a partner. Can you think of any other questions you would ask about this study?

3 Using appropriate pronunciation and language when agreeing and disagreeing

3a Work in pairs. What would be an appropriate way of agreeing and disagreeing with the comment, below, in the following situations?

1 an informal conversation with a friend

2 a formal seminar discussion with students from your course

> I think the appearance of the university, what its buildings look like, is an important factor in choosing where to study.

3b Work in pairs. You are going to listen to a group of students discussing research findings. Before you listen, complete this transcript with these words and phrases.

how certain can you be	can't say that	a similar point	can still see
we can say	would you say the link is	the results	is it possible that
results seem to suggest	the results could have been affected	are accurate	it not possible that

Andrew: … OK, thank you. So, are there any questions at all? Anyone?

Becky: Yes, I have. How strong **1)** _____ between lighting levels and creativity?

Andrew: Well, I think **2)** _____ we have here suggest that natural light is a bit better than artificial light, but we would probably need to do more research as this was a fairly small study.

Becky: But the thing I wonder is, there was natural light in all of the rooms. Even rooms two and three had small windows. So **3)** _____ that the results from rooms two and three **4)** _____ ?

Andrew: Well, that's a good question – yes, there was some natural light coming through the small windows in rooms two and three, so we **5)** _____ we're testing purely natural versus purely artificial light, but I think what **6)** _____ is that we were looking at completely natural light, in room one, and restricted natural light in rooms two and three, and the **7)** _____ that having purely natural light is better. Are there any other questions?

Clare: Yes, on **8)** _____ , do you think it's possible that **9)** _____ by changes in the lighting condition?

Andrew: Well, we controlled everything and had the same lighting condition in each room. Can you explain what you mean?

Clare: Yes, for instance, in room one, there was natural light, but **10)** _____ there were changes in that light – for example, there might have been bright sunshine at one point, and cloud at another. Is **11)** _____ this could have affected the scores?

Andrew: Yes, yes, I suppose it could. I know we didn't do anything to control for that, but perhaps that's something we could do in a future study. To make sure that we did it in such a way that the quality of the natural light coming in wasn't changing. Nevertheless, I think we **12)** _____ , though, that despite any changes in the natural light, that was still the room where people, both male and female, scored highest on the creative thinking test.

4.11

3c Listen to the conversation and compare your answers with the original conversation.

3d Becky and Clare ask questions which are potentially criticising the research. Find these questions in the transcript above.

3e Now listen to the extract of one of the questions and the response.

4.12

1 How is the question asked so that it remains polite? Think of
- language (vocabulary and grammar)
- speed (fast or slow)
- stress (Which words are emphasized?)
- pitch and tone (Does the tone generally rise or fall?).

2 What makes the response polite?

3f Work in pairs. Read the following extracts from the discussion. Identify the language (vocabulary and grammar) the speakers use to soften criticism or to sound more polite and indirect.

1 But the thing I wonder is, there was natural light in *all* of the rooms. Even rooms two and three had small windows. So how certain can you be that the results from rooms two and three are accurate?

2 Well, that's a good question – yes.

3 … do you think it's possible that the results could have been affected by changes in the lighting condition?

4 Can you explain what you mean?

5 Is it not possible that this could have affected the scores?

6 Yes, yes, I suppose it could. I know we didn't do anything to control for that, but perhaps that's something we could do in a future study.

4.13

3g Listen to six phrases of agreement and disagreement. For each phrase, decide whether it expresses agreement or disagreement and whether it is direct or indirect by ticking (✓) the correct column. Then listen again and write the phrase you hear in the last column.

	Agree	Disagree	Direct	Indirect	Phrase
1		✓	✓		I totally disagree with you
2					
3					
4					
5					
6					

3h Work in groups of four. Each member of the group should choose one of the statements below and imagine that it is their own opinion. Spend a few minutes thinking of arguments that you could use to defend the opinion in a discussion.

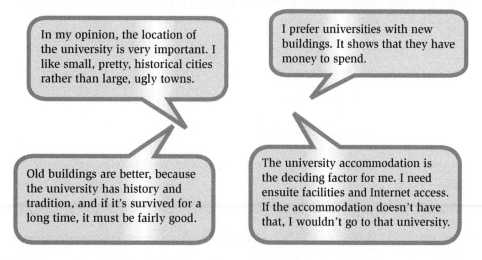

In my opinion, the location of the university is very important. I like small, pretty, historical cities rather than large, ugly towns.

I prefer universities with new buildings. It shows that they have money to spend.

Old buildings are better, because the university has history and tradition, and if it's survived for a long time, it must be fairly good.

The university accommodation is the deciding factor for me. I need ensuite facilities and Internet access. If the accommodation doesn't have that, I wouldn't go to that university.

3i Discuss each of these opinions, using appropriate pronunciation and language and agreement and disagreement phrases.

> **LESSON TASK**   **4   Conducting a class survey**

In groups, you are going to carry out a class survey. You will need to prepare questions, interview your classmates, report back on your findings, then ask questions or respond to other groups' questions appropriately.

4a Read this question.

Does your college or university accommodation help or hinder your studies?

Work in groups of four. Discuss which questions you could ask students about their accommodation in order to answer the question. Try to use a range of question types (Wh-questions, Yes/No questions, etc.).

4b Practise asking the questions using an appropriate rise or fall tone, depending on the question type.

4c Form new groups. Join another group and take turns to interview each member of the other group individually, using appropriate intonation.

4d Return to your group. Discuss the data you have collected and create simple visual aids to represent the questions you used, and your findings. Think of potential questions the class may ask you.

4e Present this information to the class using descriptive and comment language.

1   the questions you used, and why you decided to use them

2   the results you got

3   any problems with the questions you chose

4   what you think the results show

4f Give feedback to each group on these points:

1   how effectively the students described and commented on the findings

2   how effective their questions were for getting the information they needed

5   Review and extension

Intonation in questions

4.14

5a Listen to some questions students asked in a survey on student accommodation. Which tone do you hear: rising or falling?

Question	Tone	
	↘	↑
1 Could you tell me your nationality?		
2 Do you live in a house or a flat?		
3 Does your accommodation have enough natural light?		
4 Is your accommodation quiet enough?		
5 Would you like to live in the centre of town?		
6 Would you mind sharing?		

4.15

Polite agreement and disagreement

5b Listen to six phrases of agreement or disagreement and write them down in the table. Listen more than once if necessary.

Phrase
1 I think you might be right about that.   I   Higher pitch / quick
2
3
4
5
6

4.16

5c Study the graph below. Then listen to four questions about the data. Write the questions in the first column of the table on p.202.

Proportion of population living in households considering that they suffer from noise %

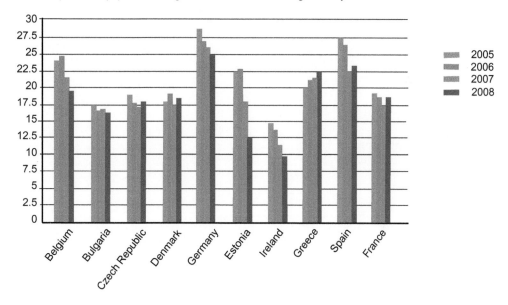

Source: European Union / Eurostat, 2011

	Question	Possible answers
1		
2		
3		
4		
5		
6		

5d Work in pairs. Think of possible answers to the questions and complete the second column of the table. Consider the following points to help you:

- The method used for the research

- Different environments or contexts in each country

5e Work in small groups. Discuss the possible answers and decide which ones are probably most likely. Use polite language to agree and disagree.

Reporting in writing

1 Recognizing and using the structure and grammar of abstracts

1a Work in pairs. Discuss these questions.

1 What are the different purposes of an *abstract* and an *introduction*?

2 What information does an abstract commonly include?

1b Ignoring the letters A–E for now, read the abstract below and answer these questions.

1 What was the purpose of the research?

2 What method(s) did the researcher use to carry out the research?

3 What were the results?

4 How does this compare to other research?

5 What recommendations does the writer make?

ABSTRACT

(A) Physical design and decoration elements in the work environment are known to have an effect on occupants' moods, concentration and work output. However, relatively little research has been conducted to establish the link between physical space and creative thinking. (B) In this study an experimental approach was used to investigate individuals' perceptions of how well different offices could promote a creative atmosphere. (C) 30 participants working in digital design (m=18, f=12) rated pictures of different rooms for their 'creativity potential'. Scores were given for rooms as a whole, as well as individual environmental features. (D) It was found that there was a slight preference for 'natural'-looking rooms, with wall decorations and warm colour schemes. (E) Lighting was found to be less significant than in other studies. The findings suggest that some investment in room features specifically for the enhancement of creativity may have a benefit for work output in the creative industries.

1c Five different features are commonly found in abstracts, each performing a different function. Match a section of the abstract (A–E) with the five functions described below. Then make a note of the order the different functions appear in this abstract.

- Background (to the topic)
- Discussion (of (i) recommendations for future projects or further research; (ii) the contribution of this research to knowledge on the topic)
- Method
- Purpose (of the current research)
- Results

1d Work in pairs. Read the abstract, and underline the different features from 1c that you find. How is the structure of this abstract similar to or different from the one in 1b?

Existing theories about creativity focus on the social nature of creative thought, and how creativity arises from, or is hindered by, collective interactions and the social environment. By contrast, this study investigates how physical environment impacts individual creativity in the creative industries. Twenty in-depth interviews were conducted with workers in computer and industrial design industries in the UK, North America and Sweden to analyze the way that particular features of a room or work location are perceived to promote a sense of creative potential or inspiration. This study examines individual feelings about where creative inspiration comes from and finds that (1) those working in the creative industries believe that physical attributes of a place are important in fostering a sense of creativity, and (2) the location of the place where creative work occurs also has an impact.

> There are variations in the way that abstracts are written in different academic disciplines, although the features identified above are relatively standard. The rest of this section explores some of the language commonly used in each of the separate sections.

1e Read the two abstracts below. Identify the different features of each abstract. Then check your ideas with a partner.

A

In the first laboratory study on the subject, Pressey (1921) found no difference in psychological or physiological effect between rooms decorated in warm or cool colours. However, a large body of subsequent research has indicated that there may be psychological effects related to environmental colour. In this study, the effect of brightly coloured room interiors on psychological state is described. 30 participants completed a range of cognitive tasks in rooms painted or decorated in various colour schemes. The results support the claim that room colours may have effects on mood, concentration, sense of well-being and task performance. The emotions and functioning ability of those occupying a room can be significantly impacted by choice of colour scheme. While neutral or cool colours are associated with calmer states, stronger colours such as red tend to cause heightened excitement. These can lead to severe effects on task performance and achievement. The findings imply that there is a practical benefit in deliberate room design which incorporates use of effective colour features. Future research on room design should place more emphasis on colour and its impact on mood and task performance.

B

In this study, we investigated the effect of an indoor plant on task performance and on mood. Three room arrangements were used as independent variables: a room with (1) a plant, or (2) a magazine rack with magazines placed in front of the participants, or (3) a room with neither of these objects. Undergraduate students ($M = 35$, $F = 55$) performed a task of associating up to 30 words with each of twenty specified words in a room with one of the three room arrangements. Task performance scores showed that female participants performed better in view of the plant in comparison to the magazine rack ($p < 0.05$). Moreover, mood was better with the plant or the magazine rack in the room compared to the no-object condition ($p < 0.05$). However, the difference in task performance was highly influenced by the evaluation about the plant or the magazine rack. It is suggested that the compatibility between task demand and the environment is an important factor in facilitating task performances.

Source: Shibata, S., & Suzuki, N. (2004). Effects of an indoor plant on creative task performance and mood. *Scandinavian Journal of Psychology, 45*, 373–381.

Background section

> The background section provides the context for the study. This can include:
>
> 1 reference to other research on the topic:
>
> a references to specific researchers. These are often in the past simple tense: e.g. *Cox (1994) **demonstrated** the link between indoor plants and mood.*
>
> b general references to unnamed 'other' research. These are often in the present perfect tense:
>
> *Researchers **have identified** a link between lighting levels and task performance.*
>
> 2 general comments about the topic. These are frequently in the present simple tense:
>
> *The physical environment **affects** creativity.*
>
> 3 the use of attitude adjectives:
>
> *Lighting is an **important** element in room design.*

1f Look back at abstract A in 1e. Underline any of the features (1–3) that you find in the Background section.

Purpose section

> In the purpose section, the writer presents their own research. This includes:
>
> 1 the use of general references to the research (*this research, this report, this paper, this study, this investigation*) or plural pronouns (*we*) in place of personal pronouns (*it, I*)
>
> 2 the use of both the present and past simple tenses to explain the purpose of the research: e.g. *this study **examines** the relationship between architectural design and task performance / this study **investigated** the effect of bright colours on creativity potential.*

1g Look back at the abstracts in 1e and complete these activities.

    a Identify the particular phrases used to refer to the author's research in place of a personal pronoun.

    b What tense does each abstract use to explain the purpose of the research?

Method section

> In the method section, the writer briefly summarises how the research was done. This includes:
>
> 1 descriptions of the researcher's actions. These are frequently written in the past simple passive: *twenty in-depth interviews **were conducted**.*
>
> 2 descriptions of the actions of any test subjects. These are frequently written in the past simple tense: *The participants **rated** pictures of different rooms.*

1h Look back at the abstracts in 1e. Underline any descriptions of the researcher's actions. Circle any descriptions of the test subjects' actions.

1i Work in pairs. Discuss why researchers often prefer to describe their actions in the passive voice.

Results section

In the results section, the writer briefly summarises the key findings of the study.

1 Both present and past tense, and active and passive voices, can be used in this section: (a) *This study **finds** that the location of the place where creative work occurs **has** an impact*; (b) *It **was found** that there **was** a slight preference for 'natural'-looking rooms.*

2 Modal verbs can also be used: *mood **can** be strongly affected by the presence of plants in a room.*

1j Work in pairs. Look back at the abstracts in 1e. Complete these activities.

  a Identify the tenses used in this section of each abstract.

  b Discuss with a partner which tense is better for

      1 giving an impression of objective reporting of observed facts

      2 giving a sense that the results from this study are generally applicable.

Discussion section

In the discussion section, the writer explains how the current study relates to other research on the topic and/or makes recommendations for possible uses of the information, or future research based on the findings. This includes:

1 the use of the present simple tense to describe generalised findings (*The findings **suggest** that some investment in room features specifically for the enhancement of creativity **may have** a benefit for work output in the creative industries*).

2 the use of modal verbs (*Investment **may** have a benefit*), modal adjectives (*Poor lighting is believed to be a **possible** cause of lowered mood*) and attitude adjectives (*Lighting was found to be less **significant** than in other studies*) to express the writer's claims.

3 the use of reporting verbs followed by *that* clauses to introduce ideas (*The study **reveals that** ..., The findings **suggest that** ...*) and recommendations (*it is **suggested that** investments should be made; it is **suggested that** more research be carried out to determine the cause of the anomaly*).

1k Look back at the abstracts in 1e. Underline any of the features (1–3) that you find in the discussion section.

1l Do the abstracts in 1e make any recommendations? How are these recommendations expressed?

2 Writing an abstract using concise language

When writing an abstract, the author normally tries to express the information as concisely as possible. Typical abstracts vary between 100 and 200 words in length, depending on different academic disciplines.

2a Work in pairs. Match these methods for making writing more concise (1–4) with the examples (a–d).

Method	Example
1 Replacing one word or phrase with another	**a** In the first laboratory study ~~which was conducted~~ on the subject, the researcher Pressey (1921) found that...
2 Omitting an auxiliary verb	**b** We ~~studied and recorded~~ **investigated** the effect of an indoor plant.
3 Omitting a word, phrase or sentence	**c** The results support the claim that room colours may have effects on mood~~. They may also have effects on~~, concentration, sense of well-being and task performance.
4 Joining sentences together	**d** This ~~can~~ help**s** to improve concentration.

2b Work in pairs. The abstract on room design and creativity in 1b is 150 words long. Imagine you are the writer of this abstract and that you have been given a word limit of approximately 100 words. Reread the abstract and then discuss which words and phrases could be omitted or changed to make the abstract shorter.

2c Work in pairs. Look at a reduced version of this abstract in **Appendix 15**. Compare the two abstracts to examine what has been deleted or modified.

2d Work in pairs. Reduce this student abstract from 155 words to 100. Write notes on the actions you have used to reduce the word length.

Abstract	Action
Digital music has been particularly popular since the introduction of the MP3 audio format in the 1990s. However, there are many digital formats, and as new ones are invented, incompatibility among them increasingly confuses consumers and the market in general. This essay aims to analyze technical aspects of three formats and their marketing influence. In the essay, secondary research is used and several articles related to the topic are discussed. The findings show that there are advantages in the fact that MP3 has no copyright protection, for example that a greater number of companies are involved in the development of the format; however, it can also lead to increased levels of piracy. A possible solution which is suggested in this essay is that companies can reach an agreement on a compatible format or standard. The difficulty is that they are competing in the market and want to increase their profits by using their own standards.	

2e Compare your 100-word abstract with the example in **Appendix 16**. Have you changed and omitted the same parts of the abstract?

> **► LESSON TASK** **3** **Writing an abstract**

3a Work in small groups. Discuss these questions.

1 How important is creative thinking for success in higher education?

2 How might higher education courses be designed to enhance creative thinking in students?

3b Read the introduction, method and conclusion from a piece of research about the design of study spaces (**Appendix 17**), and write notes on the key points it makes.

3c Work in pairs. Use your notes to write a draft abstract for the study, of no more than 200 words. Use this table to check that it covers the main functions of an abstract.

Details from abstract	Function
	Background
	Reason for research
	Method
	Results
	Contribution to knowledge
	Recommendations

3d Exchange extracts with another pair of students, and all pairs reduce the extracts to no more than 150 words. Then pairs give the abstracts back to the original writers.

3e Write an appropriate title for this research.

3f Work in groups of three. Compare your titles and abstracts. Which is the most successful and why?

4   Review and extension

Writing abstracts

4a Read the three abstracts below. What academic field does each abstract appear to come from?

A This article explores whether the manager's physical office work environment can stimulate the manager's creativity. A total of 60 managers from a large manufacturing company participated in the study. They rated the creativity potential and physical elements of office environments shown in 25 photographs. The results indicate that offices differ in terms of creativity potential. Compared to offices with low creativity potential, offices with high creativity potential have lower complexity, more plants, bright lighting conditions, windows, cooler colours, and a computer facility. The results suggest that a good interior design of manager's office environment could stimulate a manager's creativity and could therefore contribute to an organization's innovation.

Source: Ceylan, C., Dul, J., & Aytac, S. (2008). Can the office environment stimulate a manager's creativity? *Human Factors and Ergonomics in Manufacturing, 18*(6), 589–602.

B

A basic analysis of a patient's gait and posture provides information about the body and the capability of the musculoskeletal system to adjust to physical stressors. An understanding of normal gait and posture is essential for identifying and treating musculoskeletal pain. This article discusses normal gait and how to assess gait. It also outlines common musculoskeletal conditions and their association with abnormal gait and posture. General practitioners can detect faulty postural syndromes and abnormal gait by visual scanning and awareness of pain referral patterns. Awareness of pain that can arise from faulty gait and posture will assist GPs to shift their focus away from structural diagnoses and unhelpful radiological investigations. The GP can become an effective facilitator of the prevention and rehabilitation of pain problems where abnormal gait and posture are found to be a main contributing factor.

Source: Sweeting, K. & Mock, M. (2007). Gait and posture – Assessment in general practice. *Australian Family Physician, 36*(6)

C

Immunofluorescence microscopy offers a highly specific analytical tool for unambiguous recognition and mapping of proteins in complex matrices. In the present work, the analytical potentials of immunofluorescence microscopy have been exploited to provide recognition of proteinaceous binders in painting cross-sections. An optimised analytical protocol is proposed for the identification of ovalbumin and of bovine serum albumin as markers of egg white and casein, respectively. The study has been carried out on laboratory model samples simulating both easel and mural paintings. The obtained results demonstrated the effectiveness of the method, suggesting the potential future use of immunofluorescence microscopy as a routine diagnostic tool in conservation science. Possible developments of the proposed methodology in order to improve the specificity of the method and its detection sensitivity are presented and discussed.

Source: Vagnini, M., Pitzurra, L., Cartechini, L., Miliani, C., Brunetti, B.G., & A. Sgamellotti. (2008). Identification of proteins in painting cross-sections by immunofluorescence microscopy. *Analytical and Bioanalytical Chemistry, 392*(1-2), 57–64. DOI: 10.1007/s00216-008-2041-9

4b Identify the sections in each part of the abstracts.

4c Identify the language used in each section. To what extent is it similar to the general rules described in this unit?

4d Look online for some journal articles from your own field. Read the abstracts for the articles, and complete these activities.

   1 Record the word count of the abstracts you review. Is it the same, or more or less than the guidelines given in this unit?

   2 Identify the sections included in the abstracts.

   3 Identify the language features used in each section of the abstracts. To what extent do they follow the same pattern as the general rules described in this unit?

Appendices

Appendix 1: Example tables of numerical data

Student A

Table 1: Proportion of senior academic staff who are female by age group, 2007

	<35	35–44	45–54	55+	Total
EU Average	25%	23%	21%	18%	19%
Germany	28%	17%	14%	7%	12%
Italy	*	20%	20%	18%	19%
UK	15%	17%	20%	15%	17%

Source: European Commission She Figures, 2009

Student B

Table 2: Female PhD researchers as a percentage of total, by field

Field	2001	2006
Education	55%	64%
Humanities and Arts	48.9%	52%
Science, Maths and Computing	35.7%	41%
Health and Social Services	49%	54%
Engineering, Manufacturing and Construction	20.6%	25%
Social Science, Business and Law	39.3%	47%

Source: European Commission She Figures, 2006

Appendix 2: Three extracts

Extract 1

Results in the financial sector showed that while women's pay compared to men's has increased steadily over the last twenty years, their bonuses are growing far more slowly than their male counterparts'. Women's bonuses have gone up marginally since 1990, with yearly increases of about 0.3%, whereas many men's bonuses shot up fast, particularly in the boom years of the early 2000s. Bonuses have dropped considerably in the financial crisis, with average reductions of around 3%, but again women have been worse hit, with their bonuses falling dramatically since 2005.

Extract 2

Women working at lower pay scales in education confirmed that although their pay has increased gradually over the last twenty years, there have been some periods where salaries have fluctuated somewhat. Women working at higher pay scales reported that pay has increased moderately, going up more sharply in recent years. However, they claim that men's pay in similar positions had risen more markedly still. The male–female pay gap has increased by 6%.

Appendix 3: Gender gap graph 1

Female job satisfaction in nursing ages 20–60

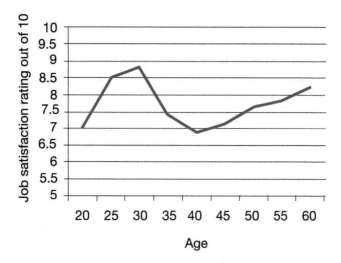

Figure 2: Female nurse job-satisfaction rating / 10

Appendix 4: Gender gap graph 2

Average hours worked per week by public sector females ages 20–60

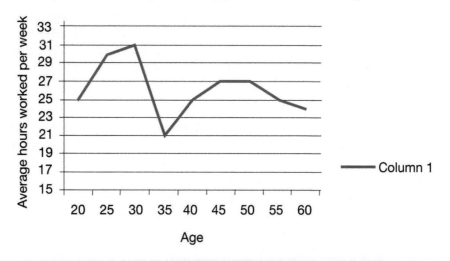

Figure 3: Average hours worked per week by public sector females aged 20–60

Appendix 5: Audio transcripts and excerpts

1.7

1 There seems to be a commonly held stereotype that women prefer 'soft' subjects. I wondered where this <u>had come</u> from.

2 I found some quite early reports – from the 1970s and 80s – which show that women <u>had been choosing</u> arts and social science courses like English, history and education for years.

3 … more and more women <u>have been choosing</u> STEM over the last few decades …

4 Cameron's report <u>shows</u> that 3% more women each year are currently turning from subjects such as education to STEM.

5 … by 2030 the proportion of women studying STEM <u>will have reached</u> 50% overall …

6 … as many women <u>will be studying</u> STEM as men.

7 This could come even quicker <u>if</u> the effects of some initiatives <u>are seen</u>.

8 For example, the government <u>has invested</u> a lot of money in STEM recently.

9 But surely those <u>will encourage</u> boys to study STEM too?

10 Yes, I read about them, and how <u>they are helping</u> social attitudes to change.

11 … in the 1980s 34% of families still <u>considered</u> STEM subjects inappropriate for their daughters …

12 Doesn't it seem amazing to think that even when we were children many girls who <u>were hoping</u> to study STEM found their plans met with so much resistance?

Appendix 6: Literature review

Job satisfaction can be defined as a worker's subjective assessment of their happiness with the work they do. An understanding of what factors influence job satisfaction is critical for two reasons. Firstly, it can guide policy-makers and those involved in the campaign for better working conditions, but also because higher job satisfaction is likely to lead to better work performance and lower turnover costs for employers.

Clark and Oswald (1996) <u>were</u> the first to create a model of the factors involved in job satisfaction. They <u>drew</u> a link between earned income and satisfaction, but also <u>introduced</u> the importance of expectations: greater job satisfaction <u>is found</u> where the gap between actual and expected wages is small. Clark and Oswald therefore <u>claimed</u> that the amount of money earned <u>is</u> not, by itself, the most important element of job satisfaction. This <u>has become</u> particularly significant in the debate about the sources of women's satisfaction at work, and explanations for the so-called gender/job satisfaction paradox.

It <u>is</u> widely accepted that women <u>tend</u> to have greater job satisfaction than men. This <u>is</u> often explained in part as being due to women having low expectations of what they will be able to earn, or how likely they are to be promoted. If women do not have such high expectations of salary or career advancement as men do, then it follows that they will be more satisfied with less-attractive earnings and career outcomes. However, as Hammermesh (ibid) <u>notes</u>, job expectations and actual work experiences <u>change</u> during the course of a career, and so it is unlikely that male and female expectations <u>are</u> uniformly different. This would seem to undermine Clark and Oswald's claim for low expectations, though findings from a large body of studies following Clark and Oswald <u>suggest</u> that it is at least part of the reason.

Quite separately from the issue of low expectations, Clark and Oswald (ibid) <u>suggest</u> that another possible reason for women's higher job satisfaction despite lower earnings <u>is</u> because men and women value specific aspects of their work, such as pay or flexible work arrangements, differently (Clark, 1997). However, it is again unlikely that this <u>is</u> sufficient explanation for the gender satisfaction gap, and <u>may</u> even underestimate the importance of the similarities between the genders. In a study of job attitudes among US lawyers, Mueller and Wallace (1996) <u>find</u> that the perception of fair pay between male and female workers <u>is</u> a significant element of female job satisfaction.

Furthermore, women's work experience levels <u>are</u> not uniform: for instance, younger female workers <u>tend</u> to have work experiences and expectations which <u>are</u> similar to male colleagues of the same age. This is particularly evident among workers in professional jobs and with higher education (Royalty, 1998), which would seem to be supported by the findings of Mueller and Wallace (ibid). It therefore <u>seems</u> that different job expectations cannot account fully for the gender/job-satisfaction difference.

In conclusion, there <u>is</u> widespread agreement that a gender/job-satisfaction gap does exist. Following early studies by Clark and others (see, for example, Hodson, 1989), it <u>has long been assumed</u> that this <u>is</u> a result of male and female workers having different expectations of their career success, or indeed having significantly different opinions about what aspects of a job are important for a feeling of contentment. However, these theories <u>are challenged</u> by studies which <u>show</u> that levels of expectation differ between women of different age, occupational type and educational level. While most studies of age-dependent differences of expectations <u>have been carried out</u> in the United States, little <u>has yet been done</u> to investigate whether this is true in the UK. The aim of the present study, therefore, is to explore in more detail whether young female workers in the UK share career progress expectations with their male colleagues.

Appendix 7: Audio transcripts

2.2

Mark: I thought we were going to get asked to look at earthquakes, or volcanic eruptions, as the worst natural disaster. I couldn't believe we've got to look at drought.

Jennifer: I don't mind, <u>to be honest</u>. I read ages ago this article about a group of experts who were asked to rank natural events in terms of the problems they caused, and I remember they came to the conclusion it was drought.

Mark: <u>It's weird</u>. It seems the least problematic.

Jennifer: <u>Yeah</u>, but it's because it goes on for so long. Droughts can last for years.

Mark: <u>Actually</u>, I was reading about a place where it hadn't rained in four years.

Jennifer: <u>That's nothing</u>. I heard there was a drought in parts of Northern Africa that lasted from 1968 to 1980 – that's twelve years!

Mark: <u>So</u>, let's start with a definition of what drought is.

Jennifer: Well, that's obvious. It's when it doesn't rain, or when there isn't enough rain or a lack of rain,<u> to be precise</u>.

Mark: <u>Yeah</u>, but it's not just any old time it doesn't rain. There has to be a problem as a result of it not raining. It hasn't really rained here for the last month or so, but there aren't any real problems yet because it poured so much the month before.

Jennifer: <u>I get it</u>. <u>OK</u>, go with your definition. So what kind of problems do you want to include? I think it's when there's a problem with water supply to people. They haven't got enough to drink or use for washing and stuff.

Mark: <u>True</u>. Or maybe when plants start dying?

Jennifer: Hmm, I guess if plants won't grow and you can't eat you'd have no choice but to leave and move to somewhere it is raining, don't you think?

Mark: That's easier said than done. You'd probably spend ages waiting, trusting that it will rain eventually.

Jennifer: <u>Right</u>. If it's always rained in the past, you'd think it would do the same again this year. And it'd be a hard decision, to leave your home for somewhere else. I guess it's easier if you have family in the city or something.

Mark: Maybe there is just nowhere else to go.

Jennifer: <u>You mean</u> the cities have problems too?

Mark: No, <u>I mean</u> that maybe the only other place is to move to a different country, where you wouldn't be welcome.

Jennifer: Most places would take in refugees, wouldn't they?

Mark: Yeah, <u>I suppose so</u>. <u>Anyway</u>, apart from refugees, what else do we think about drought and how it's important? Didn't it say in the reading that lack of rain often causes conflicts? A lot of fighting is over resources. I found that really surprising. I mean, I get it over things like oil. But everywhere has some form of rain.

Appendix 8: Water for future urban populations

Seminar: Junichiro Takahashi

Date: 15 January, 2012

Water for future urban populations

Introduction

There has been a large increase in the number of people with access to clean, safe drinking water. In the 1980s and 1990s, much of the discussion focused on the differences between urban and rural populations. Various projects have successfully introduced safe drinking water to villages and to urban populations. Of the 1.8 billion people who gained access to safe water over the period 1990–2008, around 60% were living in urban areas. However, this has had limited success, as during the same period, urban populations have grown at a faster rate than the water supply, leaving more and more people without access year on year. In a changing world, new solutions will be needed.

This seminar aims to explore the following issues:

1 What personal and economic benefits are there to improving access to water?
2 What are the main costs of funding a regular supply of water?

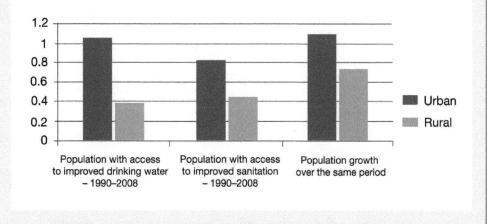

Figure 1: Changes in access to water and sanitation in urban and rural areas

Appendix 9: Opportunities in rainwater harvesting

Helmreich, B., & Horn, H. (2010). Opportunities in rainwater harvesting. *Desalination, 251*, 118–124

1. Introduction

According to UNESCO (2008) some 840 million people still suffer from undernourishment, and one billion people do not have access to safe drinking water. Indeed, most developing countries are classified as water-scarce countries, characterized by low, erratic rainfall. This results in high drought risk, intra-seasonal dry spells and frequent food insecurity. Most rainfall is in the form of storms, with very high rain intensity and extreme spatial and temporal rainfall variability (Ngigi, 2003). Evaporation rates tend to be high with potential evapo-transpiration of between 1500 and 2300 mm per year, three times the average annual rainfall in semi-arid areas. Typically, rainfall rates only exceed evapo-transpiration rates in 2.5–4 months of the year, thereby creating a very short growing season (Falkenmark et al, 2001).

In arid and semi-arid areas, between 70% and 85% of rainfall is "lost" from the agricultural system as soil evaporation, deep percolation and surface run-off. In such areas it is necessary to increase the amount of water available for agricultural purposes above the actual amount of direct rainfall. This report assesses the potential value of rainwater harvesting (RWH) to help reduce water scarcity in such regions.

2. Rainwater harvesting techniques

Rainwater harvesting has been in use for thousands of years. It is a technology used for collecting and storing rainwater from rooftops, land surfaces or rock catchments using simple techniques such as natural and/or artificial ponds and reservoirs. After collecting and storing, the rainwater is used in households for drinking, cooking and sanitation, as well as for productive use in agriculture.

There are three major forms of RWH:

- In situ RWH - collecting the rainfall on the surface where it falls and storing it in the soil.

- External water harvesting - collecting run-off originating from rainfall elsewhere and stored offsite.

Both of these are used for agricultural RWH.

- Domestic RWH (DRHW) - water is collected from roofs and street and courtyard run-offs.

2.1. Agricultural RWH

Irrigation of rainfed crops by the use of RWH is a viable option to increase crop yields. Rainfed agriculture in arid and semi-arid areas contributes to up to 90% of the total cereal production of these regions (Mwenge et al, 2005). However, in many countries, productivity remains low due to unreliable rainfall, unfavourable land conditions and lack of proper management of these resources. Increasing productivity of rainfed areas by RWH would increase food security, improve livelihoods, and reduce irrigation frequency. However, apart from climate, the landscape must also be suited for RWH agriculture in the following ways:

- The landscape surface must have a high level of run-off.

- There must be differences in elevation so that the run-off generated by rainfall can flow into the RWH collection points.

- The run-off receiving part must have sufficiently deep soils of suitable texture and structure to retain and store the run-off water.

Storage can be achieved by various types of surface and sub-surface storage systems which depend largely on the financial resources available. The following systems are common:

- Microcatchment systems: These are specially sloped areas designed to increase run-off from rain and concentrate it in a planting basin. Here it infiltrates the soil and is "stored" therein. The water is available for plants but protected from evaporation. Microcatchments are simple and inexpensive and can be rapidly installed using local materials and manpower.

- Sub-surface dams, sand dams or check dams: Water is stored underground in an artificially raised water table or local sub-surface reservoir.

- Tanks of various forms made of plastic, cement, clay, soil, etc. They can be built underground or above ground, depending on the space, technology and money available.

2.2. Domestic rainwater harvesting

For DRWH, rainwater is collected from rooftops, courtyards and streets with water being stored, either underground or above ground, close to these. Smaller storage, tanks are commonly made of bricks, stabilized soil, rammed earth, plastic sheets and mortar jars. For larger quantities, rainfall tanks can be made of pottery, concrete or polyethylene.

Precautions required in the use of DRWH storage tanks include the provision of an enclosure to minimize contamination from humans and animals and a tight cover to prevent algal growth and breeding of mosquitoes. Open tanks are not recommended for collecting drinking water.

The stored water can be used for domestic purposes such as garden watering and small-scale productive activities. The main advantage of DRWH is in providing water close to the household, minimising the distance walked to collect water. The costs for DRWH depend on the on-site requirements. Capital costs are high but neither operation nor maintenance usually involves significant expenditure. The investment costs depend on the size, the material and whether the tank is built underground or over ground. Storage costs for smaller tanks are low, e.g. for a 2 m3 jar made from pottery or cement about 20–40£. The costs for a concrete tank with a size of about 20 m3 are between £120 - 140 (Development Technology Unit, 2001).

3. Quality of harvested rainwater

All rainwater contains low levels of pollution from the atmosphere. Atmospheric pollutants include particles, microorganisms, heavy metals and organic substances. However, rainwater in rural areas – far from atmospheric and industrial pollution – is fairly clean except for some dissolved gases. Urban rainwater is more polluted.

In addition, the catchment surfaces themselves may be a source of pollutants. Relatively clean rainwater can be collected from roofs constructed with tiles, slates and aluminium sheets (Gould, 1992). However, roofs with bamboo gutters, zinc and copper roofs or roofs with metallic paint have high levels of pollutants.

Although rainwater harvested from most roof catchment systems generally matches the WHO standards for drinking water, rainwater collected from roads may be polluted by heavy metals from brakes and tyres, and by organic compounds like polycyclic aromatic hydrocarbons (PAH) and aliphatic hydrocarbons. To obtain drinking water the removal of these hazardous compounds is necessary.

Bacteria, viruses and protozoa may originate from faecal pollution by birds, mammals and reptiles. (Evans et al, 2006). Although the presence of microbial indicators and pathogens has been found to vary greatly Sazakli et al (2007) found harmful coliforms in 80.3% of rainwater samples. Therefore, harvested rainwater is often unsuitable for drinking without any treatment and needs disinfection to improve microbiological quality.

4. Rainwater treatment for DRWH

The basic requirement for developing countries is a practicable treatment method for clean water which is inexpensive. Initially, rainwater quality can be improved by cutting out the first waters of a rain event by water diverters. They are easy to install, operate automatically and are available in a number of different sizes. In addition to the improvement of rainwater quality they help reduce tank maintenance.

For disinfection the easiest and most common practice is chlorination. Chlorine kills most microorganisms and it is relatively cheap. Chlorination should be applied after the removal of the harvested rainwater from the storage tank, because chlorine may react with organic matter in the tank. One problem of chlorination is that some parasitic species have shown resistance to low doses of chlorine.

Slow sand filtration is another cheap method to improve the bacteriological quality of water (Palmateer et al, 1999). Filters are carefully constructed using graded sand layers and develop a thin biological layer i.e. a biofilm, on the filter surface. An effective slow sand filter may remain in service for many weeks, or even months. However, in order to be effective, a constant flow of water through the filters is essential and some microorganisms still remain.

Pasteurization by solar technology, combining UV-A radiation with heat, is also a cheap disinfection method (Wegelin et al, 1994). Since the sun is a free natural source of energy plentiful in most developing countries, this technique is a reliable and effective low cost treatment. Pasteurization by solar technology can be done in plastic bottles or bags or with continuous flow (SODIS) reactors. It is most effective with a water temperature of at least 50°C which can be achieved by using sun energy (Joyce et al, 1996). However, this method has limitations when the concentration of suspended solids is more than 10 mg/L., in which case other techniques like filtration may be added.

Filtration techniques are often necessary for the removal of hazardous substances from rainwater, with the most common type being the rapid sand filter. Water moves vertically through sand which is covered by a layer of activated carbon or anthracite coal. The top layer removes organic compounds, while other impurities are removed on their way through the filter. Effective filtration therefore depends on the depth of the filter.

For drinking water, membrane filter systems can effectively remove protozoa, bacteria, algae and other microorganisms. A membrane filter functions like a fine-meshed sieve. It consists of about 10,000 porous plastic fibres that form a web. A pump propels contaminated water through the membrane to the inside and any particle exceeding 0.1 mm – which includes all bacteria – gets stuck. However, the treated water may still contain some viruses which are smaller, so these filter systems are therefore coupled with a disinfection system. They are also expensive and require a great deal of maintenance.

5. Problems and constraints hampering RWH

Even though RWH is a useful technique for increasing water supply in areas with scarce water resources, there are problems hindering its integration and implementation. Often the technology used is inadequate or else is too expensive. Sometimes there is a lack of acceptance, motivation and involvement among users. Hydrological data and information for confident planning, design and implementation of RWH systems are lacking. Additionally there is often an insufficient attention to social and economic aspects such as land tenure and unemployment. In many cases local knowledge with regard to RWH and use is inadequate and outdated and the absence of long-term government strategies is also a handicap (Safapour & Metcalf, 1999). In some areas DRWH is actually illegal if water purity legislation is strictly applied (Mwenge et al, 2007). To help improve the success of RWH projects, Geographic Information Systems (GIS)-based models, which combine physical, ecological and socio-economic data, could be used.

6. Conclusions

Rainwater harvesting seems to offer considerable benefits for minimising water scarcity in developing countries. However, it is essential that local materials and manpower is used to identify catchment areas and build harvesting systems. For agricultural use most of the harvested water can be stored underground in natural systems protecting it from evaporation. On the other hand, rainwater harvested for domestic use may be polluted by bacteria and hazardous substances requiring a more careful choice of catchment area. For disinfection purposes there are many techniques available, but those utilizing natural sources such as solar energy may have more long-term potential. To develop and sustain successful RWH systems human and economic factors as well as climatic factors need to be considered, with GIS technology playing a major role.

References

Development Technology Unit. (2001). *Recommendations for designing rainwater harvesting system tanks.* Domestic Roofwater Harvesting Research Programme, O-DEV Contract No. ERB IC18 CT98 027, Milestone A6: Report A4, University of Warwick.

Evans, C.A., Coombes, P.J., & Dunstan, R.H. (2006). Wind, rain and bacteria: the effect of weather on the microbial composition of roof-harvested rainwater, *Water Research*, 40, 37–44.

Falkenmark, M., Fox, P., Persson, G., & Rockström, J. (2001). Water Harvesting for Upgrading of Rainfed Agriculture, (SIWI Report 11). Stockholm International Water Institute, Sweden. ISBN: 91-974183-0-7.

Gould, J.E. (1992). Rainwater catchment systems for household water supply. *Environmental Sanitation Reviews*, No. 32, ENSIC, Asian Institute of Technology, Bangkok.

Mwenge Kahinda, J., Boroto, J.R., & Taigbenu, A.E. (2005). Developing and integrating water resources management and rainwater harvesting systems in South Africa. *Proceedings of the 12th SANCIAHS Symposium*, Johannesburg, South Africa.

Mwenge Kahinda, J., Boroto, J.R., & Dimes, J. (2007). Rainwater harvesting to enhance water productivity of rain-fed agriculture in the semi-arid Zimbabwe, *Physics and Chemistry of the Earth*, *32*, 1068–1073.

Ngigi, S.N. (2003). What is the limit of up-scaling rainwater harvesting in a river basin? *Physics and Chemistry of the Earth*, *28*, 943–956.

Palmateer, G., Manz, D., Jurkovic, A., McInnis, R., Unger, S., Kwan K.K., & Dutka, B.J. (1999). Toxicant and parasite challenge of Manz intermittent slow sand filter. *Environmental Toxicology*, *14*, 217–225.

Safapour, N., & Metcalf, R.H. (1999). Enhancement of solar water pasteurization with reflectors. *Applied and Environmental Microbiology*, *65*, 859–861.

Sazakli, E., Alexopoulos, A., & Leotsinidis, M. (2007). Rainwater harvesting, quality assessment and utilization in Kefalonia Island, Greece. *Water Research*, *41*, 2039–2047.

Joyce, T.M., McGuigan, K.G., Elmore-Meegan, M., & Conroy, R.M. (1996). Inactivation of fecal bacteria in drinking water by solar heating. *Applied and Environmental Microbiology*, *62*, 399–402.

United Nations Educational Scientific and Cultural Organization. (2008). *Official Homepage*. Retrieved from http://www.unesco.org.

Wegelin, M., Canonica, S., Mechsner, T., Fleischmann, F., Pescaro E., & Metzler, A. (1994). Solar water disinfection: scope of the process and analysis of radiation experiments, *Journal of Water Supply: Research and Technology-AQUA*, *43*, 154–169.

Appendix 10: short passages about the Panama Canal

Student A:

The Panama Canal

History

The Panama Canal is located in the narrowest stretch of land to link the Pacific and the Atlantic Oceans. It was built by the US Army Corps of Engineers between 1904 and 1914. It provided a route for ships through the Americas, avoiding the lengthy and dangerous route around the tip of Argentina. During its construction, the infrastructure in the area around the canal benefited from an injection of finance and this was used to provide some much-needed services. Safe drinking water, sewage and garbage disposal were introduced in both the Canal Zone and some of the cities in Panama as a result of the canal's construction. Despite this, the company carrying out the work was heavily criticised for its treatment of the local people, in comparison to the treatment American workers received.

The Canal Zone was administered by the US government, and was seen as an important military base throughout most of the last century. Following a treaty enforced after 31 December 1999, the United States withdrew its military installations from the area, but not before signing a treaty with Panama to guarantee the canal's neutrality in war. However, there is also a clause in the treaty giving the United States the right to position military vessels in the area in times of war.

Student B:

Justification for the expansion of the Panama Canal

The Panama Canal is a key transportation route between the Atlantic and Pacific Oceans and is therefore one of the most widely used shipping routes in the world. The canal consists of three locks, the Gatun Lock, Pedro Miguel Lock and Miraflores Lock, two artificial lakes and several artificial channels. Lake Alajuela acts as a reservoir for the canal, feeding it with the water it needs. There are four trains either side which help steer large ships through the canal. Smaller ships use hand lines to steer.

The canal locks are 108 feet wide, considerably smaller than the width of modern container ships and cruise liners. Tankers from the oil platforms of South America are also unable to navigate the route. The growth of shipping between China and other countries in the industrial parts of Asia and the Eastern Coast of the United States, and the expansion in the popularity of cruise ships, has meant that there has been an increase in the pressure to modernise and expand the 100-year-old canal.

The plan is to build another set of locks alongside the existing structure to accommodate these larger ships. The project will cost $5.2 billion, but this will be largely financed by the taxes paid by shipping companies that use the canal. There will also be considerable environmental benefits resulting from a canal extension. Using the canal will decrease distances travelled. Since most large ships use oil-based fuels, this will therefore decrease fuel consumption, thereby helping to extend the life of dwindling world oil reserves.

Student C:

Against the expansion of the Panama Canal

The project to expand the Panama Canal is expected to double the amount of traffic coming through the canal. This will largely benefit multinational manufacturing companies and large international corporations, many of which will take any profits they make to the countries in which they are based.

The area immediately around the canal is densely populated, with a number of large settlements. The new plans laid out by the Interoceanic Regional Authority for the expansion of the canal make no provision for the individuals, organizations and companies currently living and working in the region. It is likely that a number of these will be displaced and problems of homelessness or unemployment may result.

In particular, there has been no mention of compensation for those who will be evicted by the project. Many people lack the financial ability to move from their current location. Also, anyone claiming against the eviction would need to proceed in the cheaper Panamanian courts, not under the US legal system, which pays higher damage payments. This has been disadvantageous to the many companies in the area which are unlikely to be awarded full payments for any losses they make.

The area around the canal has also developed an important ecosystem. It is now strongly dependent on tourism, with people visiting the nature management and conservation projects around the canal. Much of this area will need to be destroyed to provide for the new locks. In addition, the new locks will require feeding from alternative water sources, as the existing lakes will be inadequate. This pressure on water supply could have disastrous consequences for areas, not only those close to the canal. The risk of an increase in earthquake activity in the area is also unclear.

Appendix 11: Lesson task on processes

Lesson task – Student A:

Describe the process the HR department in the printing company Inkspress uses to recruit new staff.

Use time expressions, rhetorical questions and repetition and/or reformulation.

1   Confirm job and person specification with relevant department.

2   Fix interview dates and start dates.

3   Advertise position in local and national press and specialist websites.

4   Shortlist candidates for interview.

5   Hold first round of interviews.

6   Shortlist candidates for final interview in conjunction with relevant department.

7   Hold final interviews with the relevant department.

8   Offer job to the preferred candidate.

9   Check the preferred candidate's qualifications and references.

10 Draw up a formal contract for the new post holder.

Notes

Lesson task – Student B:

Describe the process by which electricity is produced in a hydroelectric plant.

Use time expressions, rhetorical questions and repetition and/or reformulation.

1 A suitable location, usually around an existing river or lake, is identified and a dam is built to raise the water level.

2 A gate in the dam is opened to allow water to fall through a channel.

3 The water gains kinetic energy as it flows to a turbine.

4 The water hits the turbine and the kinetic energy becomes mechanical energy.

5 The water flows downhill or is pumped back into the original source.

6 The turbine is connected to a generator, which converts the mechanical energy into electricity.

7 Transformers increase the voltage of the electricity.

8 Transmission wires carry the high-voltage current into the power supply.

9 Local substations and transformers reduce the voltage again.

10 The electricity is used in our homes.

Notes

Appendix 12: Student summaries of research methods

Author: Burke, P.

Study carried out: 2003

Published: 2004

Method: Postal questionnaires about use of herbs were mailed to
                    4,000 people. The respondents were asked to estimate how
                    much they thought they had spent on herbal medicines in
                    the past year. The results were used to make an estimate of
                    total expenditure for the UK population.

Response rate: 55% (2,200) of the respondents replied. Of that number,
                    80% (1,760) were women.

Author: Johnson, D.

Study carried out: 2007

Published: 2009

Method: Semi-structured interviews about use of natural remedies
                    were carried out on a random sample of 50 students.
                    Participants were asked how often and for which ailments
                    they used natural remedies, as well as how successful
                    they believed these remedies to be. Data was analyzed
                    qualitatively and quantitatively in order to ascertain the
                    reasons why UK students may use natural remedies over
                    modern medicine.

Author: Rodriguez, M.

Study carried out: 2001

Published: 2002

Method: Online questionnaires were completed by 2,000 people. The
                    questionnaire design was based around a rating scale used
                    to gauge participants' awareness of ten herbal treatments for
                    common ailments. The data was analyzed quantitatively to
                    inform a marketing campaign for a producer of alternative
                    remedies.

Author: Allen, F. P.

Study carried out: 2005–6

Published: 2007

Method: A longitudinal case study was carried out on a health-
                    food store to assess the impact of a marketing campaign
                    for natural skin-care products. Weekly sales figures for
                    the products were collected and quantitative analysis was
                    performed, showing a 230% increase in sales over the
                    period.

Author:	Frosch, M.
Study carried out:	1997
Published:	1999
Method:	Face-to-face interviews were conducted on a sample recruited in an allergy clinic. Participants were asked which alternative remedies they had used to treat their allergies. They were then treated weekly with hypnotherapy for one month. Participants were then interviewed again to see if the treatment had had any effect. A control group, which did not receive any treatment, was also interviewed.

Appendix 13: Research articles for lesson task

Text A

The effect of powdered ginger on osteoarthritic joint pain

A growing body of evidence supports the medical effect of ginger on a number of ailments. Records dating back to ancient times attest to its use in easing digestive problems and relieving nausea, as well as its circulatory benefits. Recent studies have started to confirm even more wide-ranging benefits, from lowering cholesterol (for example Luo and Zhang, 2007), to fighting certain cancer cells (for example Pietersen, 2009 and Piqueras, 2010). There seems little doubt that the spice deserves its "superfood" reputation.

This paper adds to the growing body of clinical research into ginger's anti-inflammatory properties. Recent research has led to a much deeper understanding of the link between gingerols and the relief of pain and swelling from inflammation. Our study draws particularly on Akinyemi and Jackson's research (2008), which through sound research methods found a significant correlation between the ingestion of 2 grams of powdered ginger root daily and the reduction of joint pain in osteoarthritis sufferers. Our study sought to repeat Akinyemi and Jackson's experiment and to investigate whether the use of fresh ginger may be more effective. In line with findings of other research, we hypothesized that fresh ginger root would have a greater effect.

Participants were recruited through the osteoarthritis clinic at the local hospital. Participants who had recently changed their daily routines, dietary habits or any course of medical treatment were excluded from the study. A total of 360 suitable participants were recruited. These participants were then divided into two categories: those who were currently taking regular prescribed medicine to control their pain (314 of the 360 participants), and those who had not yet started a course of medication (the remaining 46 participants). Each group was then split again (giving two groups of 23 and two groups of 157). Finally, 25% of participants of each of these groups was selected as the control.

Before beginning the experiment, data was gathered through a questionnaire (self-administered at the clinic) using rating scales to assess their pain levels in various contexts (at different times of day, after various activities, etc.: for more information see Appendix 1) and answering a mixture of closed and open questions regarding how long they had been suffering from arthritis and, in the case of those taking medication, the drugs they used and their ratings of the effectiveness of these.

With the exception of the control groups, one group of participants was then instructed to add 2 grams (approx. ½ teaspoon) of powdered ginger root to their food/drink each day for two months. The other group was instructed to add 2 grams of fresh ginger for the same period of time.

All participants returned to the clinic every two weeks to complete a second questionnaire (again self-administered at the clinic) using rating scales to assess their pain levels. Interviews were also carried out on a sample of participants to gather qualitative data regarding the exact nature of any changes in condition experienced.

Our results further support Akinyemi and Jackson's conclusion that powdered ginger root is an effective means of pain management for osteoarthritis sufferers. Data regarding our own hypothesis is inconclusive: participants taking fresh ginger also found it an effective means of pain relief, but with the exception of the under-50 age group there was no significant difference between their responses and those taking powdered ginger root. A clear flaw revealed in the method was, however, the lack of instructions given to participants regarding how to prepare fresh ginger and in what ways it could easily be incorporated into one's daily diet.

Text B

Do oranges boost the immune system?

Many people consume oranges through the winter months in the belief that they will strengthen their immune system against colds. This belief isn't entirely without scientific reason: citrus fruits have a relatively high concentration of vitamin C, which has been proven to have some effect on the body's immunological system by increasing numbers of white blood cells (whose role in fighting infection is well documented) and interferon, which helps block viruses.

The two most recent studies into the benefits of oranges in particular on the immune system (Gelb, 2008 and Itou and Hayes, 2009) have seen their results widely discredited due to flawed methods. In addition, those studies only researched the consumption of orange juice, whose vitamins may be differently absorbed than those in the fruit.

This research used a longitudinal and a cross-sectional study to judge the effects of eating oranges on contraction of the common cold virus. Both studies were conducted on 300 male pupils (participating voluntarily) aged 16–18 at a boarding school. Boarding school pupils were selected due to their controlled diets: all participants consumed the same meals throughout the study. A control group of 100 pupils was selected randomly and received no supplements to the standard diet. The remaining 200 pupils ate two additional oranges daily (one at breakfast and one after their evening meal).

In the longitudinal study, all students were asked to self-report the number of colds they came into contact with (e.g. when close friends or roommates were suffering from colds), and the number of colds they caught over the six-month time period. Self-reporting may admittedly distort data, but previous studies have suggested that error margins are small (notably Mason, 2004 and Henders, 1996).

The cross-sectional study took place in March. A group of 20 participants from the orange-eating group, and 20 from the control group, were selected at random. The cold virus was then administered into the noses of these participants in laboratory conditions. Participants were then monitored over the course of the following two weeks to note whether any symptoms were displayed, and if so to assess their severity and duration.

Results suggest that eating two oranges daily does slightly decrease both infection rates and the severity and duration of symptoms from colds.

Appendix 14: Texts for lesson task

Text A

Advances in modern medicine in recent years have seen huge improvements in the treatment of rheumatoid arthritis. Treatment is now started earlier, and this, alongside new generations of drugs, slows the development of symptoms and greatly improves patients' quality of life. The disease is tackled in three ways: through education, drugs and surgery.

Firstly, patients and families are better educated about the disease. Lifestyle changes may be recommended, particularly where patients are overweight and/or inactive. In particular, light physical exercise has been proven to reduce pain and inflammation. Swimming is a particularly beneficial form of exercise. For those whose suffering is severe, physical and occupational therapy are offered. Many centres also have qualified trainers who can develop exercise programmes for sufferers of rheumatoid arthritis. Some patients also try various complementary therapies, in particular dietary supplements and relaxation therapies, but there is very little evidence suggesting that these have any positive effect.

Secondly, medical treatments are administered. These are divided into two groups. The first is those that reduce inflammation short term: non-steroid anti-inflammatory agents (NSAIDs). The second, disease modifying anti-rheumatic drugs (DMARDs), control the root of the disease long term and need to be taken for several weeks before effects are seen. These drugs are not without their side effects. NSAIDs may lead to a variety of conditions ranging from stomach upsets to increased blood pressure to reduced kidney function. DMARDs may also lead to a number of side effects, some of which may be severe. However, there are a great many varieties of NSAIDs and DMARDs on the market, meaning that if a patient reacts adversely to one, they may accept another.

In addition, patients are monitored closely for side effects, so that any potential problems are detected early and can be combated by alternative courses of treatment or by further medication. Furthermore, a new generation of biological drugs is currently replacing more traditional DMARDs, leading to a faster and more dramatic reduction in symptoms. These biological drugs tend to have fewer, and less severe, side effects. Unless future clinical trials prove that they may safely be taken alongside these modern medicines, patients are strongly advised not to take additional supplements. These need not be approved by any regulatory body and may have extremely damaging side effects, such as dangerous reactions with existing drugs.

Finally, in more advanced cases, surgical intervention is recommended in order to correct abnormalities. Inflamed tissue may be removed, or part or all of the joint may be replaced in order to restore function. However, the need for this is becoming less and less, due to improvements in medications.

Garcia, D. (2006). *The control and management of disease*. Birmingham: Napier. (p.207)

Text B

Patients suffering from rheumatoid arthritis who approach their GPs are generally given little choice in the treatment route they follow. Though modern medicine is aware of some complementary approaches to ease the symptoms of rheumatoid arthritis, the official line is that the effectiveness of such treatments is unproven, despite anecdotal evidence from thousands of sufferers worldwide. As a result, most patients are pushed into a regime of multiple drug-taking which has potentially serious – even life-threatening – consequences. Even the 'mild' side effects which most people will suffer from, such as weight gain or hair loss, can have a significant effect on a patient's self-esteem and quality of life. Furthermore, we should be extremely cautious in hailing the new generation of biological drugs, whose long-term safety has not been proven and which may lead to extremely debilitating auto-immune disorders.

Complementary and alternative medicine offers a natural, and safe, approach to those suffering from rheumatoid arthritis. It need not be seen as an addition to the chemicals of modern medicine, but can be successful in reducing the symptoms of rheumatoid arthritis as the sole course of treatment. A number of different therapies are available, which can be split into two main groups: dietary supplements and relaxation therapies. In treating the disease holistically, the best results are seen when elements of both are combined.

While even modern medicine will advocate the need for a balanced diet in reducing the symptoms of rheumatoid arthritis, particularly in patients who are overweight, little clinical research has been done into individual supplements which anecdotal evidence suggests can be hugely beneficial. If taken following the guidelines of a qualified herbalist or homoeopathist, a variety of herbal extracts, and Omega 3 and Omega 6 fatty acids obtained through fish and plant oils, can have an extremely encouraging effect, reducing inflammation and improving joint function. Even common spices such as turmeric and ginger may also be effective in combating swelling. In addition to its other health benefits, recent studies have also suggested that drinking green tea may help both prevent and reduce the severity of rheumatoid arthritis due to its antioxidant effects.

The safety of relaxation therapies is undisputed. A number of therapies have been shown to reduce the symptoms of rheumatoid arthritis, affording patients a great deal of choice and enabling a therapy to be chosen which matches the patient's lifestyle. Mind–body relaxation techniques such as tai chi, meditation and hypnotherapy have long proven effective in relieving pain in a variety of conditions, but seem particularly effective in musculoskeletal disorders. Further physical therapies may also be successful in minimising the symptoms of rheumatoid arthritis, notably hydrotherapy or balneotherapy, acupuncture, magnet therapy and crystal therapy. Magnet therapy is a particularly interesting field of research, as sufferers are able to wear magnets on their person, or place them in shoes or clothing, in order to feel constant alleviation of symptoms.

Smith-Watson, G. (2010). An alternative approach to treating arthritis.
International CAM Journal, 16(3), 124.

Appendix 15: Abstract on study into 'Creative rooms'

Physical design and decoration in the workplace affect occupants' moods, concentration and work. Little research has been conducted to link physical space and creativity. This study investigates individuals' perceptions of how well offices foster a creative atmosphere. Thirty participants working in digital design (m = 18, f = 12) rated pictures of rooms for their 'creativity potential'. They gave scores for whole rooms, as well as individual features. The findings suggest a preference for 'natural'-looking rooms, with wall decorations and warm colour schemes, but little effect from lighting. The findings suggest room features which enhance creativity may benefit work output in the creative industries.

Appendix 16: Abstract on study into MP3 format

Digital music has been popular since the introduction of the MP3 audio format in the 1990s. However, the variety and incompatibility of new digital formats can be confusing. This essay uses secondary research to analyze technical aspects and the marketing influence of three formats. The findings indicate that the lack of MP3 copyright protection encourages the involvement of more companies in the format's development; however, it can also encourage piracy. A possible solution is an industry-wide agreement on a compatible format or standard, though this would have to overcome resistance from companies which want to preserve standards from their competitors.

Appendix 17: Elements of a research article about creativity and study

Introduction

Creativity is an important element in relation to education and societal growth. As the degree of complexity and the amount of information in our society continue to increase, society's problems require more creative solutions. For this reason, all sectors of society are requiring leaders who can think critically and creatively (Isaksen & Murdock, 1993). Although this important construct has not been universally defined, defining creativity as "the production of novel thoughts, solutions, or products based on previous experience and knowledge" (Gandini cited in Carter, 1992, p.38) seems to capture the essence of creativity.

In terms of education, creativity is an essential element necessary for learning. Starko (1995) suggests that learning is a creative process that involves students making information relevant by linking prior knowledge and new knowledge in an individually meaningful format. She attributes this meaningfulness to the individual's creativity. Unfortunately, most school environments do not support, and many actively suppress, creative expression. Torrance and Safter (1986), for instance, assert that teachers are often ill equipped to develop, support, or evaluate creativity in their students. In addition, much theory and research shows that creative students often lose their creative potential (Shaughnessy, 1991). If education strives to prepare children for a productive life in society, the educational system must accept responsibility for supporting and developing creativity. The purpose of this study was to explore the characteristics comprising a supportive classroom environment for creativity. Within this context, we focused on the teacher's role in creating this supportive environment.

Method

Graphics communication course

This study was conducted during the spring semester of 1996, within the context of an advanced-level graphics communication course offered at a large Midwestern University. The course was oriented toward junior and senior journalism majors, and a total of eighteen undergraduate students varying in class standing and artistic ability were enrolled in the class. The instructor possessed several years of experience in offering this particular course, and also had two decades of experience in reporting photography, copy editing, picture editing, and graphics editing. The major course objectives outlined in the course syllabus in order of importance were (a) creative process, (b) graphic design theory, and (c) computer skills. Enabling students to synthesize these elements was a long-term goal of the class emphasized by the instructor. The classroom in which this course was taught seated a total of twenty students. Each desk contained a graphic design computer equipped with the appropriate software for producing assignments in this course.

Data Collection

This study was conducted in a naturalistic setting where the following qualitative methods were employed as data collection methods: document review of the course syllabus, instructor interview, six student interviews, and classroom observations. The syllabus was examined with the assumption that it provides the student with the instructor's intentions and directions for the course. This data provided information on student–teacher relationships, methods of assessment, communication of this assessment, creative processes taught, and students' responses to these processes. Observations and the syllabus provided information useful in devising questions for the interviews. Separate sets of questions for both the instructor and students were used for the interviews. We analyzed the data by coding units of information and developing categories emerging from this data.

We triangulated our findings by conducting multiple data collection and by conducting our study as a team. All three researchers were equally involved in the data collection, analysis, and interpretation phase. The major limitation of this study is that no follow-up interviews or survey data were collected to provide member checks of the interpretations we made. However, each member of the research team first independently analyzed the data before joining the team with their summaries and interpretations of the findings.

Conclusion

This study was framed with the purpose of identifying characteristics comprising a supportive environment for creativity in a college classroom. However, future development of this environment would also benefit from research at both the individual student level and classroom community level. Future research at the student level should concentrate on the creative development of individual students. The current study revealed differences in individual needs for the creative processes taught in this class. Second, these findings indicated the need to investigate methods of designing group work supportive of the creative process, and the need for accurate evaluation of group work, from the students' perspectives.

Third, further investigation, at the broader classroom level, should explore dynamics of teacher–student interaction and examine students' influence on shaping the classroom environment. Because this study focused on the professor's influence, students' impact on shaping the environment was not discussed. Fourth, research determining the effects of various assessment methods on creativity is needed, especially considering the importance of assessment in influencing all aspects of the college classroom. If research finds that non-traditional grading significantly enhances creativity, policy measures will need to address issues of standardization and grading, and changes in post-secondary institutions will be necessary. In the meantime, teachers are responsible for giving grades to students, and therefore need to cope with current policies. For this reason and our final implication, research examining additional methods for coping with this requirement while simultaneously implementing low-risk assessment methods as part of a supportive environment for creativity will also be needed.